REELECTION 1996

REELECTION 1996

How Americans Voted

Edited by

Herbert F. Weisberg
The Ohio State University

Janet M. Box-Steffensmeier
The Ohio State University

CHATHAM HOUSE PUBLISHERS
SEVEN BRIDGES PRESS, LLC
NEW YORK · LONDON

Reelection 1996: How Americans Voted

Seven Bridges Press, LLC
P.O. Box 958, Chappaqua, New York 10514-0958

Copyright © 1999 by Chatham House Publishers
of Seven Bridges Press, LLC

Publisher: Robert J. Gormley
Cover design: Inari Information Services, Inc.
Managing editor: Katharine Miller
Production supervisor: Melissa A. Martin
Composition: Bang, Motley, Olufsen
Printing and binding: Versa Press, Inc.

Library of congress cataloging-in-publication data

Reelection 1996 : how Americans voted / edited by Herbert F.
  Weisberg and Janet M. Box-Steffensmeier.
      p. cm.
    Includes bibliographical references and index.
    ISBN 1-56643-068-2
    1. United States. Congress—Elections, 1996. 2. Presidents
  —United States—Election—1996. 3. Elections—United States
  I. Weisberg, Herbert F.   II. Box-Steffensmeier, Janet M., 1965–
  JK1968 1996f
  324.973'9-0929—dc21
                                                              98-40158
                                                              CIP

Manufactured in the United States of America
10   9   8   7   6   5   4   3   2   1

To

John Kessel

Our Colleague, Mentor, Friend

Contents

Figures and Tables

Figures

Tables

Preface

Our collective endeavor to analyze the 1996 elections brings together some of the best voting behavior scholars conducting research today. The chapters are united by viewing the 1996 elections through the lens of reelection—the reelection of President Bill Clinton and the reelection of the Republican Congress.

Each chapter uses a great national resource, the National Election Study (NES) surveys, which are unique in the number, depth, and continuity of questions over time that focus on political opinions. We are indebted to the NES for continuing to pursue this important electoral data collection, to David Legee, board chair, Steven Rosenstone, principal investigator, Larry Bartels, planning committee chair, Kathryn Cirksena, director of studies, and Leslie Jo Scott and Zoanne Blackburn, the Survey Research Center's study directors for fieldwork, and to the National Science Foundation for funding those surveys. We are fortunate that these individuals and organizations continue to put so much effort into these surveys, and we are among the many who hope that they are able to continue this invaluable resource in perpetuity.

Books are always collective activities. This book certainly is. As editors, we owe a considerable debt to the authors of the several chapters who responded with considerable speed to many of our urgings and deadlines. We would also like to give special thanks to Justin Zeefe, who provided suggestions and excellent editorial assistance while working on this book, and to Sara Dunlop for assistance with indexing and processing the final manuscript. We thank Chris Kelaher, Melissa Martin, Katharine Miller, and Phillip Martin for their careful work on the book. Special appreciation is to be given to the late Ed Artinian, founder of Chatham House, for his support of this project. We also want to thank our spouses, Judy Weisberg and Mike

Steffensmeier, who would easily be reelected, and our families, who inspire us to work hard and play hard.

On behalf of the authors of these chapters, we want to thank those who reviewed parts of this book, including Herb Asher, Paul Beck, Barry Burden, Damarlys Canache, Robert Erikson, Tobin Grant, John Kessel, David Kimball, Dean Lacy, Carl McCurley, Steve Mockabee, Jeffery Mondak, Quin Monson, Anthony Mughan, Steve Nichols, Dick Niemi, Barbara Norrander, Samuel Patterson, George Rabinowitz, Peter Radcliffe, Charles Smith, Harold Stanley, Andy Tomlinson, and Nancy Zingale.

Finally, a sincere thank-you to John Kessel, professor emeritus of political science at The Ohio State University, whose outstanding work has profoundly influenced us as scholars and whose guidance and friendship has touched our lives. Even though he is a contributor, we dedicate this book to him because of his importance to those of us here at Ohio State. Most of the authors of this book have or have had associations with the Ohio State Department of Political Science, and we share the distinct pleasure of having John as a colleague, mentor, and friend.

Reelection:
The 1996 U.S. Election

Herbert F. Weisberg and
Janet M. Box-Steffensmeier

REELECTION provides the rhythm of democracy. The usual discussion of the "electoral cycle" misses the large extent to which reelection drives the system. Incumbents must face the electorate again if they want to keep their positions. Voters are given the opportunity to decide whether they want to keep the incumbents in place or give the other team a chance. Campaigns are often fought along these lines, giving the voters a choice between two slogans: "Don't change horses in midstream" and "Throw the bums out."

Presidential incumbents and their designated successors are familiar to voters, who are able to judge their performance in office. The opposition party must try to convince the public either that the incumbent party has mismanaged the country (especially its economy) or that the opposition party's leaders are better suited to be president. Neither of these claims has been an easy argument to sell to the public in the twentieth century. The typical result has been reelection, with Bill Clinton's success in 1996 replicating the successes of Ronald Reagan in 1984, Richard Nixon in 1972, Dwight Eisenhower in 1956, Franklin Roosevelt in 1944, 1940, and 1936, Woodrow Wilson in 1916, and William McKinley in 1900. The few exceptions were George Bush's defeat in 1992, Jimmy Carter's failure in 1980, Herbert Hoover's in 1932, and William Taft's in 1912. Overall, reelection should be considered democracy's steady beat.[1]

Why do some reelection attempts succeed and others fail? In part, the reasons have to do with the public's limited attention span for politics. Just as the stockholders of a successful company are usually willing to reelect the board of directors without examining the details of the company's financial statement very closely, American voters are usually willing to vote for the re-election of a president (or a retiring president's designated successor) if the country seems to be running smoothly. If the general picture is positive, details rarely matter. If the public recognizes that the country and the economy are doing well, it is hard to hold the public's attention long enough to dislodge a sitting president. Only when the country and the economy are doing poorly does the public focus on politics enough to want to change leadership teams.

This argument is both correct and overly facile. It is correct in part because strong potential candidates decide whether or not to run for the presidency based on their perception of their chances. Strong candidates often decide not to run against an incumbent when the economy is doing well, whereas they are more likely to run when there is no incumbent and when the economy is doing poorly. Yet this argument is overly facile because elections are decided on the margin. One mistake by an advantaged incumbent might be enough to allow the challenger to win. And a challenger can always try to shift the nature of the debate away from a prospering economy toward other issues, especially if the challenger has a more appealing personal story than does the incumbent. From this perspective, reelection still provides the steady, underlying rhythm of democracy, but other notes can arise to offset that rhythm.

Our theoretical understanding of American presidential elections should be modified to give greater emphasis to the reelection theme. These elections are generally not occasions on which the electorate weighs the relative merits of two competing candidates as if they have just emerged in presidential politics. In nearly every presidential election of the twentieth century there was either an incumbent or an heir apparent running for the presidency, and this should be taken into account more explicitly in our voting models.[2] In this book, we consider the 1996 presidential election from this perspective, using the National Election Study surveys to examine the determinants of Bill Clinton's reelection, particularly in contrast to George Bush's failure to be reelected four years earlier.

The National Election Study Surveys

The National Election Study (NES) mission "is to produce high quality survey data on voting, public opinion, and political participation" (http://www.umich.edu/~nes/, 6 March 1998). The surveys are conducted in both presidential and midterm election years, in time series dating back to 1948. The continuity of questions is a prominent feature of the surveys because it allows for comparisons and contrasts to be drawn across elections. This aspect is central to the examination of reelection in this book.

Headquartered at the University of Michigan, the NES has been funded since 1977 by the National Science Foundation. Prior to that time, scholars at the University of Michigan were responsible for running and conducting the surveys. The Board of Overseers obtains a wide range of input from the research community and consults with the principal investigators, the NES staff, and planning committees. Although continuity is emphasized in the NES surveys, specific themes are also highlighted to gauge the significance of political changes. For example, major substantive themes in the 1996 study included an evaluation of the performance of the first Republican Congress elected in 1994 in four decades and an evaluation of President Clinton.

The 1996 study, like previous presidential-election-year studies, consisted of preelection and postelection interviews. Both pre- and postelection surveys were seventy minutes long, with a national sample of 1,750 and 1,490 respondents, respectively. In the past, NES interviews were conducted in person. The 1996 postelection survey, however, included an experiment where half the interviews were conducted in the homes of respondents and the other half were done by telephone. The intent was to reduce the cost of the surveys. It was deemed a success, and plans are for the vast majority of interviews to be conducted by telephone in the future (http://www.umich. edu/~nes/overview/spproces.htm, 2 October 1998). The 1996 survey was part of a panel design, which means that some of the respondents were interviewed in previous years as well. The panel part of the survey has not been released as of this writing, but this study design will allow for even greater leverage on questions of continuity across the 1992, 1994, and 1996 elections.

As Weisberg points out, the number of interviews has implications for statistical generalizations (1995, 7). Specifically, sampling error occurs because we have surveyed a sample rather than the entire population. This error affects the confidence we have in our conclusions, which are based on the statistical results. In the 1996 survey, the maximum sampling error is estimated to be 3.25 percent for a full sample (see Weisberg, Krosnick, and Bowen 1996 for the formula for the margin of error and the 1996 NES codebook for details relating to the specific sampling design used in 1996). Also keep in mind that when analyses are conducted on only part of a sample, the sampling error increases.

An analysis of the NES data is necessarily highly statistical. The authors of the following chapters report on a series of topics from the study, giving results for 1996, drawing comparisons with 1992, and often showing trends since the 1950s or 1960s. Their analysis usually begins by presenting "marginal distributions" showing what percentages of the respondents fall into each category on the variables they are examining, followed by "bivariate" (two-variable) analysis that indicates how this variable directly affected the vote. Voting, however, is a complicated topic to study, with many causes operating simultaneously. Therefore, it is necessary to move to "multivariate" analysis to estimate properly the effects of each presumed cause while taking into account the other likely causes. Regression analysis is the classic procedure for such analysis when the variable being analyzed (the "dependent variable") is numeric. The main dependent variables in the study of voting are instead just categories—such as voting Republican or Democrat, or voting versus not voting on election day. The authors of several chapters in this book use special procedures for dealing with such two-category dependent variables, generally logit or probit analysis (which are actually similar techniques). The basic logic behind this procedure is explained most thoroughly in chapter 4.

The NES surveys are much longer than the typical short phone polls that the media take before elections. This permits a thoroughness that cannot be obtained when looking at media polls. Yet, it is never possible to include questions on all possible topics in a survey. The 1996 NES questionnaire does cover most of the important issues raised in the campaign, but inevitably it does not touch every base.

The NES studies are unique in a world of an increasing number of surveys because of the depth of questions focusing on enduring facets of elections, public opinion, and political participation over time. This feature of the NES surveys makes them particularly valuable for scholarly analysis. In contrast, media polls, while conducted more often, tend to focus on topical, "headline news" issues. The overall format of the NES surveys is also unique in the number of open-ended questions. Open-ended questions, which are more difficult to analyze, allow respondents to answer as they choose instead of being limited to the response categories provided by the interviewer. In chapter 5, Kessel and Weisberg contrast closed-ended and open-ended approaches and explore the similarities and differences in results found in chapters 3 and 4. The content of the NES voting surveys reflects a social-psychological emphasis on attitudes, which is the primary framework used by scholars to examine voting behavior in the United States.

The Framework for Studying Voting

The two dominant theoretical approaches to the study of voting behavior are social-psychological and rational choice (see Niemi and Weisberg 1993b, esp. chap. 1, for more details). The social-psychological approach of the Michigan School attributes electoral outcomes to voters' political attitudes and identifications. The classic study in this tradition is *The American Voter* (Campbell, Converse, Miller, and Stokes 1960). In contrast, rational choice emphasizes self-interest and was introduced by Anthony Downs in *An Economic Theory of Democracy* (1957).

The NES surveys were begun by scholars of the University of Michigan and retain much of the original focus on the social-psychological theoretical framework.[3] Three primary attitudes are emphasized as explanatory variables for determining the vote by this framework: partisanship, candidates, and issues (Niemi and Weisberg 1993a, 8). The current literature views partisanship as a long-term attachment and candidate and issue attitudes as more short-term. It is also common to ask which factors are important given particular circumstances. This question is particularly useful for drawing comparisons across elections, as is done in each of the chapters here. The current literature also focuses on how these attitudes affect voting instead of asking whether issue or candidate attitudes affect voting.

The literature gives remarkably little attention to reelection at the presidential level. This minimal attention to reelection as a separate concept in the presidential election literature is in marked contrast to the congressional election literature, which gives considerable emphasis to incumbency effects. As an attempt to examine the bases of reelection more, the chapters in this volume on the presidential election compare the 1996 election with the 1992 election.

The central question in voting behavior is what determines the vote. Most often, this question is asked in the study of presidential voting. Weisberg and Mockabee in chapter 3 and Smith, Radcliffe, and Kessel in chapter 4 provide sophisticated analyses of the NES data to answer the question of who reelected Clinton. Weisberg and Mockabee find that partisanship aided the Democrats in 1996 as did the economy (though less so than in 1992), while the perception of Clinton as caring for people offset any perceived defects in his character. Using responses to open-ended questions, Smith, Radcliffe, and Kessel also show that candidate attributes were important factors and that partisanship, ideology, and the economy affected presidential voting in 1996. In contrast to 1992, they find that instead of the economy playing the dominant role in Clinton's reelection, a combination of lifestyle issues, social benefits, and economics prevailed. Kessel and Weisberg compare the methods and conclusions of chapters 3 and 4 and highlight the nuances of the election that can be learned using the NES data.

Mughan and Burden examine a new attitudinal influence on voting: feelings about the candidates' wives. They show that in both 1992 and 1996 Hillary Clinton had a greater impact on the vote than either Barbara Bush or Elizabeth Dole. Short-term issue factors are central to the studies of Asher and Tomlinson and of Lacy and Grant. Asher and Tomlinson conclude that the Clinton campaign team made 1996 a repeat of 1992 by their success in defining the campaign issues and setting the agenda. The single most prominent issue studied in the literature is the role of economics in elections (Fiorina 1981; Lewis-Beck 1988). Lacy and Grant continue in this tradition, showing that the economy affects presidential candidate choice and extending the literature by demonstrating that economic perceptions also affect voter turnout.

The study of voting decisions is clearly paramount, but prior to the decision of which candidate to vote for comes the decision whether to vote in the first place. The study of voter turnout is an area of active scholarly debate. Specifically, the parallel trends of decreasing turnout and increasing education levels are labeled as a puzzle of participation (Niemi and Weisberg 1993b, 14; Brody 1978). Nichols, Kimball, and Beck examine turnout in 1996 and ask whether the increase in turnout in 1992 was a turning point in American electoral participation.

Which groups support which party is an enduring topic in voting behavior. The shifting alliances of groups have had a large impact on the U.S. political system in the past (Key 1955; Burnham 1970; Sundquist 1973; Beck 1979) and are of vital importance to our current understanding of present and future politics. Stanley and Niemi find evidence that processes begun in the past several decades are continuing, such as the movement of native southern whites from the Democratic Party. Several watershed changes have also occurred recently, such as Hispanics becoming a substantial fraction of the Democratic coalition. Stanley and Niemi's conclusions highlight what the implications of the data trends are for the parties. Norrander concentrates on gender differences, documenting the development of the current gender gap in partisanship, issue positions, and presidential candidate choice. She argues that the gender gap developed as the changing preferences of men led them to desert the Democratic Party for the Republican Party. The 1994 journalist label "Year of the Angry White Male" is more accurate than the 1992 slogan "Year of the Woman" or 1996's "Year of the Soccer Mom."

The 1996 election was the first election since the 1920s in which a Republican-controlled Congress was retained by voters. Mondak, McCurley, and Millman sort out the differential impact of parties, candidates, and issues. They extend the debate in voting behavior between those who assert the dominance of national factors (Tufte 1975; A. Campbell 1960; J. Campbell 1987) and those who place more weight on local factors (Ragsdale 1980; Erikson 1990) with their innovative measure of candidate quality. Specifically, they bring new insights into the classic topic of "attitudes toward the candidates."

Patterson and Monson also study the reelection of the Republican Congress. Consistent with the thesis of the social-psychological approach, they find that partisanship has a powerful influence on both congressional voting and congressional performance evaluations. Their discussion of congressional performance reflects a growing concern in the literature about institutions. Their work highlights the stark contrasts among the 1992, 1994, and 1996 congressional elections.

The 1996 Election

Reelection provided the dominant rhythm of the 1996 U.S. election. Bill Clinton was easily reelected president, while the Republicans maintained their majorities in both houses of Congress. Reelection was so much the theme of the year that continued Democratic control of the White House was rarely in doubt throughout the campaign period. Poll after poll showed Clinton well ahead of his Republican challenger, Bob Dole. Whenever an occasional poll seemed to show that Clinton's lead was diminishing, the numbers returned to prior levels within a few days. All the usual trappings of presidential election campaigns were present in 1996, from contested primaries at the beginning of the year to national nominating conventions in the summer and televised debates in the fall, but the country seemed to pay little attention. Reelection was the dominant theme in the presidential contest, and the Republicans could not stop that.

THE PRESIDENT

It would be a mistake to assume that Bill Clinton's reelection was preordained from the start of his presidency. Indeed, his administration started off in an unusually rocky fashion. He had been elected with only 43 percent of the popular vote (to 38 percent for George Bush and a surprising 19 percent for H. Ross Perot). His first actions as president were attacked as ultraliberal, especially his changing the policy against gays in the military. His early cabinet appointments hit trouble. Clinton's top legislative priority was passage of a health-care-reform plan developed by a special task force headed by his wife, Hillary, but this plan died in the Democratic Congress. Republican attacks on the Clintons' ethics over the Whitewater real estate deal and related matters further eroded the president's position. The low point was reached when Republicans stunned political experts by winning control of both houses of Congress in November 1994, for the first time since 1946. There was little reason, at that point, to expect that Clinton could be reelected in 1996.

Yet, as often happens, public sympathies soon began to swing again, this time toward the president. The new Republican 104th Congress started off on a collision course with the Democratic president (Weisberg and Patterson 1998). House Speaker Newt Gingrich behaved as though he were the country's leader. The House passed most of the Republican Contract with America in its first 100 days. The initial impression of Republican invulnerability began to fade when parts of the Contract were slowed down and/or defeated in the Senate. More serious problems developed when the president and Congress sparred on a deficit-reduction package. Finally, the federal government was shut down twice in November and December 1995 because of an impasse between Clinton and Congress on appropriations bills. The president won the resultant public relations battle, with the country blaming the Republican Congress for closing down the government. Meanwhile, Clinton was getting high marks for his leadership in the aftermath of the summer 1995 terrorist bombing of the Oklahoma City federal building. As 1996 began, the president's approval ratings climbed and his chances for reelection soared.

THE CHALLENGERS

The structure of the presidential campaign became defined as various possible challengers decided whether or not to enter the race. No Democratic opponent to President Clinton emerged. Incumbent presidents generally have no difficulty winning renomination by their parties. Some have been so bloodied in divisive primaries, however, that they either dropped out of the race or were too weakened to win the general election. Clinton escaped this potential problem when his improved poll standings and his success in raising a large campaign war chest deterred an intraparty challenge. Also, while many liberal Democrats might have preferred a candidate other than the moderate Clinton, they did not want to risk hurting their party's chances to keep the presidency.

Clinton also benefited from the lack of a new minor-party challenger. Several potential independent candidates were mentioned—including Jesse Jackson, former Democratic senator Bill Bradley (N.J.), and former Republican senator and governor Lowell Weicker (Conn.)—but they ultimately decided against running. Ralph Nader did run on a Green Party ticket, but he attracted little notice outside California. Ross Perot ran again, receiving the nomination of his Reform Party over former governor Richard Lamm (Colo.) in a manner that struck many as heavy-handed. Perot, however, was unable to rekindle the spark of his 1992 campaign.

Several potentially strong Republican candidates also decided against running in 1996, including many who had participated in the Reagan and/or Bush administrations—former vice-president Dan Quayle, former secretary of state James Baker, former secretary of defense Richard Cheney, former education secretary William Bennett, former HUD secretary Jack Kemp, and most notably former chairman of the joint chiefs of staff Colin Powell—as well as moderate Massachusetts governor William Weld and House Speaker Newt Gingrich (Ga.). California governor Pete Wilson joined the race but had to drop out before the primary season even began. Several senators did run for the nomination, including Bob Dole, a long-time Washington insider and the Republican Senate majority leader, plus conservative Phil Gramm (Tex.), Richard Lugar (Ind.), and Arlen Specter (Pa.). The other active Republican candidates were conservative commentator Pat Buchanan, billionaire publishing magnate Steve Forbes, former Tennessee governor and education secretary Lamar Alexander, and a few lesser-known contenders (radio talk-show host Alan Keyes, conservative Republican congressman Bob Dornan, and millionaire businessman Morry Taylor) who seemed to specialize in trying to hurt the chances of the Republican front-runners.

THE REPUBLICAN PRIMARY SEASON

The 1996 Republican primary season moved quickly. Bob Dole was seen as the early front-runner. He had raised much more money than the other candidates had, and his campaign was much better organized. The early nomination events were not favorable to Dole, but his main competitors peaked too early.

The 1996 primary season differed from earlier years in that the primaries were "front-loaded." That is, many states moved their primaries earlier so that they could affect the race. In 1996 the primary season functionally was only five to six weeks long. This is a more compact time than in recent years and much shorter than a generation ago. Also, many primaries were held on the same dates, such as "Junior Tuesday" (5 March), "Super Tuesday" (12 March), and "Big Ten Tuesday" (19 March). The Iowa caucuses and New Hampshire primary were still the first main events in February, but many other primaries followed quickly in March. This put a premium on organization, since a candidate had to spend a lot of time in Iowa and New Hampshire and then could not spend much time in the remaining states. Also, most Republican primaries, after the first few, were winner-take-all, so that a candidate who could win 25–30 percent of the vote in all these states would win no delegates from these states if the race had boiled down to two contenders.

A possible complication was that every major candidate receiving public funding (which meant everyone but billionaire Forbes) was limited in total campaign expenditures. Buchanan and Alexander did not spend much money in the early primaries because they had not raised much, which meant that they would be permitted to spend large amounts of money in later primaries if they could stay in the race that long. Dole, in contrast, spent a lot of money in the initial campaign events, so this limitation would have hurt him badly had he not put a lock on the nomination early.

There was considerable early attention to Steve Forbes and his flat-tax idea. But this attention peaked a couple of weeks before the primaries and resulted in a consensus that the flat tax would not be fair and that Forbes was a one-issue candidate. Forbes's negative television blitz also backfired. He had relied on an expensive advertising campaign instead of developing a precinct organization in the early states and personally campaigning heavily in those states. As a result of these factors, Forbes faded by the Iowa caucuses and the New Hampshire primary. He won the Delaware primary on 24 February and the Arizona one on 27 February, but those were to be his

TABLE 1.1. 1996 REPUBLICAN PRESIDENTIAL PRIMARY RESULTS

Event	Date	State	Winner	Percent	Second place	Percent
Early primaries	20 Feb.	New Hampshire	Buchanan	27	Dole	26
	24 Feb.	Delaware	Forbes	33	Dole	27
	27 Feb.	Arizona	Forbes	33	Dole	30
		North Dakota	Dole	42	Forbes	20
		South Dakota	Dole	45	Buchanan	29
	2 Mar.	South Carolina	Dole	45	Buchanan	29
	3 Mar.	Puerto Rico	Dole	98		
Junior Tuesday	5 Mar.	Colorado	Dole	44	Buchanan	22
		Connecticut	Dole	54	Forbes	20
		Georgia	Dole	41	Buchanan	29
		Maine	Dole	46	Buchanan	25
		Maryland	Dole	53	Buchanan	21
		Masachusetts	Dole	48	Buchanan	25
		Rhode Island	Dole	64	Alexander	19
		Vermont	Dole	40	Buchanan	17
	7 Mar.	New York[a]	Dole			
Super Tuesday	12 Mar.	Florida	Dole	57	Forbes	20
		Louisiana	Dole	48	Buchanan	33
		Mississippi	Dole	60	Buchanan	26
		Oklahoma	Dole	59	Buchanan	22
		Oregon	Dole	51	Buchanan	21
		Tennessee	Dole	51	Buchanan	25
		Texas	Dole	56	Buchanan	21

Big Ten Tuesday	19 Mar.	Illinois	Dole	65	Buchanan	23
		Michigan	Dole	51	Buchanan	34
		Ohio	Dole	66	Buchanan	22
		Wisconsin	Dole	52	Buchanan	34
Pacific Tuesday	26 Mar.	California	Dole	66	Buchanan	18
		Nevada	Dole	52	Forbes	19
		Washington	Dole	63	Buchanan	21
Late primaries	23 Apr.	Pennsylvania	Dole	64	Buchanan	18
	7 May	District of Columbia	Dole	76	Buchanan	10
		Indiana	Dole	71	Buchanan	19
		North Carolina	Dole	71	Buchanan	13
	14 May	Nebraska	Dole	76	Buchanan	10
		West Virginia	Dole	69	Buchanan	16
	21 May	Arkansas	Dole	76	Buchanan	24
	28 May	Idaho	Dole	62	Buchanan	22
		Kentucky	Dole	74	Buchanan	8
	4 Jun.	Alabama	Dole	75	Buchanan	16
		Montana	Dole	61	Buchanan	24
		New Jersey	Dole	82	Buchanan	11
		New Mexico	Dole	75	Buchanan	8

SOURCE: "Guide to the 1996 Republican National Convention," *Congressional Quarterly*, 3 August 1996, 63.

a. New York primary was for election of delegates only.

last hurrahs. Forbes withdrew a couple of days after Super Tuesday and endorsed Dole for the nomination.

Pat Buchanan did well in the early campaign events. He beat Phil Gramm in a preseason event in Louisiana to become the main conservative candidate. He then finished second in the Iowa caucuses and won the New Hampshire primary (see the listings of caucus and primary results in tables 1.1 [pp. 10–11], 1.2, and 1.3). This led to front-cover treatment by the newsmagazines, but greater attention to Buchanan painted him as an extremist. After winning the New Hampshire primary, he faded quickly. Dole had the support of party leaders and Ralph Reed's Christian Coalition in South Carolina, and he defeated Buchanan there on 2 March. Next, Buchanan lost to Dole on all the Junior Tuesday (5 March), Super Tuesday (12 March), and Big Ten Tuesday (19 March) states, with Buchanan's only victory being in the Missouri caucuses on 9 March. Buchanan generally was limited to 25–30 percent of the vote, a percentage that put him near the top when there were nine candidates in the race but that brought him little notice when the race became essentially a Dole–Buchanan contest.

Lamar Alexander, by finishing a strong third to Dole and Buchanan in the Iowa precinct caucuses and the New Hampshire primary, positioned himself to be the mainstream candidate if Dole faltered. But the party establishment backed Dole over Alexander after Buchanan won New Hampshire, and Dole was then able to consolidate his position. Alexander had hoped to do well in southern primaries, but he finished fourth in South Carolina and only third in Georgia and had to drop out of the race.

TABLE 1.2

1996 REPUBLICAN PRESIDENTIAL PRIMARY TOTALS

| Candidate | Percentage of vote | Best showing | |
		State	Percentage of vote
Dole	59.1	New Jersey	82.3
Buchanan	21.3	Michigan	33.9
Forbes	10.1	Arizona	33.4
Alexander	3.5	New Hampshire	22.6
Keyes	3.2	New Jersey	6.7
Lugar	.9	Vermont	13.6
Gramm	.5	North Dakota	9.4
Dornan	.3	New Mexico	1.2
Taylor	.1	New Hampshire	1.4
Other	1.0		

SOURCE: "Guide to the 1996 Republican National Convention," *Congressional Quarterly,* 3 August 1996, 64.

TABLE 1.3

1996 REPUBLICAN CAUCUS RESULTS

Date	State	Winner	Percent-age	Second place	Percent-age
12 Feb.	Iowa	Dole	26	Buchanan	23
2 Mar.	Wyoming	Dole	40	Buchanan	20
5 Mar.	Minnesota	Dole	41	Buchanan	33
9 Mar.	Missouri	Buchanan	36	Dole	28

SOURCE: *Congressional Quarterly Weekly Report,* various issues, 1996.

Dole was only third in the delegate count at the end of February, with 27 delegates won versus 31 for Buchanan and 57 for Forbes (using figures from *Congressional Quarterly Weekly Report,* 2 March 1996, 577). His victories in South Carolina and in the Wyoming caucuses on 2 March plus the Puerto Rico primary on 3 March started his forward movement. He won in all eight primaries and the Minnesota caucus on 5 March, all seven primaries on 12 March (including delegate-rich Florida and Texas), and all four primaries on 19 March. Victory in California on 26 March guaranteed him enough delegates to be nominated. Dole had been able to use his greater funding in the unusually front-loaded presidential primaries to secure the nomination by the end of March. Yet he had been bloodied in the early primaries, he was nearly broke, and his nomination victory with near-record speed did not signal a united party.

Further perspective on the Republican contenders can be gained by looking at their popularity ratings. In particular, it is useful to compare the "thermometer ratings" of those who fought for the Republican nomination in 1996 or at least considered running. The NES survey asks respondents to rate these candidates on a 0–100 thermometer scale according to how cold or warm they feel toward the candidates. Some candidates were not very well known, and potential candidates would likely have lost some of their popularity had they faced the other candidates and media in the primaries, but the comparisons are still telling.

Table 1.4 (p. 14) shows the preference rankings of ten prominent Republicans based on these thermometer scores.[4] The left half of the table shows results for the full sample, while the right half of the table includes only those respondents who were able to place all ten people on the feeling thermometer scale so that comparisons are guaranteed to be for the same respondents. Colin Powell clearly emerges as the most popular figure, with a mean rating more than 10 points above that of Clinton and 15 points above that of Dole. Indeed, Bob Dole finishes a distant fourth among the Republicans. In fact, Senator Dole may not have been the strongest candidate from the Dole household; Elizabeth Dole ranks a strong second to Powell. Of course, if Powell or Elizabeth Dole or Kemp had run in the primaries, each would have been subjected to the same kind of negative advertising assault that Bob Dole faced from the Alexander, Buchanan, Forbes, and Clinton forces. Yet it is clear from table 1.4 that the two party nominees were not as exciting to the public as were some other political personalities and, especially, that there were Republicans who were more popular than Bob Dole.[5]

TABLE 1.4

1996 PREFERENCE RANKINGS (BASED ON THERMOMETER
MEANS) OF PROMINENT REPUBLICANS AND
OTHER POLITICAL LEADERS

	Including all respondents' answers			Including answers only of respondents who placed all ten Republicans on the feeling thermometer		
	Mean	Standard deviation	N	Mean	Standard deviation	N
Colin Powell	69.85	19.07	1573	71.74	18.67	705
Elizabeth Dole	60.18	21.18	1567	64.22	21.54	705
Jack Kemp	56.95	20.02	1450	60.63	20.91	705
Bob Dole	52.15	23.38	1682	55.60	23.83	705
Lamar Alexander	50.81	17.27	940	50.47	16.83	705
Steve Forbes	50.35	17.64	1296	51.75	18.44	705
Phil Gramm	49.29	19.16	1123	48.30	20.24	705
Pat Robertson	44.82	22.85	1293	42.19	23.34	705
Pat Buchanan	44.29	21.94	1545	41.14	23.55	705
Newt Gingrich	39.58	26.34	1526	41.40	29.09	705
Bill Clinton	58.82	29.61	1707			
Al Gore	57.67	24.67	1641			
Hillary Clinton	52.27	29.92	1692			
Ross Perot	39.99	23.73	1660			

SOURCE: 1996 National Election Study.

The ratings in table 1.4 are obviously confounded by partisanship. What the table does not show is that Bob Dole was popular only among Republicans. Colin Powell received a higher average rating than did Dole across all three categories of party identification and higher than Clinton among Republicans and Independents. He even posts a strong 68 rating among Democrats—a figure close to Dole's rating among Republicans.

Wrapping up the Republican nomination by the end of March meant that Dole's candidacy received less attention at a point in the campaign when Clinton was ahead in the polls. In addition, Dole was essentially out of prenomination funds by 1 April, yet he had to make it to August before receiving more money. This time frame was longer than usual because of the front-loaded primaries and the later convention date brought on by the Olympics. Regaining attention would require dramatic moves by Dole—particularly three free publicity moves. First, he surprised everyone in May by announcing that he would step down as Senate majority leader and resign his Senate seat in June. That move brought many public accolades, as leaders praised him for his distinguished career of public service. It also took him out of the line of fire in the Senate, where business had bogged down; the Democrats had not wanted to assist the Dole campaign by helping him build a record of success in legislative output. But resigning from the Senate also took away Dole's public platform. Second, he came out in favor of a 15 percent income tax cut in a manner that was reminiscent of Reagan's support for a tax cut in the 1980 campaign. Dole's stance, however, was seen as overtly political because he had not previously been a strong advocate of tax cuts and because the public was still concerned about the budget deficit. Third, Dole surprised everyone by choosing Jack Kemp as his running mate. This move again momentarily energized the Dole campaign, at least until commentators began to point out how the two men had differed on important issues over the years. Meanwhile, Clinton had virtually all of his prenomination money available, and he used it on ads and campaigning that cemented his lead in the polls.

The Republican convention came first in 1996 and provided the usual "bump" in the polls in favor of the party. The television networks gave the conventions less coverage than usual, however, because of the lack of surprises. The Democratic convention a few weeks later was equally uneventful, but it gave the Democrats enough publicity to regain the full edge they had in the polls prior to the Republican convention.

THE GENERAL ELECTION

The setting of the fall election campaign was a strong economy and no serious crises either domestic or foreign. The Republican campaign mostly emphasized the "character issue," the accumulated charges against Bill Clinton as a person of questionable integrity whose word could not be trusted —charges which continued to plague Clinton in his second term, especially regarding whether he committed perjury in his testimony about his relationship with Monica Lewinsky. By contrast, Dole was depicted as a World War II hero who had proved his leadership in the Senate. Yet Dole's age was a disadvantage (see chapter 4); had he been elected, he would have been the oldest person to take the presidential oath of office (Knox 1996). The Clinton staff targeted married people and women voters, and a combination of the two that became known as "soccer moms," with a series of campaign initiatives regarding "family issues" (Weisberg and Kelly 1997).

Televised presidential debates took place in October between Clinton

TABLE 1.5. PRESIDENTIAL VOTES BY STATE, 1996 AND 1992

	1996 Electoral vote		1996 Percentage of popular vote			1992 Percentage of popular vote			Change in Clinton's margin[a]
	Clinton (Dem)	Dole (Rep)	Clinton (Dem)	Dole (Rep)	Perot (Indep)	Clinton (Dem)	Bush (Rep)	Perot (Indep)	
Alabama		9	43	50	6	41	48	11	0
Alaska		3	33	51	11	32	41	27	−9
Arizona	8		47	44	8	37	39	24	5
Arkansas	6		54	37	8	54	36	11	−1
California	54		51	38	7	47	32	21	−2
Colorado		8	44	46	7	40	36	23	−6
Connecticut	8		53	35	10	42	36	22	12
Delaware	3		52	37	10	44	36	21	7
District of Columbia	3		85	9	3	86	9	4	−1
Florida	25		48	42	9	39	41	20	8
Georgia		13	46	47	6	44	43	13	−2
Hawaii	4		57	32	8	49	37	14	13
Idaho		4	34	52	13	29	43	28	−4
Illinois	22		54	37	8	48	35	17	4
Indiana		12	42	47	11	37	43	20	1
Iowa	7		50	40	9	44	38	19	4
Kansas		6	36	54	9	34	39	27	−13
Kentucky	8		46	45	9	45	42	14	−2
Louisiana	9		52	40	7	46	42	12	8
Maine	4		52	31	14	39	31	30	13
Maryland	10		54	38	7	50	36	14	2
Massachusetts	12		51	28	9	48	29	23	4
Michigan	18		52	38	9	44	37	19	7
Minnesota	10		51	35	12	44	32	24	4

Mississippi		7	44	49	6	41	50	9	4
Missouri	11		48	41	10	44	34	22	−3
Montana		3	41	44	14	38	36	26	−5
Nebraska		5	35	54	11	30	47	24	−2
Nevada	4		44	43	9	38	35	27	−2
New Hampshire	4		49	39	10	39	38	23	9
New Jersey	15		54	36	9	43	41	16	16
New Mexico	5		49	42	6	46	38	16	−1
New York	33		59	31	8	50	34	16	12
North Carolina		14	44	49	7	43	44	14	−4
North Dakota		3	40	47	12	32	44	23	5
Ohio	21		47	41	11	40	39	21	5
Oklahoma		8	40	48	11	34	43	23	1
Oregon	7		47	39	9	43	32	25	−3
Pennsylvania	23		49	40	10	45	36	18	0
Rhode Island	4		60	27	11	48	29	23	14
South Carolina		8	44	50	6	40	48	12	2
South Dakota		3	43	46	10	37	41	22	1
Tennessee	11		48	46	6	47	43	10	−2
Texas		32	44	49	7	37	40	22	−2
Utah		5	33	54	10	26	46	29	−1
Vermont	3		53	31	12	46	31	23	7
Virginia		13	45	47	7	41	45	14	2
Washington	11		50	37	9	44	31	24	0
West Virginia	5		52	37	11	49	36	16	2
Wisconsin	11		49	38	10	41	37	22	7
Wyoming		3	37	50	12	34	40	26	−7
Total	379	159	49	41	8	43	38	19	3

a. Values = (1996 Clinton vote − 1996 Dole vote) − (1992 Clinton vote − 1992 Bush vote).

and Dole, after the usual preliminary skirmishes about the inclusion of third-party candidates, timing, and other ground rules. The first debate followed the usual moderator format, the second one involved the two vice-presidential candidates, and the final one used a town-meeting format with questions from the audience. Clinton and Gore did well in the debates and held on to their advantage in the polls.

There was talk of an "October surprise," but the two changes in the campaign in October were different from what that phrase was intended to suggest. First, Republicans began to air campaign commercials that emphasized the importance of retaining a Republican Congress as a check on the Clinton White House, as if they were conceding the presidential race. Second, a scandal broke out about the Clinton campaign's accepting money from foreign contributors (which, if true, would be illegal), and the result was a slight erosion of support for Clinton in the polls. Clinton could still win handily, but not with the landslide required to pull in a Democratic Congress—particularly as the Republican ads played up the need for a Republican Congress.

In the end, Bill Clinton won reelection by a fairly solid margin. He won only 49 percent of the popular vote, but that compared to just 41 percent for Dole and 8 percent for Perot, with the remaining 2 percent split between other minor candidates. As usual, the victor's margin was exaggerated in the Electoral College totals, which broke 379 to 159 for Clinton over Dole (see table 1.5, pp. 16–17).

On the one hand, Clinton's 8 percent margin over the other major-party nominee could be viewed as solid, only a couple of points below the 10-point lead that would usually be considered a landslide, and his 49 percent of the popular vote was well above the 43 percent that he obtained in his 1992 victory. On the other hand, 49 percent is still less than a majority. This "on the one hand, on the other hand" victory margin turns out to be replicated in the individual-level analysis of the vote in the following chapters. The Clinton victory is apparent in every aspect of the analysis, but often with a lack of decisiveness. Clinton may have led in virtually every preelection poll, but there is no indication in the data of true depth to his victory. Furthermore, this weak victory made his situation particularly vulnerable when the Monica Lewinsky affair became public knowledge in 1998.

Clinton was reelected, but Republicans managed to keep down his victory margin enough to maintain their control of Congress. On the Senate side, Republicans increased their majority from 53–47 at the beginning of the 104th Congress to 55–45 at the beginning of the 105th, a solid majority but not filibuster-proof. On the House side, the Republicans lost nine seats, with their majority falling from a 230–204 margin to a 227–207 margin, a majority so slim as to be vulnerable to factional tensions. The Republicans edged the Democrats in the national congressional vote by a slight 48.9 percent to 48.5 percent margin. This was to be a reelection victory without being a mandate election, confirming the status quo of divided government.

Winning the presidency requires more than deterring strong challengers and maintaining a lead. It requires assembling a strong support coalition. This moves our focus to how reelection plays through at the level of the mass public. How did Clinton appeal successfully to individual voters? And what accounts for the changes since 1992, when an incumbent president was defeated? What is the impact of national forces, such as the reelection of the president, on congressional elections and congressional approval? The chapters that follow explore these important questions.

Conclusion

Reelection provides the rhythm of democracy, but it is not based on notes from a single instrument. Partisanship, ideology and issues, and candidate factors all share in the orchestration. The continuities and nuances of the reelection of President Clinton and the Republican Congress are discussed in the following chapters, with particular emphasis on comparisons with 1992. The ability of Clinton to get reelected in 1996 regardless of Republican television advertising attacks on his character, stands in marked contrast to Bush's failure to be reelected in 1992 even after his success in the Gulf War. Thus, this is an important comparison of elections if we are to understand the bases of presidential reelection.

At the same time, Clinton's reelection in 1996 was very different from other recent presidential reelections. Ronald Reagan was reelected in 1984 in a landslide over Walter Mondale, as was Richard Nixon in 1972 over George McGovern and Dwight Eisenhower in 1956 over Adlai Stevenson. Most of those elections were marked by popular incumbents, weak challengers, and healthy economies. Although the economy was very healthy in 1996, and the challenger did not prove to be strong, the incumbent was not as popular as a Reagan, a Nixon, or an Eisenhower. The result was reelection but without a majority of the vote.

Overall, we see continued emphasis on the volatility of the electorate and candidate-centered campaigns amid the continuity of reelection. Volatility is tied to disengagement of a large part of the electorate, as shown by decreasing turnout (see Nichols, Kimball, and Beck, chap. 2 in this volume), the loosening of traditional ties to the parties (see Norrander, chap. 9; Stanley and Niemi, chap. 10), and decreasing approval and increasing cynicism in government institutions (see Patterson and Monson, chap. 11). The influence of the media (see Asher and Tomlinson, chap. 8), candidate-centered campaigns, and emphasis on candidate traits in elections for both Congress (see Mondak, McCurley, and Millman, chap. 12) and the presidency (see Weisberg and Mockabee, chap. 3; Smith, Radcliffe, and Kessel, chap. 4; Mughan and Burden, chap. 7) virtually assure us of volatility in the future. John DiIulio's (1997) argument that the 1996 elections moved even more toward valence politics—politics based on symbols that almost all voters would approve of, such as a strong defense, economic prosperity, decisive leadership, or family values—suggests that our electoral setting is becoming more volatile, rather than less (see also Stokes and DiIulio 1993).

What could reverse the trend of an increasingly volatile electorate, a theme of voting behavior research for the last several decades? Clearly, voter realignment between the two major parties or the introduction of a new party could do the trick, leading to increased turnout, strengthened ties to the newly constituted parties, and renewed confidence in governing institutions. Electoral changes that fundamentally alter candidate-centered campaigns or that are aimed at reducing the high levels of cynicism toward politics may also reverse the trend. Perhaps campaign finance reforms and media innovations could have such an impact, but these possibilities are all for the future.

Along with the volatility of the electorate and the potential for valence issues to result in wide public opinion swings in 1996 came reelection—reelection of Democratic president Bill Clinton and reelection of the Republican Congress. Regardless of the tempo, reelection still provides the steady rhythm of American democracy. The chapters that follow examine in greater detail the themes that combined to produce the reelections of 1996.

PART I

The Presidential Election Outcome

2

Voter Turnout in the 1996 Election:
Resuming the Downward Spiral?

STEPHEN M. NICHOLS, DAVID C. KIMBALL,
AND PAUL ALLEN BECK

ALTHOUGH low by the standards of other democracies and nineteenth-century America, the 55 percent voter turnout achieved in the 1992 election marked a significant increase in participation from that in the 1988 election and ran against a thirty-year trend of declining turnout. Did 1992 represent a break point in American turnout, the beginning of an era of higher, maybe even rising, electoral participation?

Or was it merely a temporary phenomenon, a pause in the continuing decay of voter involvement in elections?

Writing on this subject four years ago, we expressed doubts about the staying power of this burst of electoral involvement in the United States. Noting that our evidence pointed to forces specific to the 1992 contest —heightened interest in the election and concern about the result, intertwined with what was then the novelty of Ross Perot's independent candidacy—we offered the following caution:

> Unless short-term factors emerge again to enhance voter turnout in future years, 1992 will have been merely a brief respite from the long trend of declining political participation, rather than the onset of a new era of high turnout. (Nichols and Beck 1995, 30)

This prediction was borne out in President Bill Clinton's reelection in 1996. In the absence of an interesting, competitive race and without a credible alternative to the major-party offerings, turnout in 1996 fell to 49 percent[1]—its lowest level since 1924, the first election in which women were eligible to vote in all states. Put another way, over 8 million fewer votes were cast in 1996 than in 1992. In short, more of the eligible electorate stayed home in 1996 than voted.

This chapter focuses on some of the interesting aspects of the sharp turnout decline in 1996, coming on the heels of an equally striking increase just four years earlier. Drawing on evidence from both aggregate vote totals and survey-based individual perspectives, we find that factors specific to the 1992 and 1996 contests account for much of the turnout difference between them. The 1996 election, in which Clinton's reelection seemed assured from the outset, failed to interest the citizenry to the extent that the competitive 1992 race did. Ross Perot, meanwhile, had suffered such a substantial loss of credibility as a viable presidential aspirant since 1992 that he could do little to rally voter enthusiasm in 1996. Turnout therefore fell sharply, in spite of significant efforts by the parties to mobilize their adherents, and despite recent changes in voter registration efforts and procedures that may have prevented an even more precipitous participatory decline in 1996.

This chapter concludes with our thoughts on the future of voter turnout in American national elections. We can state at the outset of this chapter that the increase in voter turnout in 1992 now appears, as we suggested four years ago, to have been but a brief respite. The election of 1996 quite likely marks the resumption of a long and steady downward spiral in U.S. political participation.

Previous Scholarship on U.S. Voter Turnout

The 1996 decline in U.S. voter turnout was startling by any measure. Relative to 1992, turnout fell by more than 6 percentage points—among the steepest four-year drops on record. The decrease was seen throughout the country: turnout fell in each of the fifty states. Despite the fact that the voting-age population increased in all but two states between 1992 and 1996, the number of ballots cast in 1996 declined in every state but two. The 49 percent turnout rate is the lowest in a U.S. presidential election in seven decades and marks the first time in the modern era that less than half of the eligible electorate voted in the country's most important national election.

The ebbs and flows of voter participation have long been an inviting target for scholarly analysis, and there is no dearth of explanations for the considerable variation in U.S. turnout levels. Observers have long established, first, that some citizens are more likely to vote than others (for fuller treatment of these differences and their longitudinal patterns, see Nichols and Beck 1995, 35–56). In terms of sociodemographic categories, research shows that those of higher socioeconomic status (generally assessed as some blend of education, income, and occupational status) vote with considerably greater regularity than do lower-status citizens (Verba and Nie 1972).

Other groups evince consistently high voting rates, too. Whites vote more than minorities; middle-aged and older citizens invariably participate more than the younger generation; males had long shown higher turnout than females, but the gender gap in turnout now seems to have vanished. Southerners and Protestants, in the aggregate, turn out less than do non-southerners and Catholics. Cultural changes in modern American society have left their imprint on national voter turnout as well: increases in residential mobility and in the number of nontraditional families have contributed to the turnout decline, as a result of weakened connections to the social structure and political system (Teixeira 1987).

Twentieth-century turnout is noticeably lower than participation rates in the latter half of the 1800s. Some (Burnham 1965) explain the decline by contending that industrial elites successfully safeguarded their interests against the possible encroachment of mass influence by fostering local and state party monopolies throughout the country. Lacking the mobilizing force of a strong workers' party, many citizens grew disenchanted with the political process, leading to a decline in electoral participation. Others (e.g., Rusk 1970; Converse 1972) point to changes in voting institutions and procedures as the cause of the early twentieth-century decline. The introduction of voter registration requirements and the implementation of the secret ("Australian") ballot, both of which occurred between 1890 and 1910, reduced electoral fraud and made voting more burdensome for honest citizens as well, thereby reducing the involvement in election for those with the weakest motivations and lowering aggregate turnout levels. Indeed, some scholars have pointed to our relatively onerous voter registration requirements as the primary reason that voter turnout in the United States has been among the lowest of all advanced democracies (Powell 1986).

Changes in individual political attitudes, rather than in voting laws or levels of interparty competition, stand out as a likely cause of the steady decline in turnout since the 1960s. Over this period, the number of Americans who profess a strong tie to a political party has waned, while the number who report a frustrating sense that citizens hold little influence over our political institutions has risen. Some believe that this combination of declining partisanship and political efficacy has contributed heavily to the post-1960 turnout drop (Abramson and Aldrich 1982; but see Cassel and Luskin 1988). By contrast, voting laws have been changed during this period to make voting easier, and competition between the Democrats and Republicans is tighter in most states than it had been earlier in this century.

Turnout in recent elections, though, evinces a volatility that cannot likely be attributed to incremental changes in long-term political attitudes. Today, it seems, changes in turnout levels hinge more on features specific to individual elections. Our previous analysis (Nichols and Beck 1995) found that interest in the election and concern about the outcome, both probably intertwined with Perot's presence in the race, elevated 1992 turnout to a twenty-eight-year high. But the dependence of turnout levels on such election-specific forces is a double-edged sword. The evidence shows that while heightened voter interest sparked a rise in participation in 1992, in 1996 the absence of this interest led to a sharp drop in voting—and the decline would likely have been even greater were it not for various efforts by political parties and interest groups to mobilize voters and to make the voter registration process easier.

The Turnout Decline

As noted earlier, the decline in turnout from 1992 to 1996 was seen in every state and the District of Columbia. As table 2.1 indicates, however, that statement masks considerable variation between states. Wyoming, for example, experienced a slight decline—from 62.3 percent in 1992 to 60.1 percent in 1996. Utah, in contrast, witnessed a turnout drop of more than 15 percentage points, from 65.1 percent in 1992 to a paltry 50.3 percent in 1996. As a first cut at explaining turnout decline, we offer some state-level tests of our expectation that low voter interest in the election, combined with Perot's loss of credibility as a viable alternative candidate, contributed to the fall in participation in 1996.

DECLINING INTEREST

One way to compare voter interest levels in the 1992 and 1996 campaigns is to examine ballot roll-off rates in the two elections. "Roll-off" refers to the well-documented decrease in the number of votes cast as one moves down the ballot. Generally, more votes are cast in the presidential contest than in races that appear farther down the ballot, presumably because the presidential campaign receives more media attention than any other contest, and the prestige of the presidency usually means that the stakes are higher. Voters, then, are relatively more interested in the presidential contest than in any other race on the ballot. The degree of roll-off from presidential to congressional races may thus be regarded as an indicator of the extent to which interest in the presidential contest exceeds interest in the congressional campaigns. If, as we argue, citizens were relatively less interested in the presidential election in 1996 than they were four years earlier, we should see evidence of this in the form of lower ballot roll-off between the presidential and congressional contests in 1996 than in 1992.[2]

This was indeed the case: the gap between presidential and congressional turnout was significantly greater in 1992 than in 1996. In 1992, roughly 8.2 million more votes were cast in the presidential contest than

TABLE 2.1. VOTER TURNOUT IN 1992 AND 1996 PRESIDENTIAL ELECTIONS,
BASED ON STATE-REPORTED TOTALS[a] (IN PERCENTAGES)

State	1992	1996	Change	State	1992	1996	Change	State	1992	1996	Change
Alabama	55.2	47.7	-7.5	Kentucky	53.7	47.5	-6.2	Ohio	60.6	54.3	-6.3
Alaska	65.4	56.9	-8.5	Louisiana	59.8	56.9	-2.9	Oklahoma	59.7	49.9	-9.8
Arizona	54.1	45.4	-8.7	Maine	72.0	64.5	-7.5	Oregon	65.7	57.5	-8.2
Arkansas	53.8	47.5	-6.3	Maryland	53.4	46.7	-6.7	Pennsylvania	54.3	49.0	-5.3
California	49.1	43.3	-5.8	Massachusetts	60.2	55.3	-4.9	Rhode Island	58.4	52.0	-6.4
Colorado	62.7	53.1	-9.6	Michigan	61.7	54.5	-7.2	South Carolina	45.0	41.5	-3.5
Connecticut	63.8	56.4	-7.4	Minnesota	71.6	64.3	-7.3	South Dakota	67.0	61.1	-5.9
Delaware	55.2	49.6	-5.6	Mississippi	52.8	45.6	-7.2	Tennessee	52.4	47.1	-5.3
District of Columbia	49.6	42.7	-6.9	Missouri	62.0	54.2	-7.8	Texas	49.1	41.2	-7.9
				Montana	70.1	62.9	-7.2	Utah	65.1	50.3	-14.8
Florida	50.2	48.0	-2.2	Nebraska	63.2	56.1	-7.1	Vermont	67.5	58.6	-8.9
Georgia	46.9	42.6	-4.3	Nevada	50.0	39.3	-10.7	Virginia	52.8	47.5	-5.3
Hawaii	41.9	40.8	-1.1	New Hampshire	63.1	58.0	-5.1	Washington	59.9	54.7	-5.2
Idaho	65.2	58.2	-7.0	New Jersey	56.3	51.2	-5.1	West Virginia	50.6	45.0	-5.6
Illinois	58.9	49.2	-9.7	New Mexico	51.6	46.0	-5.6	Wisconsin	69.0	57.4	-11.6
Indiana	55.2	48.9	-6.3	New York	50.9	46.5	-4.4	Wyoming	62.3	60.1	-2.2
Iowa	65.3	57.7	-7.6	North Carolina	50.1	45.8	-4.3				
Kansas	63.0	56.6	-6.4	North Dakota	67.3	56.3	-11.0	United States	55.2	49.0	-6.2

SOURCE: Scammon and McGillivray 1993, 1997.

a. Percentages of voting-age population.

in House races. In 1996, turnout in presidential races exceeded that in House races by approximately 6 million votes. Thus, ballot roll-off was about 2 million votes lighter in 1996. When calculated as a percentage of presidential-race turnout, ballot roll-off was roughly 8 percent in 1992, compared to 6 percent in 1996. The decline in ballot roll-off was not confined to a few states, either: when House roll-off is calculated as a percentage of the presidential vote, thirty-nine of the fifty states experienced more roll-off in 1992 than in 1996.[3]

Aggregate patterns of ballot roll-off support our contention that the 1996 turnout decline was in part a consequence of the view that the 1996 presidential campaign was relatively less interesting than the 1992 contest. We explore declining interest in the 1996 presidential campaign in much greater depth with survey data in the pages to follow, but a few additional tidbits are illuminating here. The television audience for party conventions, presidential debates, and election-night coverage dropped substantially in 1996. For example, the combined election-night audience for network television coverage of election returns produced a Nielsen rating of 28.7 in 1996, compared with a rating of 39.8 in 1992 (*New York Times*, 7 November 1996, B7).[4] Furthermore, the amount of network news coverage devoted to the presidential campaign declined in 1996 (Sabato 1997, 151).

PEROT'S FALL

The most obvious reason for low voter interest in the 1996 campaign is that the presidential outcome seemed apparent well in advance of election day, as Bob Dole never managed to cut into Bill Clinton's healthy lead in the polls. Another contributing factor, however, was Ross Perot's inability to position himself in 1996 as a viable alternative to the major-party offerings, at least to the extent that he had done in 1992.

Perot was a unique and intriguing presence in the 1992 race, and some evidence suggests that his efforts enhanced participation levels in that contest—perhaps not directly, by drawing out supporters who otherwise would not have voted (see Rosenstone, Behr, and Lazarus 1996, 254, for evidence that this did not occur), but indirectly, by stimulating greater interest in that contest among otherwise unlikely (i.e., uneducated or apathetic) voters (Nichols and Beck 1995, 64). Perot's presence, especially in the spring and summer, made the 1992 presidential contest closer and less predictable than previous elections. By 1996, however, Perot's stock had fallen considerably: public opinion polls registered increasingly negative assessments of him, probably in response to his erratic behavior and various high-profile embarrassments, particularly his poor showing in a nationally televised NAFTA debate with Vice-President Al Gore.

If Perot's attractiveness helped produce a participatory increase in 1992, one might reasonably expect his diminished personal appeal to be associated with the drop in turnout in 1996. To explore this possibility, we correlated the state-level voter turnout decline from 1992 to 1996 with the change in Perot's share of the vote in each state. There is a modest positive relationship between the two (r = .40, p < .01), indicating that statewide voter turnout fell most from 1992 to 1996 in those states in which Ross Perot's vote total saw the greatest declines between the two elections. Here, then, is circumstantial evidence suggesting that Perot's declining popularity is associated, in part, with the drop in voter participation in 1996. It is also worth mentioning here that Perot spent roughly $63.5 million on his 1992 presidential bid (at least $45 million on media advertising); in 1996 he and the Reform Party together spent $41 million. As shown later, mobilization efforts contributed substantially to turnout in both 1992 and 1996, and Perot, like his major-party rivals, mobilized supporters in both contests through the efforts financed by this money. That he spent less in 1996 suggests that his mobilization efforts were likely less effective that year, and one might reasonably conclude that this contributed to the 1996 turnout decline.

THE MOTOR VOTER LAW AND
VOTER REGISTRATION EFFORTS

Our look at aggregate patterns evident in the drop in turnout in 1996 would be incomplete if we failed to note forces that likely lessened the extent of the decline. In the spring of 1993 President Clinton signed the National Voter Registration Act (NVRA) into law. Widely known as the "motor voter" law, after a feature that allows people to register to vote at driver license agencies, the program has increased voter registration across the country, and it had boosted voter turnout in states that adopted the program before the 1993 law (Knack 1995; Rhine 1995; Ayres 1995).

While overall voter turnout declined between 1992 and 1996, we expect the drop in turnout to be smaller in states that recently implemented motor voter programs than in those that did so some time ago. Knack (1995) finds that motor voter programs provided the largest boost in registration and turnout in the first two or three elections after implementation because the voter rolls were expanded most and probably included the most motivated of the previous nonvoters. In the thirty states that adopted motor voter programs after the 1990 elections, the average drop in turnout from 1992 to 1996 was 6.2 percentage points. For the twenty states that had already adopted motor voter provisions by 1990 or were exempt from the NVRA because they already had permissive registration laws or no registration at all, the average drop in turnout from 1992 to 1996 was 7.7 percentage points. A statistical significance test shows the difference in average turnout decline of 1.5 points to be statistically robust (t = 1.78, p = .081).[5] Thus, motor voter programs may have helped lessen the drop in turnout in 1996.

We can further explore the relationship between voter registration efforts and turnout by looking at state-level changes in voter registration (measured as the percentage increase in a state's registered voters between 1992 and 1996) and the extent of turnout decline over the same period. There is a healthy negative correlation ($r = -.34$, $p < .05$) between statewide increases in registration and the drop in turnout from 1992 to 1996. In other words, the turnout decline in 1996 was the smallest in states where voter registration increased the most.

Finally, we end our aggregate analysis with a multivariate examination of statewide declines in turnout as a function of all of our explanatory variables plus the presence of Senate contests, which might have stimulated more interest. This enables us to control simultaneously for the effects of the Perot candidacy, registration changes, Senate contests, and motor voter law on state-level changes in voter turnout from 1992 to 1996. Table 2.2 presents the results of an ordinary least squares regression analysis of state-level turnout decline across the two elections.[6]

The results for equation 1 suggest that Ross Perot's waning candidacy is a principal reason for the drop in turnout in 1996. The regression coefficients in the table predict that a 10-point decline in Perot's share of the

TABLE 2.2

STATEWIDE DECLINE IN VOTER TURNOUT, 1992 TO 1996

Independent variable	Equation 1 Coefficient (Standard error)	Equation 2 Coefficient (Standard error)
Constant	5.515 ***	6.173***
	(.926)	(1.073)
Decline in Perot's share of the vote	.201 ***	.183 ***
from 1992 to 1996	(.074)	(.074)
Increase in percentage registered	−.141 ***	−.145 ***
from 1992 to 1996	(.055)	(.055)
Senate race in 1996	−1.110 **	−.979 *
but not in 1992	(.645)	(.646)
Motor voter registration implemented	—	−.850 *
after 1990		(.627)
N	51	51
Adjusted R^2	.25	.26
Standard error of estimate	2.15	2.14

SOURCE: Knack 1995; Duncan 1997; Scammon and McGillivray 1993, 1997.

NOTE: The dependent variable is statewide drop in voter turnout in percentage points from 1992 to 1996. The District of Columbia is included in the analysis.

*$p < .1$, one-tailed; **$p < .05$, one-tailed; ***$p < .01$, one-tailed.

vote—and note that Perot experienced a decline of that magnitude in over half the states in 1996—was associated with about a 2-point decline in state-wide turnout. Given that Perot's share of the vote nationwide dropped from 19 percent in 1992 to 8 percent in 1996, the Perot effect on turnout was rather important.

The multivariate results also suggest that increases in voter registration helped stem the tide of turnout decline in 1996. The regression coefficient for the registration variable indicates that a 5-point increase in voter registration reduced the drop in turnout by roughly .8 percentage points. Since nearly half the states improved voter registration by at least 5 percentage points from 1992 to 1996, it seems safe to conclude that registration programs played an important role in limiting the magnitude of turnout dropoff from 1992 to 1996.

The presence or absence of a U.S. Senate race on the ballot also accounts for some of the variation in statewide turnout, as high-visibility Senate contests can motivate voters to go to the polls. The findings in table 2.2 indicate that the turnout decline in 1996 was about 1 percentage point smaller in the seventeen states that featured Senate contests in 1996 but not in 1992. This phenomenon sheds some light on turnout in two states discussed earlier. For example, voter turnout hardly declined at all in Wyoming, partly because the state featured a competitive Senate contest in 1996, while no Senate contest graced Wyoming's ballot in 1992. By the same token, the absence of a Senate race in Utah in 1996 (after Utah held a Senate contest in 1992) partially explains that state's precipitous drop in turnout.

Finally, a second equation was estimated by adding motor voter laws to the preceding variables. As shown in equation 2 of table 2.2, even after taking into account the increased voter registration that the new law helped foster, a recent move to motor voter provisions boosted turnout. The regression coefficient indicates that the drop in voter turnout in 1996 was almost 1 percentage point lower in states that adopted motor voter programs after 1990. While motor voter programs did not increase turnout in 1996, as perhaps some had expected, these programs may have prevented turnout from dropping farther than it actually did in 1996.

An Individual-Level Look at the 1996 Turnout

The task before us now is to determine whether the differences among states in aggregate turnout patterns seen to this point are paralleled when the analytic focus turns to variations at the level of the individual voter. For this we rely on survey data collected in the biennial National Election Study (NES) series conducted by the University of Michigan's Center for Political Studies.

Bivariate Correlates of Turnout

We first explore variation in voter-participation levels in terms of the many traits and attributes long associated with turnout. The first of these, socioeconomic status (SES), clearly reflects the large participatory disparities between the traditionally low- versus high-turnout categories (see table 2.3).[7] Citizens of higher socioeconomic standing, whether assessed in terms of education, income, or occupation, went to the polls at a much higher rate than their lower-SES counterparts. The turnout difference between those of highest versus lowest education and income levels is particularly startling: in both cases the disparity was roughly 35 percentage points.

The sociodemographic correlates of turnout (see table 2.4) are equally unsurprising. As is always the case, young people were less reliable voters than were their elders; participation in the South trailed that of the rest of the nation; voting rates among Protestants were lower than among other denominations, but higher than among those professing no religious ties; and the domestically stable—married or long-time residents of an area—went to the polls in greater numbers than did the residentially mobile and the unmarried. Gender differences in participation rates, once sizable, are now statistically insignificant, and the gulf between black and white voter turnout levels is narrowing (and, as we demonstrate later, the racial disparity disappears altogether once differences in education levels are taken into account).

The attitudinal correlates of electoral participation indicate that stable, long-standing political attitudes (see table 2.5)—partisanship, external political efficacy,[8] and one's sense of citizen duty—remain reliable predictors of voter turnout. The more election-specific attitudes (see table 2.6, p. 34)—interest in the campaign (along with its behavioral counterpart, following the campaign in the newspapers) and concern about the outcome—also go a long way toward separating participants from bystanders. The lone exception

TABLE 2.3

SOCIOECONOMIC STATUS
CORRELATES OF VOTER
TURNOUT IN 1996
(IN PERCENTAGES)

	Reported turnout in 1996
Education[a]	
Less than high school	55.7
High school	69.3
Some college	80.7
College degree	89.7
Income[a]	
0–16th percentile	60.7
17–33d percentile	67.1
34–67th percentile	74.6
68–95th percentile	87.3
96–100th percentile	96.5
Occupational status[a]	
Blue collar	66.1
White collar	78.3
Professional / manager	88.9

SOURCE: 1996 National Election Study.

a. Turnout differences are statistically significant at $p < .01$.

TABLE 2.4 SOCIODEMOGRAPHIC CORRELATES OF VOTER TURNOUT IN 1996 (IN PERCENTAGES)	*Reported turnout in 1996*
Marital status[a]	
Married	83.7
Unmarried	65.9
Age[a]	
18–29	57.8
30–69	79.7
70+	85.0
Gender	
Female	76.4
Male	77.6
Race	
White	78.1
Black	70.4
Region[a]	
South	71.8
Non-South	79.3
Religion[a]	
Jewish	93.5
Catholic	80.4
Protestant	77.8
No affiliation	63.0
Residential mobility[a]	
Same residence	81.7
Moved in last four years	70.7

SOURCE: 1996 National Election Study.

a. Turnout differences are statistically significant at $p < .01$.

TABLE 2.5 LONG-TERM ATTITUDINAL CORRELATES OF VOTER TURNOUT IN 1996 (IN PERCENTAGES)	*Reported turnout in 1996*
Strength of partisanship[a]	
Strong partisans	91.1
Weak partisans, leaners	73.4
Independents	53.3
Strength of external political efficacy[a]	
High	89.6
Medium	78.2
Low	64.0
Citizen duty: willing to serve on jury[a]	
Yes	83.3
No, rather not	68.5

SOURCE: 1996 National Election Study.

a. Turnout differences are statistically significant at $p < .01$.

to this pattern is the perception regarding the closeness of the presidential race: those who foresaw a comfortable victory were no less likely to turn out than were those anticipating a narrow margin. The turnout differential between the high and low categories of the interest variable are especially striking: very interested observers voted at a rate nearly double that of the uninterested.

TABLE 2.6

ELECTION-SPECIFIC
ATTITUDINAL CORRELATES OF
VOTER TURNOUT IN 1996
(IN PERCENTAGES)

	Reported turnout in 1996
Interested in campaign?[a]	
Very much	92.4
Somewhat	75.2
Not much	49.6
Read about campaign in news-paper?[a]	
Yes	88.7
No	69.5
Will presidential race be close?	
Yes	76.1
No	77.9
Care who wins the presidency?[a]	
Yes, care	83.4
No, don't care	53.3

SOURCE: 1996 National Election Study.

a. Turnout differences are statistically significant at $p < .01$.

TABLE 2.7

MOBILIZATION CORRELATES
OF VOTER TURNOUT IN 1996
(IN PERCENTAGES)

	Reported turnout in 1996
Worked with others in the community?[a]	
Yes	91.0
No	72.6
Was contacted about registering?[a]	
Yes	80.8
No	74.6
Contacted by one of the parties?[a]	
Yes	90.8
No	71.2
Contacted by a religious group?[a]	
Yes	92.5
No	74.6
Campaign information provided at church?[a]	
Yes	89.5
No	76.1
Don't attend church	69.5
Union member in household?[a]	
Yes	83.6
No	75.6

SOURCE: 1996 National Election Study.

a. Turnout differences between yes and no responses are statistically significant at $p < .01$.

Lastly, efforts by the political parties, labor unions, and churches to mobilize the electorate appear to have enhanced voter turnout in 1996 (see table 2.7): participation rates were between 15 and 20 percentage points higher among those who were reached by such efforts. Moreover, having a union member in the household increased turnout by about 8 percent.

A MULTIVARIATE ASSESSMENT

To this point, we have examined the correlates of voter turnout in isolation. In reality, though, individuals are swayed by the concurrent influence of various forces. To assess more realistically the determinants of turnout, we must examine the suspected causal factors while taking into account the effects of the other determinants of participation. This may be achieved statistically through multivariate analysis; the results of such an analysis on 1996 voter turnout are displayed in table 2.8 (p. 36).[9]

The multivariate results give rise to a number of intriguing observations. First, note that while two of the three components of socioeconomic status emerge as significant turnout predictors—and education's effect on the probability of voting is especially powerful—only age and marital status stand out among the sociodemographic variables as reliable determinants of voter participation, once the effects of other factors are considered. In other words, the bivariate indications that the young and the unmarried vote at a lower rate than others are sustained in the multivariate analysis, but the racial, gender, regional, and religious differences in individual-level turnout behavior disappear when the simultaneous effects of the various forces affecting the turnout decision are considered. Simply put, there appear to be no meaningful turnout differences in terms of race, gender, region, and religion; these factors do nothing to account for variation in turnout once other voter characteristics are included in the same analysis.

Turning to the long-term attitudinal predictors of participation, we see that party loyalists and those with a stronger sense of their obligations as citizens were more likely to vote than were independents and those with weaker feelings of citizen duty. The turnout disparity between strong partisans versus political independents was quite large: the probability of voting among the former was fully one-third greater than among the latter. Political efficacy levels did not reliably distinguish voters from nonvoters in 1996, but this does not necessarily mean that political efficacy was unrelated to the turnout decline. Indeed, as suggested earlier (and we return to this theme in our concluding thoughts), a case can be made that the decline in efficacy since the 1960s carries a great deal of responsibility for the steady decrease in voter turnout since then (Abramson and Aldrich 1982), and 1996 may provide more evidence for this thesis. Both of the measures we used to assess political efficacy experienced rather sharp declines between 1992 and 1996. For example, only 24 percent of the 1996 NES respondents disagreed with the statement that "public officials don't care what people like me think," compared to the 38 percent in 1992. Similarly, the percentage of survey participants who felt that they had a say in what government decides fell from 58 percent in 1992 to 45 percent four years later. This is significant, for although political efficacy evinced no direct impact on 1996 turnout, efficacy is moderately correlated with our measures of interest in the campaign and

TABLE 2.8.

DETERMINANTS OF REPORTED VOTER TURNOUT IN 1996

Independent variable	Coefficient (Standard error)	P value	Change in probability
Constant	$-6.72***$ (.84)	.000	—
Socioeconomic variables			
Education	.44*** (.11)	.000	.23
Occupational status	.14 (.13)	.259	n.s.
Income	.19* (.09)	.042	.12
Sociodemographic variables			
Race	$-.18$ (.23)	.439	n.s.
Gender	.23 (.17)	.167	n.s.
Age	.68*** (.17)	.000	.20
South	$-.29$ (.18)	.119	n.s.
Religion	$-.01$ (.13)	.920	n.s.
Married	.62*** (.19)	.001	.10
Residential mobility	$-.24$ (.18)	.169	n.s.
Long-term political attitudes			
Strength of partisanship	.95*** (.16)	.000	.33
Strength of external political efficacy	.25 (.17)	.146	n.s.
Sense of citizen duty	.41** (.17)	.016	.07
Election-specific political attitudes			
Interest in election	.62*** (.14)	.000	.19
Concern about outcome	.68*** (.19)	.000	.12
Read about campaign in newspaper	.48*** (.19)	.010	.07
Perceived closeness of election	.11 (.17)	.499	n.s.

TABLE 2.8 — CONTINUED

Independent variable	Coefficient (Standard error)	P value	Probability change
Mobilization variables			
Union member in household	.37*	.098	.06
	(.22)		
Contacted by a political party	.69***	.002	.10
	(.22)		
Contacted by a religious group	.83**	.019	.10
	(.35)		
Attends religious services	.60***	.002	.10
	(.19)		
Works in a community organization	.62***	.013	.09
	(.25)		

N	1325
χ^2	462.2 (22 df/$p < .001$)
−2 log likelihood	955.9
Pseudo-R^2	.45
Percentage correctly predicted	83.2
Percentage baseline prediction	77.6

SOURCE: 1996 National Election Study.

NOTE: Dependent variable is coded 1 for voters, 0 for nonvoters. The independent variables are coded such that the higher turnout categories of the variables are given higher scores (with the exception of the South [coded 1 for South, 0 for the rest of the country], residential mobility [coded 1 for moved in the last four years, 0 for same residence], and race [coded 1 for nonwhites, 0 for whites]).

The probability change column indicates the difference in probability of voting between people in high-turnout versus people in low-turnout categories of each variable. The abbreviation "n.s." means that the explanatory variable was not statistically significant; therefore no probability change score was calculated.

*$p < .1$, two-tailed; **$p < .05$, two-tailed; ***$p < .01$, two-tailed.

attention to election news coverage—and thus the decline in efficacy may have been an indirect contributor to the fall in participation: citizens who felt they had no influence over government decisions may have taken little interest in the campaign and may in turn have seen little point in voting.

Finally, perhaps the most noteworthy result of this analysis is the fact that all but one of the election-specific attitudinal and mobilization variables survive this stringent multivariate test and remain substantial predictors of 1996 voter turnout. The lone exception, perceived closeness of the race, is no surprise because it was not linked to participation in the bivariate test; furthermore, polls taken throughout 1996 suggested that the presidential contest would not be very close. This finding serves as the springboard for our main argument about the decline in turnout in 1996 and thus warrants more discussion. It is particularly important to note the difference in the probability of voting between those in the high-turnout versus those in the low-turnout categories of these variables. This analysis suggests, for example, that someone contacted by a political party over the course of the 1996 campaign was about 10 percent more likely to vote than someone the parties missed; contact with religious organizations and community groups elicited similar effects, as did concern over the election results and attending to the proceedings in the papers. Interest in the election, though, looms especially large: the "very interested" were almost a fifth more likely to vote than the "not much interested."

At this juncture, we should compare the findings from our multivariate model of 1996 turnout with a similar analysis of voter participation in 1992. This contrast, presented in table 2.9, allows us to assess whether or not the nature of the relationship between our predictor variables and voter turnout changed across the two election contests.

With minor exceptions,[10] the independent variables used to predict turnout in both elections are essentially the same as those employed in our earlier multivariate analysis (see table 2.8, p. 36). In comparing the logit models for 1992 and 1996 turnout, we see that most of the explanatory factors have largely comparable effects on turnout in both elections, although some exceptions do emerge. The coefficient for a recent move, for example, is large and significant in the 1992 analysis, but small and insignificant in 1996—perhaps an indication that the motor voter law and other registration efforts have indeed made a difference; a move to a new state usually entails a new driver's license and registration, and many who undertake such a move can now also register to vote with little additional effort.

Also, the effects of age and strength of partisanship appear weaker in 1992 than in 1996; both disparities may well be explained by the greater relevance of a third party contender in 1992. Young people and independents, often one and the same, were more likely to have voted in 1992 than in 1996, and Perot drew sizable support from these groups. In 1996, some of these Perot supporters may have opted to stay home on election day.

We are particularly intrigued by the effects of the election-specific turnout factors across the two contests. In both elections, the impact of interest in the campaign (and related forces) and voter mobilization efforts is substantial. There are some differences here, of course: it appears that religious groups were more effective at mobilizing voters in 1996 than had been the case four years earlier, but that the reverse was true for labor unions. On the whole, though, mobilization and interest factors had comparable effects on turnout in both 1992 and 1996; the coefficients for the interest variables, in particular, are quite similar across the two elections. As we demonstrate shortly, however, those relatively stable coefficients mask the pronounced impact of these short-term political attitudes on the 1996 turnout decline:

TABLE 2.9

COMPARING DETERMINANTS OF VOTER TURNOUT,
1992 AND 1996

Independent variable	1992 Coefficient (Standard error)	1996 Coefficient (Standard error)
Constant	−5.47***	−7.23***
	(.50)	(.67)
Socioeconomic variables		
Education	.65***	.47***
	(.08)	(.10)
Income	.18**	.25***
	(.07)	(.09)
Sociodemographic variables		
Race	.06	−.22
	(.19)	(.23)
Gender	.47***	.23
	(.14)	(.17)
Age	.30**	.68***
	(.13)	(.17)
South	−.35**	−.27
	(.16)	(.18)
Religion	.08	−.02
	(.12)	(.13)
Married	.13	.56***
	(.15)	(.18)
Residential mobility	−.79***	−.26
	(.15)	(.18)
Long-term political attitudes		
Strength of partisanship	.57***	.94***
	(.12)	(.16)
Strength of external political efficacy	.30**	.25
	(.13)	(.17)
Sense of citizen duty	.47***	.43***
	(.14)	(.17)
Election-specific political attitudes		
Interest in election	.60***	.62***
	(.11)	(.14)
Concern about outcome	.67***	.69***
	(.16)	(.19)
Read about campaign in newspaper	.59***	.50***
	(.15)	(.19)
Perceived closeness of election	.15	.12
	(.17)	(.17)

TABLE 2.9 — CONTINUED

Independent variable	1992 Coefficient (Standard error)	1996 Coefficient (Standard error)
Mobilization variables		
Union member in household	.44**	.35
	(.21)	(.22)
Contacted by a political party	.98***	.79***
	(.24)	(.22)
Attends religious services	.13	.61***
	(.16)	(.19)
Works in a community organization	.42**	.63***
	(.21)	(.24)
N	1863	1337
Percentage correctly predicted	84.0	83.7

SOURCE: 1992 and 1996 National Election Studies.

NOTE: Dependent variable is coded 1 for voters, 0 for nonvoters. The independent variables are coded such that the higher turnout categories of the variables are given higher scores (with the exception of the "South" variable, which is coded 1 for South, 0 for the rest of the country).

*$p < .1$, two-tailed; **$p < .05$, two-tailed; ***$p < .01$, two-tailed.

the effect of interest and related forces was relatively constant across the two elections, but the proportion of interested citizens was not.

DIFFERENT ELECTORAL CONTEXTS: 1992 AND 1996

In our multivariate analysis, then, we find few surprises among the SES, sociodemographic, and long-term attitudinal predictors of voter turnout. With respect to these factors, citizens in certain categories and those holding particular attitudes were more likely to vote than others; education, age, and strength of partisanship evinced particularly strong effects on the likelihood of voting.

But the composition of the American electorate in terms of most of these attributes and attitudes fluctuates very little over a single four-year span, and thus we cannot look to changes in them as the culprit behind the 6-percentage-point decline in participation from 1992 to 1996. Instead, we should consider whether things changed from 1992 to 1996 with respect to the important turnout determinants that can vary significantly from election to election: the short-term attitudes and features specific to a particular presidential contest. Doing so (see table 2.10), we see that 1992 and 1996 provided very different electoral contexts, and here we find compelling evidence of the causes of the 1996 participatory downturn.

TABLE 2.10

DIFFERING ELECTION CONTEXTS: 1992 VERSUS 1996
(IN PERCENTAGES)

	1992	1996
Interest in the campaign		
Very interested in the presidential campaign[a]	39	27
Believe the presidential contest will be close[a]	79	52
Read about presidential campaign in the news-paper[a]	66	58
Strong preference for one's presidential selection[a]	80	69
Care a good deal who wins the presidency	75	79
Mobilization		
Contacted by either party[a]	20	29
Contacted to register or vote	37	37
The Perot factor		
Mean Perot feeling thermometer rating[a] (post-election survey[b])	52.8	43.3

SOURCES: 1992 and 1996 National Election Studies.

a. Difference between 1992 and 1996 is statistically significant at $p < .01$.

b. Perot's mean thermometer score in the 1996 pre-election survey (40.0) was only a hair above that of Newt Gingrich (39.6), the least popular potential candidate. Perot's score ranked behind those of even Pat Buchanan (44.3) and Hillary Clinton (52.3).

The lack of a competitive presidential contest, compounded by the absence of a viable third-party alternative, clearly dampened the electoral enthusiasm of the American public; the proportion of citizens in the high-interest categories declined significantly in four of the five interest variables assessed in both the 1992 and 1996 NES surveys (and the increase in the one exception was modest). In three of the four categories, in fact, the decrease was greater than 10 percentage points. Opinions of Perot (measured by his average "feeling thermometer"[11] score) likewise fell by a similar margin.[12] Note, though, that the level of party mobilization increased substantially in 1996, suggesting that the decline in turnout could have been even greater were it not for the mitigating influence of increased efforts to motivate citizens to go to the polls.

The evidence in tables 2.8 through 2.10 should be considered in tandem as the linchpin for our explanation of the 1996 turnout decline. Our examinations of the 1992 and 1996 elections indicate that very little changed in terms of the determinants of voter turnout in either contest. What did change over four years, and therefore what caused participation levels to wane in 1996, was the relative proportion of the American electorate falling in the election-specific categories most conducive to high turnout.

In sum, the individual-level findings fit neatly with our state-level con-clusions. Factors specific to particular elections—interest in the contest, the presence of an attractive third-party option, efforts to mobilize the elector-ate—went a long way toward determining turnout levels in both 1992 and 1996. The difference between the two contests was that far fewer citizens were intrigued by the 1996 race in general, and Perot in particular could do little to generate interest. As a result, turnout declined, though not as much as it probably would have were it not for the combination of (1) efforts of political parties and other organizations to get out the vote, and (2) easier voter registration procedures owing to the motor voter law.

The Implications of Declining Voter Turnout

In their classic study of the patterns and consequences of political participa-tion, Sidney Verba and Norman Nie (1972) liken democratic politics to a system of inputs and outputs, and note that bias in the participatory input will be reflected in biased policy output. The relevance of this point to our analysis is clear: one implication of falling voter turnout is a shrinking voice in the policy process for those who choose not to vote. When the proportion of those who so choose reaches majority status in a nation, as it apparently now has in the United States, one might rightly view the situation as a seri-ous breakdown in representative democracy.[13] This may suggest, in turn, that the solution to this problem is as simple as getting out to vote. Indeed, rare is the discussion of the ills of American democracy that lacks such fa-miliar and facile refrains as "If you don't vote, don't complain!"

But one might also view the steady fall in voter participation over re-cent decades, interrupted only temporarily in 1992, as a rational response on the part of citizens who no longer regard the political arena as a legitimate and worthwhile venue for addressing their concerns. Public opinion polls provide unmistakable evidence that large proportions of Americans have lost faith in their government: the public harbors greater distrust and cyni-cism about politics and government today than even during the Watergate scandals of the 1970s (Lewis 1996, 223). The almost-daily revelations of widespread abuses involving campaign finance in 1996, along with the ap-parent unwillingness of elected officials in both the White House and Con-gress to address the problem, surely cannot help matters. Indeed, the lasting image of the 1996 election and the subsequent investigations stemming from it may well be the perception that elected officials represent those who bank-roll their campaigns and that voting is therefore an exercise of greater sym-bolic than substantive meaning. The Center for Public Integrity, one of sev-eral nonpartisan organizations keeping watch on the growing intrusion of money into the U.S. political system, notes that close to $1.5 billion was contributed to campaigns for federal elective office in 1992—in 1996, some estimate that as much as half a billion dollars was spent contesting the presidency alone—and that fewer than 1 percent of the population produced more than three-fourths of that money (Lewis 1996, 221). Charles Lewis, director of the Center, asserts that a direct link exists between this situation and the decline in citizen participation in the political process:

> As passive participants watching and thereby allowing our elected officials to assume and maintain power in a money-dependent manner, we detach ourselves as citizens from the process because it all seems overwhelming. . . . The candidates too frequently speak in soothing, irrelevant bromides, and unless you are a wealthy donor, they are difficult to talk to directly before or after the election. We either go to the polls mumbling about our limited choices, or we don't bother to vote at all. The distrust and disenchantment about politics in America today are not particularly mysterious. (1996, 222)

The long-term decline in voter participation, briefly interrupted in 1992 but apparently back on track now, seems a clear reflection of the rising discontent with the American political process. In addition, there is evidence that the increasingly common negative campaigning "demobilizes" voters in particular contests and contributes to discontent even more (Ansolabehere, Iyengar, Simon, and Valentino 1994). This is no minor problem, for an increasingly and perpetually disaffected citizenry poses a serious threat to the health of a democracy. The lessons of history suggest that citizens who feel powerless within the confines of normal political processes are susceptible to mobilization by demagogues and may eventually vent their frustrations in decidedly nondemocratic and even violent ways.

Low voter turnout also has implications for the political capital wielded by those elected by a comparatively small percentage of the citizenry. Indeed, much has been made of the fact that Clinton's election and reelection were both achieved with pluralities of the popular vote, rather than by outright majorities. Such a discussion usually centers on the difficulty of winning more than 50 percent of the vote in a three-way contest, but the problem is exacerbated further when the mere plurality behind the winner is drawn from less than half of those eligible to vote in the first place. In Clinton's case, his reelection was delivered by just 24 percent of the electorate (he won 49 percent of the ballots, cast by the 49 percent of those eligible to vote). Claims of a reelection "mandate" are hard to sustain on such grounds, and Clinton's ability to push his political agenda through Congress has undoubtedly suffered as a result.

We should also note that declining interest in politics and the resulting downturn in electoral participation raise the stakes in the partisan controversy over voter mobilization and demobilization. Democrats murmur that the line between church and state is blurred when the Christian Coalition distributes millions of voter education pamphlets at churches before election day, while Republicans complain about voter fraud when civil rights groups help register ethnic and racial minorities. Both sides criticize one another for the barbs and attacks of the negative campaign. The low level of participation has heightened concern on both sides about who actually votes and, of course, for which side they are going to vote. Given our findings that mobilization efforts appear quite successful in the face of declining voter participation, electoral mobilization will likely remain a source of partisan bickering and scholarly inquiry for some time.

Short of a dramatic reversal in the momentum of public cynicism—an unlikely event, given the failure to address the sources of that cynicism—there is little reason to expect voter turnout to increase in the foreseeable future. True, the presidential race in 2000 will feature no incumbent, and two fresh faces may spark some interest in the contest and perhaps provide another brief respite from the longer trend of declining participation. Even this possibility, though, speaks to the underlying problem: contemporary voter participation levels are highly contingent on the entertainment value of specific elections, and in the absence of such value, large segments of the citizenry see little point in going to the polls. This offers scant hope for a broad, sustained revival of electoral involvement in the United States. Instead, a continuation of low, maybe even declining, voter turnout appears far more likely.

3

Attitudinal Correlates
of the 1996 Presidential Vote:
The People Reelect a President

HERBERT F. WEISBERG AND
STEPHEN T. MOCKABEE

HOW WAS Bill Clinton reelected? Clinton's reelection was a stark contrast to George Bush's failed reelection try in 1992. Indeed, Clinton was the first Democratic president since Franklin Delano Roosevelt to win reelection. In this chapter we use National Election Study (NES) surveys to analyze voting in the 1996 presidential election. We find that all the usual suspects—parties, issues, and candidate factors—played a role in Clinton's reelection, but with particular emphasis on retrospective evaluations of the economy, on ideology, and on an empathy gap that served to mitigate the importance of the integrity issue, plus the increasing importance of religion to American elections.

It has long been common practice to study voting behavior in U.S. presidential elections by separately analyzing the effects of party identification, issues, and candidates on the electoral outcome (Campbell, Converse, Miller, and Stokes 1960; Abramson, Aldrich, and Rohde 1994). We follow that pattern in tracing the determinants of the 1996 presidential election with special attention to changes since the 1992 election. The distribution of party identification across the electorate and changes in it since the last election are examined first because they set the playing field for the election (Weisberg and Kimball 1995). Ideology and issues are next examined together because they establish the terrain for the election, especially whether the public is satisfied with the status quo on important issues such as the economy. The candidate factor is examined last because candidates project their images to the public within this constrained setting.

We find that party identification remained somewhat favorable to Clinton in 1996, but not enough to decide the election by itself. Evaluations of the national economy also worked in favor of the administration. The only way for the Republicans to offset these Democratic advantages would have been on the candidate qualities side, where Clinton's image was not especially favorable. Challenger Dole, however, also lacked a strong positive image.

The remainder of this chapter uses the 1996 National Election Study data to support these findings. We employ the closed-ended survey questions in which respondents must choose between a fixed set of answers. We show the distributions of party identification, issues, and candidate factors in 1996, along with changes in their values since 1992 and their direct relationships with the vote choice. After discussing each of these separately, we estimate their combined impact on the 1996 vote.

Party Identification

Political scientists have been monitoring the changing distribution of party identification in the electorate for more than four decades. Democratic dominance in the 1950s had fallen over the years, so the playing field had become very even among voters by 1988. A Democratic lead in partisanship returned in 1992, though well below the level of the pre-1984 period. The dramatic Republican congressional victory in 1994 was accompanied by claims of party realignment. Those early expectations, however, did not materialize as far as party identification is concerned; the Democratic lead in partisanship was maintained in 1996.

THE PARTISAN ADVANTAGE

The Democratic advantage in partisanship in 1996 was evidenced by 38 percent of the public identifying as Democrats versus 28 percent considering themselves Republicans. This Democratic advantage remains even if independents who admit they are closer to a party are considered partisans, with 51 percent of the NES sample being closer to the Democrats versus 40 percent being closer to the Republicans. Table 3.1 shows this distribution of party identification within the context of the presidential elections from 1952 through 1996. The Democratic lead in 1996 is certainly not overwhelming, but neither is there any sign of erosion in the early 1990s. This conclusion holds whether those independents who admit being closer to a party are classified as independents (Miller and Shanks 1996, chap. 6) or as partisans (Keith et al. 1992).

TABLE 3.I. PARTY IDENTIFICATION BY YEAR, 1952–96 (IN PERCENTAGES)

	1952	1956	1960	1964	1968	1972	1976	1980	1984	1988	1992	1996
Democrats	47.2	43.6	45.3	51.7	45.4	40.4	39.7	40.8	37.0	35.2	35.4	37.7
Independents	22.6	23.4	22.8	22.8	29.1	34.7	36.1	34.5	34.2	35.7	38.0	33.0
Republicans	27.2	29.1	29.4	24.5	24.2	23.4	23.2	22.4	27.1	27.5	25.7	28.4
Democratic plurality	20.0	14.5	15.9	27.2	21.2	17.0	16.5	18.4	9.9	7.7	9.7	9.3
Democrats plus leaners	56.8	49.9	51.6	61.0	55.2	51.5	51.5	52.3	47.8	47.0	49.3	51.1
Pure independents	5.8	8.8	9.8	7.8	10.5	13.1	14.6	12.9	11.0	10.6	11.5	8.2
Republicans plus leaners	34.3	37.4	36.1	30.2	32.9	33.9	32.9	32.6	39.5	40.8	38.3	39.8
Democratic plurality	22.5	12.5	15.5	30.8	22.3	17.6	18.6	19.7	8.3	6.2	11.0	11.3

SOURCE: 1952–96 National Election Studies.

NOTE: Leaners are treated as independents in the upper half of the table and as partisans in the lower half.

TABLE 3.2. POPULARITY OF PARTIES BY YEAR, 1964–96 (THERMOMETER SCORES)

	1964	1968	1972	1976	1980	1984	1988	1992	1996
Democrats	71.5	63.5	66.1	62.7	61.1	62.1	61.5	58.5	57.9
Republicans	59.4	62.1	62.9	57.4	56.9	57.9	59.2	51.7	53.4
Difference	12.1	3.2	3.2	5.3	4.2	4.2	2.3	6.8	4.5
Correlation	−0.28	−0.18	0.02	0.01	−0.23	−0.40	−0.39	−0.27	−0.42

SOURCE: 1964–96 National Election Studies.

The Democratic lead in partisanship is echoed in the NES party thermometer question (see table 3.2). Respondents are asked to rate how warm they feel toward each party on a 0-100 thermometer scale. The Democratic Party was advantaged in 1996, with people giving the Democrats a 58° average rating compared to the 53° they gave the Republicans. The Democratic average was very similar to its 1992 value, however, whereas the Republican value had climbed slightly since 1992. The Democratic advantage on the thermometers was comparable to recent years but was well below its high value during the 1964 Johnson landslide election.

POLITICAL INDEPENDENCE AND PARTY POLARIZATION

While the partisan advantage remained fairly flat between 1992 and 1996, there were more interesting changes in political independence. As shown in table 3.1 (p. 47), there was a decline in independence during the first Clinton administration. The 33 percent independents in 1996 is the lowest figure for a presidential election since 1970. The 8 percent pure independents is the first time since 1964 that less than 10 percent of the public were in this category during a presidential election year. The story of the past several decades has been one of increasing independence, so even a modest decline is worthy of some attention.

It is possible to examine the timing of this decline more closely. Figure 3.1 (p. 50) shows the distribution of independence in the CBS News/*New York Times* polls over the past several years. First, it should be observed that there was a decline in independence during the Reagan years, as party identification was moving in the Republican direction. The proportion of independents soon rose again, which may be why the early 1980s decline received little notice. Indeed, the proportion of independents kept rising through the first year of the Clinton term, but then it fell starting in late 1995. Table 3.1 shows that neither party benefited disproportionately from this decline in independents. It is more that the partisan conflict between the Republican 104th Congress and the Democratic president polarized the country, with some independents moving to the Republican side and others to the Democratic side. It is too early to tell whether this is as temporary an aberration as was the shift in the early 1980s or whether it marks a more permanent shift in public sentiment.

The decline in independents in 1996 is a sign of an increased polarization between the parties that is also evident in the correlation between the Democratic and Republican thermometers being much more negative than in 1992 (see table 3.2). The correlation between the two party thermometers was −.42 in 1996. To put this value into context, the party thermometers were actually independent of one another in the 1970s but became strongly negatively correlated in 1984 and 1988. The polarization level declined in

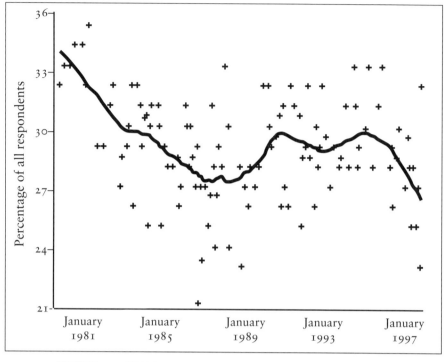

FIGURE 3.1. RESPONDENTS CLAIMING TO BE INDEPENDENTS,
1981–97

SOURCE: CBS News/*New York Times* polls.
NOTE: A Lowess smoothing function is shown (tension = .10).

1992 but went back in 1996 to the 1984–88 level. Again, there is no way to
tell at this time whether the increased polarization in 1996 will be long-term,
or whether it is just a temporary oscillation.

PARTISANSHIP AND THE VOTE

In any event, the Democratic lead in partisanship was successfully translated
into Democratic voting for president. Table 3.3 shows the relationship between party identification and presidential vote in 1996. The relationship
between party identification and vote was relatively low in 1992, especially
because of Perot's strong showing. With Perot's weaker vote in 1996, the relationship between party identification and vote returned to more familiar
territory. As expected, most partisans voted along party ties. More than 90
percent of strong partisans supported their party's candidate. Nevertheless,
short-term forces generally worked in favor of Clinton. He received a

greater vote proportion among Democratic partisans than Dole received from Republican partisans. Weak Democrats gave Clinton about 10 percent more of their votes than weak Republicans gave Dole; similarly, leaning Democrats gave Clinton about 10 percent more of their votes than leaning Republicans gave Dole. Note also that weak partisans supported their party's candidate at a greater rate than did leaners, contrary to the intransitivity that often exists in the relationship between partisanship and vote (Petrocik 1974).

TABLE 3.3.

VOTE BY PARTY IDENTIFICATION, 1996 (IN PERCENTAGES)

	Strong Dem	Weak Dem	Indep Dem	Pure indep	Indep Rep	Weak Rep	Strong Rep	Total
Dole	1.6	10.3	7.3	41.3	65.5	71.3	94.7	39.7
Perot	2.9	6.6	16.3	20.8	9.7	9.9	1.3	7.6
Clinton	95.5	83.1	76.4	37.8	24.7	18.8	4.0	52.7

SOURCE: 1996 National Election Study.

Yet table 3.3 also contains a surprise. When a candidate wins the presidency decisively, that candidate usually wins the votes of independents. Clinton did win the vote of independents, but pure independents broke slightly in Dole's favor in 1996. There were fewer pure independents than in recent presidential election years, but those who were in this category did not confirm the short-term forces that were at work in the election. This suggests a lack of depth to the Democratic victory that will be borne out as we continue through our examination of forces affecting individual voting.

In conclusion, the Democrats have grown used to having a lead in party identification, and they still benefited from that lead in 1996. But that advantage was not large enough to ensure victory for their party. Victory would still require that the issue and candidate factors not work to their disadvantage. Yet it is instructive to compare this situation with that faced by the Republicans in 1992. Bush was at a disadvantage in partisanship that year, so other factors would have had to be clearly in his favor for him to have been reelected. By contrast, Clinton in 1996 was advantaged by partisanship, so he could coast to four more years in the White House so long as the other factors were not definitively to his disadvantage.

Ideology and Issues

Elections are influenced by both long-term ideological factors and short-term issue factors. In addition to long-term predispositions that become activated in the campaign, many specific issues surface during a campaign and resonate with voters. Overall, the net impact of both ideology and more specific issues in the 1996 campaign was decidedly mixed.

LONG-TERM IDEOLOGICAL FACTORS

GENERAL IDEOLOGY — As in 1992, Clinton did not stress ideology in his 1996 campaign. The Republicans tried to tag him as a liberal, but this issue did not catch on in the campaign. Dole was seen as closer to the public on ideology, but the difference was not sizable.

The 1996 NES questionnaire asked people to locate themselves and the nominees on a 7-point ideological scale, where 1 is the most liberal response and 7 the most conservative. The average respondent was located at 4.3 on the scale, which was .8 more liberal than they saw Dole but 1.2 steps more conservative than they saw Clinton. Thus, the average respondent was .4 units closer to where Dole had been placed than to where Clinton had been placed.

The first row of table 3.4 summarizes these results, showing the average positions of the respondents as well as the average locations given to the candidates. Results are also shown for 1984 through 1992 for comparison purposes. The average respondent drifted slightly in a conservative direction from 1992 to 1996. There had been a similar drift in the liberal direction during the Republican administrations through 1992 (see also Stimson 1991, esp. chap. 6), but that was reversed during the Clinton term in office. At the same time, the ideological judgment of Clinton in 1996 was nearly identical to that in 1992. He might have tacked to the left in his first two years and tacked to the right in his second two years, but the net effect was that the public's view of his ideology had not changed. In particular, Republican attempts to tar him as a liberal failed. Meanwhile, candidate Dole was seen as similar ideologically to George Bush, rather than as conservative as Ronald Reagan had been judged in 1984. Dole was seen as slightly closer to the average respondent's position, with about the same edge on ideology as helped reelect Reagan in 1984 and helped get Bush elected in 1988. Nevertheless, this profile on ideology was not strong enough to carry Dole through to victory.

OTHER 7-POINT SCALES — The NES preelection survey asked respondents to place themselves and the nominees on 9 more specific 7-point issue scales. The results are also shown in table 3.4, with comparative results for the same scales when they were asked back through 1984. The conservative drift from 1992 to 1996 on the general ideology scale is echoed on 5 of the 6 issue scales that were asked in both surveys. The only issue on which the average respondent did not move to the right since 1992 was the role of women in society—whether they should be in the workplace or at home.

TABLE 3.4. AVERAGE PLACEMENT ON 7-POINT ISSUE SCALES, 1984–96

	1996 average position					1992 average position				1988 average position				1984 average position			
	R	Tau_c vote	Dole	Clinton	Diff.	R	Bush	Clinton	Diff.	R	Bush	Dukakis	Diff.	R	Reagan	Mondale	Diff.
General ideology	4.34	.66	5.14	3.15	-.39	4.22	5.03	3.17	-.24	4.37	5.12	3.24	-.38	4.44	5.31	3.16	-.41
Cut services or spending	4.13	.56	4.84	3.08	-.34	3.88	4.69	2.98	-.09	3.85	4.45	2.90	-.35	2.96	4.11	2.00	.19
Gov't health insurance	4.02	.52	5.10	2.83	-.11	3.41				3.84							
Guaranteed job	4.51	.50	5.09	3.25	-.68	4.28	5.14	3.49	.07	4.41	5.04	3.38	-.40	4.13	5.00	3.28	.02
Environment v. regulation	3.41	.44	4.58	3.20	.96												
Gov't should help blacks	4.87	.37	5.01	3.30	-1.43	4.69				4.68							
Defense spending	4.04	.32	4.67	3.92	.51	3.52	4.82	3.32	1.10	3.93	5.28	3.31	.73	3.99	5.67	3.39	1.08
Environment v. jobs	3.52	.30	4.56	3.43	.95												
Equal role for women	2.22	.27	3.39	2.15	1.10	2.23				2.60							
Gov't solve crime problem	4.43	.25	5.13	3.63	-.10												

SOURCE: 1984–96 National Election Studies.

NOTE: Values are the average scores on 7-point scale, where 1 is the most liberal answer. Differences indicate how much closer the average respondent (R) is to the Democratic than to the Republican candidate (larger values are closer).

This is also the question on which the public's attitudes were most liberal. The scales that were most closely related to the major party vote in 1996 (as shown by the column of Kendall's tau_c coefficients in table 3.4)[1] were the scales on general ideology, on the choice between cutting government services and spending, on government health insurance, and on government guarantees of jobs and living standards.

All in all, these scales do not show a clear advantage for either candidate. Dole was clearly seen as closer to the average respondent regarding government aid to blacks, while Clinton was closer on the role of women in society. Affirmative action was more related to the major party vote decision than was the role of women, but neither of these issues had a strong relationship to the vote. Dole was advantaged on two scales relating to the economic scope of the federal government (on guaranteeing jobs and on cutting spending versus cutting government services), while Clinton was advantaged on two scales relating to the environment. The two economic scales were more strongly related to the vote than were the two environment scales, but the candidate advantage on these scales was less. Meanwhile, crime and health insurance did not strongly advantage either candidate. These results suggest a draw, with neither candidate scoring an across-the-board advantage. Each candidate hoped that his best issues would be the most relevant in actual voting, but neither candidate was consistently favored on these issues.[2] Dole was actually viewed as closer to the average citizen's position on a majority of the specific issues in table 3.4, but winning the election clearly required more than that—voters weighed these different issues unequally in their vote decisions and/or the public cared more about other issues and factors than the 7-point scales included in the NES survey.

THE SIZE OF GOVERNMENT — Much of the domestic political debate of the past few decades has been about the proper size and role of government. Lyndon Johnson launched the Great Society in 1965 after defeating Barry Goldwater's conservative appeals in the 1964 election. Ronald Reagan's 1980 victory was seen as a victory for conservatism, but the Reagan Revolution's lasting legacy was less than seemed likely at the time. The election of a Republican Congress in 1994 was a further gain for the conservative movement, so much so that Bill Clinton himself proclaimed the end of the era of big government.

The 1992 and 1996 NES surveys contain a fascinating series of questions about the proper role of government that are useful in tracing changes during Clinton's first term. These items show a conservative shift (see table 3.5). For example, 51 percent of the public felt the government should be doing more, compared to 63 percent four years earlier. Similarly, 49 percent of the public felt that economic problems should be handled by a strong government, compared to 70 percent four years earlier. Also, when asked to

TABLE 3.5. VOTE BY VIEWS ON THE SIZE OF GOVERNMENT IN 1992 AND 1996
(IN PERCENTAGES)

| Question | 1996 vote | | | | 1992 vote | | | |
Answer	Clinton	Dole	Perot	All voters	Clinton	Bush	Perot	All voters
Proper role of government								
The less, the better	28.7	62.1	9.2	49	25.0	51.6	23.4	34
Should do more	75.1	18.7	6.0	51	62.3	21.5	16.3	63
Economic problems should be handled by								
Free market	27.9	63.1	9.0	51	24.4	51.9	23.7	25
Strong government	70.3	23.1	6.6	49	58.0	25.1	16.9	70
Why government has grown								
Doing things people should do for themselves	32.4	59.0	8.6	51	30.6	44.8	24.6	38
Problems have become bigger	73.7	19.9	6.4	49	61.1	24.4	14.5	58

SOURCE: 1992 and 1996 National Election Studies.

explain the growth of government, 51 percent blamed it for doing things that people should be doing for themselves, compared to 38 percent four years earlier.

While the proportion of conservatives had grown since 1992, Clinton's support level more than held steady among that important group. Meanwhile, liberals had little choice but to support him. Indeed, Clinton's vote rose by 10 percent among those who took liberal positions on these issues.[3] In part, Clinton's improvement among liberals may have been related to the decrease in the size of that group, with peripheral liberals who did not support him moving to the moderate camp by 1996. Nevertheless, the stable support level for Clinton among conservatives suggests that the rightward shift of the electorate did not hurt his reelection bid.

RELIGIOUS TRADITION AND COMMITMENT — The role of religion in electoral politics has garnered significant attention in recent years from both journalists and scholars (for a review, see Leege and Kellstedt 1993; Wald 1997). Much of this attention has focused on the Christian Coalition and similar groups that have been successful in mobilizing evangelical Protestants who were previously inactive in politics (Green and Guth 1988; Moen 1992; Wilcox 1992). The bulk of this conservative Protestant support has benefited Republican candidates (Miller and Shanks 1996). Studies have also emphasized the separate effects of religious commitment on voting (Miller and Shanks 1996; Layman 1997).

Religion was not an explicit issue in the 1996 election, but several campaign issues had religious connotations. For example, President Clinton had vetoed a bill that the Republican Congress had passed to outlaw a particular late-term abortion procedure described by the pro-life forces as "partial birth abortion." The Catholic church strongly supported this bill, and Republican leaders saw it as a potential "wedge issue" to draw normally Democratic Catholic voters over to their side. Similarly, the Democrats opposed school vouchers, which the Republicans favored, with this issue again being a possible "wedge issue" that could attract Catholic votes over to the Republicans.[4] Beyond these issues, the Republicans took the conservative position on such issues as prayer in the public schools that would appeal to conservative Protestant denominations.

Sharp differences in 1996 emerged when respondents are classified by religious tradition (see table 3.6) in a manner consistent with recent research on measuring religious affiliation (Kellstedt, Green, Guth, and Smidt 1996).[5] Dole did best among Protestants, winning a majority of the vote among mainline Protestants and among evangelical Protestants. Perot did better with evangelical Protestants than with other religious groups. Republican attempts to use particular issues to attract Catholic voters were partially successful—Clinton carried the white Catholic vote by only a narrow margin

TABLE 3.6

RELIGIOUS TRADITION AND THE 1996 VOTE

(IN PERCENTAGES)

Religious tradition	Clinton	Dole	Perot	All voters
Mainline Protestant	45.0	51.5	3.5	18.4
Evangelical Protestant	36.8	52.2	11.0	25.2
Catholic				
White Catholic	47.2	43.5	9.2	21.6
Hispanic Catholic	81.7	13.9	4.4	3.6
Black Catholic	100.0	0.0	0.0	.6
Jewish	86.7	6.3	7.0	2.2
Black Protestant	95.0	3.2	1.7	8.3
Orthodox	0.0	100.0	0.0	.2
Conservative nontraditional	23.7	76.3	0.0	1.2
Liberal nontraditional	68.5	0.0	31.5	.5
Other	100.0	0.0	0.0	1.2
Secular	57.6	33.4	9.0	17.0
Total	52.7	39.7	7.6	100.0

N = 1120.

SOURCE: 1996 National Election Study.

NOTE: See endnote 5.

but the Republicans lost the Hispanic vote overwhelmingly, with Dole obtaining only 14 percent of the Hispanic Catholic vote. Not surprisingly, Clinton won an overwhelming majority of the Jewish and black vote. Those in the "secular" category voted by a striking 58 percent to 33 percent margin for Clinton.

Religious commitment further intensifies these effects of religious tradition (see also Layman 1997). Clinton won a majority of the vote among those with the low to moderate levels of religious commitment, while Dole did best (65 percent) with the relatively small group at the highest level of religious commitment—people who express a religious affiliation, attend church more than once a week, pray more than once daily, and say religion provides a great deal of guidance in their lives. Religious commitment effects should be studied within the context of religious traditions, however, since higher levels of commitment could lead to different voting patterns in different traditions (Grant, Mockabee, and Monson 1997). In 1996, higher religious commitment led to more Republican voting within each of the largest religious groups: the Dole vote goes from 32 percent for evangelical Protestants with a low level of commitment to 78 percent for those with a very high commitment, from 41 percent for mainline Protestants with a low level of commitment to 83 percent at the highest level, and from 28 percent for white Catholics with a low level of commitment to 83 percent at the top level.

SHORT-TERM ISSUE FACTORS

Several issues arose during the 1996 presidential campaign. The 1996 NES survey included a number of specific issue questions. Table 3.7 summarizes the results, along with a comparison to 1992 when that is possible.

THE ECONOMIC ISSUE — The economy is always a relevant issue in elections. In the aftermath of a recession, the Clinton campaign of 1992 was encapsulated by its four-word theme: "It's the economy, stupid!" The economy actually started improving prior to the 1992 election, but President Bush received little credit for this improvement. The economic upswing continued through the entire Clinton first term, with unemployment falling sharply. Correspondingly, 44 percent of the public in 1996 thought the economy had improved in the past year, compared to only 5 percent in 1992. Also, 45 percent of the public considered themselves better off financially than a year earlier during the 1996 election season, compared to 31 percent in 1992 (see also Lacy and Grant's analysis in chapter 6).

These retrospective evaluations of the economy were strongly related to the vote in both years. Those who felt the economy had improved were more likely to vote for the incumbent, while those who felt it was worse were more likely to vote for the challenger. Consistent with the work of Donald Kinder and D. Roderick Kiewiet (1981) on economic voting, this relationship was higher in both years for sociotropic voting (row A of table 3.7) than for pocketbook voting (row B).[6] Note also that one of Perot's best showings was among the small alienated group that thought the country was worse off economically than a year earlier.

The evidence here is of a strong bivariate relationship between evaluations of the national economy and the 1996 vote. The economy had improved, and the incumbent president was able to take credit for that improvement. One interpretation of the Democratic loss of Congress in 1994 is that the Democrats did not emphasize the improvement in the economy enough and did not try to claim credit for that improvement. By 1996 they learned the need to emphasize the economic improvement and to take credit for it.

TAXES AND SOCIAL SECURITY — The NES survey also included closed-ended questions about two other economic issues: taxes and Social Security. One of Dole's major issues was his pledge to cut personal income taxes by 15 percent. Neither candidate proposed changing the Social Security pro-

TABLE 3.7. ISSUES AND THE VOTE IN 1992 AND 1996 (IN PERCENTAGES)

		1996 vote				1992 vote			
		Clinton	Dole	Perot	All voters	Clinton	Dole	Perot	All voters
A. Over the past year, the nation's economy has ...	Gotten better	70.3	23.4	6.4	44	11.9	75.1	13.0	5
	Stayed the same	42.3	50.9	6.7	43	31.1	50.7	18.3	22
	Gotten worse	28.5	57.6	13.9	14	54.7	25.9	19.4	73
B. Are you better off or worse off financially than a year ago?	Better off	60.3	31.7	8.0	45	37.3	42.6	20.2	31
	Same	42.5	48.2	9.3	22	46.8	38.1	15.1	35
	Worse off	49.3	45.0	5.7	33	57.3	21.4	21.3	35
C. Two-year limit on welfare	Favor	48.6	44.1	7.3	80				
	Oppose	69.1	22.1	8.8	20				
D. Immigrants should be eligible for gov't services ...	Immediately	64.8	23.1	12.1	12	47.7	33.4	19.0	20
	After a year	50.9	42.1	7.0	88	47.6	33.9	18.5	80
E. Abortion	Pro-life	38.5	54.6	6.9	40	37.5	47.3	15.3	39
	Pro-choice	62.4	29.4	8.2	60	53.5	25.6	20.8	61
F. Affirmative action	For	81.7	14.0	4.3	16				
	Against	47.0	44.4	8.6	84				
G. Are you a smoker?	Yes	55.2	29.3	15.6	19				
	No	52.0	42.3	5.6	81				
H. Presidential approval	Approve	78.0	14.5	7.5	68	15.6	68.5	15.8	43
	Disapprove	3.6	88.9	7.6	32	70.4	8.4	21.2	57

SOURCE: 1992 and 1996 National Election Studies.

gram, but a commonplace of recent election campaigns was Democrats attacking Republicans for trying to rein in Social Security spending.

An interesting aspect of Bob Dole's electoral weakness was reflected on the questions asking how likely the two candidates were to raise taxes or cut Social Security. Many respondents did not see a difference between the candidates on these matters. Still, 46 percent of respondents thought Dole was more likely to cut Social Security benefits (versus 19 percent answering Clinton). Furthermore, regardless of his plan to cut taxes, 29 percent of the sample thought Dole was more likely to raise taxes (versus 41 percent answering Clinton). Not only was Dole's advantage on taxes slight, but it was less than Clinton's advantage on Social Security.

SOCIAL ISSUES — Social issues dominated much of the policy debate during the Clinton administration, with issues as diverse as gays in the military, "partial birth" abortions, affirmative action, welfare reform, and tobacco regulation. The NES survey included questions on some of these issues.

The public supported conservative positions on welfare reform (row C of table 3.7), the eligibility of immigrants for government services (row D), and affirmative action (row F) by margins of at least four to one. Clinton's strongest support was among those taking liberal positions on these issues, even though his positions during his first term did not always satisfy liberal activists. At the same time, he managed to retain a small lead among those voters with conservative positions on these issues. Thus, Clinton was not damaged much even when he was not on the popular side of these social issues. There were times during Clinton's first term that it looked like the president could be severely wounded on social issues (with the wounds being largely self-inflicted), but he put this behind him by reelection time.

The public's view of abortion remained unchanged since 1992 (row E of table 3.7): 40 percent took a pro-life stand compared to 60 percent taking a pro-choice position. Dole won the pro-life vote, while Clinton won the pro-choice vote, doing 9 percent better among pro-choice voters than he had in 1992.

Another issue of the Clinton presidency involved regulation of tobacco. His administration tried to regulate the tobacco industry more than had ever been the case. During the campaign, Bob Dole expressed doubt that nicotine was addictive, or at least more so than milk, thus seeming to join the issue. The NES survey did not ask people about tobacco regulation, but it did ask if they smoked and only a fifth of the sample said they did (row G of table 3.7). Dole might have expected to win the smoker constituency, but his vote was lower among smokers than among nonsmokers. Perot's best showing in the table was among smokers, winning nearly a sixth of their votes.

OVERALL — The economy had improved since 1992, and Clinton received credit for that improvement. He was at a considerable disadvantage on some social issues, but the public did not hold those issues against him. There was a general shift to the right, but Dole had only a modest advantage on ideology. The country had moved to the right as to the proper role of government, but Clinton did not lose support among conservatives. Religious tradition and commitment were strongly related to the vote, but Clinton managed to win a plurality of all but the most committed. In short, Clinton managed to avoid severe losses on ideological and issue factors where he might have been at a disadvantage, while he benefited considerably from the economic issue. Yet one important note of caution must be introduced: this section examines effects by looking at each issue separately, without controlling for the effects of other issues or the effects of attitudes toward the candidates. Some of the issue differences found in this section may well disappear when such controls are instituted.

Candidates

The remaining factor to consider is the candidates. Political scientists largely agree that American electoral politics is now candidate-centered rather than party-dominated (Aldrich and Niemi 1996; Beck 1997). Candidates run separately from their party, and televised campaign ads focus even more attention on the candidates and their qualities. Clinton benefited from his overall job approval ratings in 1996, though his image was not very strong.

PRESIDENTIAL JOB APPROVAL

A reelection attempt rests in part on how satisfied the country is with the president's performance of his job. Reelection would be difficult to win if job approval were low, but it could be relatively easy if job approval were high.

Clinton's approval ratings were not very high through most of his first term in office, but the public's rating of Clinton as president was definitely positive by the 1996 election. Asked to evaluate Clinton's performance in office, 68 percent of the voters in the NES sample approved of his handling of his job as president. Clinton received high ratings on the environment (73 percent approving his performance), the economy (66 percent), and foreign affairs (61 percent), but weaker ratings on handling health-care reform (53 percent). These are good ratings to use as the base for a reelection campaign. By way of contrast, Bush's approval rating in the 1992 NES preelection survey was only 43 percent, with comparable ratings on foreign affairs (62 percent) but much weaker ratings on the economy (20 percent approval). As would be expected, Clinton's approval rating was strongly related to the presidential vote (row H of table 3.7).

OVERALL CANDIDATE RATINGS

Summary judgments of the party nominees showed that Clinton was somewhat more popular than Dole. As usual, the NES survey had respondents rate the candidates on a 0–100 degree thermometer scale. Clinton's preelection average thermometer rating was 59, while Dole's was only 52. Since the Democrats led in party identification, Dole needed to draw support among independents and leaners, but the Clinton lead on the thermometers is echoed among all independents, with an average rating of 57 compared to 51 for Dole.[7]

Table 3.8 places these ratings within the context of nominees since 1968. Clinton's rating was higher than his 1992 rating, but below the 60-degree rating that most winners (and even some losers) have achieved. Dole's rating was on par with Bush's 1992 rating, with these being the lowest averages of any major-party nominee during the time period in which this question has been asked. The other interesting comparison in the table is that Clinton's lead in popularity over Dole is the largest lead of any winning candidate aside from Nixon over McGovern in 1972. Weaknesses in Clinton's profile are shown by his average rating not being high for a winning candidate, but it was still substantially stronger than Dole's.

CANDIDATE IMAGES

As a presidential challenger in 1992, Bill Clinton underwent intense scrutiny regarding his personal and public character, but he overcame these damaging revelations to unseat George Bush. Clinton again faced questions about his integrity in 1996. Events during his first term—including the continuing Whitewater investigation, the White House Travel Office scandal, the improper use of FBI files by White House staff, and a highly publicized sexual harassment lawsuit filed by Paula Jones—raised the "character issue" to the fore. Part of the Republican strategy in 1996 was to turn public attention to Clinton's alleged character flaws.

The nomination of Senator Bob Dole bolstered this Republican strategy. Many analysts saw integrity as an area where Dole held a distinct advantage. He was respected as a trustworthy colleague by senators on both sides of the aisle. Furthermore, his distinguished service in World War II provided a stark contrast to Clinton's controversial draft record. The character issue was emphasized by Republicans throughout the campaign and received even more attention in the last two weeks when the discovery of foreign money being channeled into the Clinton campaign raised more questions about the White House's ethics.

The NES added two series of closed-ended questions about the candidates to its surveys in the 1980s. Respondents were asked whether the candidate ever made them feel proud, hopeful, angry, or afraid. Table 3.9 summarizes these emotional reactions. More people indicated that Clinton made

TABLE 3.8. POPULARITY OF NOMINEES, 1968–96 (THERMOMETER SCORES)

Nominee	1968	1972	1976	1980	1984	1988	1992	1996
Democratic	61.7	48.9	62.7	56.6	57.4	56.8	55.7	58.8
Republican	66.5	65.5	60.5	56.1	61.2	60.6	52.3	52.2
Independent	31.4			52.0			45.4	40.0
Winner's lead	4.8	16.6	2.2	–.5	3.8	3.8	3.4	6.6
D-R correlation	–0.18	–0.42	–0.31	–0.29	–0.54	–0.38	–0.39	–0.45

SOURCE: 1968–96 National Election Studies.

TABLE 3.9. PUBLIC FEELINGS TOWARD NOMINEES, 1984–96 (IN PERCENTAGES)

	1996		1992			1988		1984	
	Dole	Clinton	Perot	Bush	Clinton	Bush	Dukakis	Reagan	Mondale
Positive emotion									
Proud	38	49	24	57	24	33	29	55	30
Hopeful	37	58	30	48	51	39	42	60	41
Negative emotion									
Angry	34	54	27	52	26	25	29	48	30
Afraid	24	33	26	41	24	15	21	24	17
Positive minus negative	17	20	1	12	25	32	21	43	24

SOURCE: 1984–96 National Election Studies.

them feel proud and hopeful than said that Dole made them feel those ways. But more people also said that Clinton made them feel angry and afraid. Although this list of emotions is neither necessarily exhaustive nor deserving of equal weight, it is interesting to develop a net candidate image score by giving a candidate a +1 score for each positive emotion and −1 for each negative emotion. Clinton comes off only slightly above Dole on such a summary measure, and both are below all the other major party candidates since 1984 except for Bush in 1992.

Another set of closed-ended questions added to the NES surveys focuses on whether each candidate is thought to possess particular traits. Work by Kinder (1986) shows that there are four separate dimensions to these traits and that these trait questions are adequate in capturing public images of presidential nominees. Table 3.10 summarizes the results of these questions since 1984. Clinton had an edge on the leadership traits (particularly on being inspiring) and on empathy, but Dole had a large advantage on integrity. Compared with his 1992 ratings, Clinton went down a few percentage points on the leadership traits and about 10 percent on the integrity and empathy traits. Dole was perceived as better than Bush in 1992 on several traits, especially getting things done, honesty, and caring about people.

Analyses of the 1996 NES data indicate that Clinton was perceived as less trustworthy than Dole by a sizable portion of the electorate. As shown in table 3.10, 69 percent of respondents said the word "honest" described Dole extremely well or quite well, versus only 41 percent describing Clinton with that word. An even sharper divide occurred on the "moral" question, with 79 percent considering Dole moral, compared to just 39 percent for Clinton. Nevertheless, Clinton was better able to convince voters that he cared about everyday Americans. When asked how well the phrase "he really cares about people like me" described Bill Clinton, 56 percent of respondents said extremely well or quite well, compared to only 42 percent accepting that characterization of Bob Dole.

All in all, tables 3.9 and 3.10 show that neither candidate had a strong positive image in 1996. Clinton's image was better than Dole's, but Clinton was damaged goods. The conventional explanation of the factor of candidate qualities in the 1996 election has become that the public may have regarded Clinton as low on integrity but did not care about that in their voting decisions (presumably because of their pleasure with the strong economy). This would suggest that the candidate factor did not matter in voting. The results presented in this section instead show that Clinton was helped in several ways by the candidate factor: his approval rating was high and helped him get reelected, Dole was not a very popular challenger, and Clinton had a more positive image than Dole on at least some dimensions. But a true test of the effect of the integrity factor in 1996 requires that we shift to a multivariate analysis.

TABLE 3.10. PUBLIC IMAGES OF NOMINEES, 1984–96 (IN PERCENTAGES)

	1996			1992		1988		1984	
	Dole	Clinton	Perot	Bush	Clinton	Bush	Dukakis	Reagan	Mondale
Leadership traits									
Strong leader	60	59	38	56	62	54	57	71	49
Inspiring	38	52	35	39	59	39	49	59	44
Gets things done	65	57	53	41	68	—	—	—	—
Competency traits									
Knowledgeable	84	83	—	83	83	83	82	77	81
Intelligent	—	88	—	82	87	78	88	83	86
Integrity traits									
Moral	79	39	67	80	48	78	80	82	85
Honest	69	41	59	59	51	67	78	—	—
Empathy traits									
Cares about people	42	56	39	35	66	50	65	47	64
Compassionate	—	69	—	59	79	62	73	60	79

SOURCE: 1984–96 National Election Studies.

— means that the question was not asked for that candidate.

Attitudinal Basis of Reelection

As one way to summarize the several separate results of this chapter, we have developed a model of the major-party presidential vote in 1996. Our basic model consists of 8 variables, each of which has already been previewed. Party identification necessarily belongs in such a model; we use the conventional 7-point scale. The results obtained earlier suggest that ideology, the economy, and religion also should be included. We use the 7-point ideology scale, along with the retrospective sociotropic evaluation of the economy (whether the national economy has improved or gotten worse over the past year as a 5-point scale).[8] We also include a variable measuring religious commitment for evangelical Protestants.[9]

Finally, we include four candidate trait variables, measuring candidate integrity, empathy, competence, and leadership. These measures analyze the difference between voters' assessments of the qualities of the two candidates. That is, it may not matter that Clinton was seen as dishonest, for example, if Dole was seen as only slightly more trustworthy. The *integrity* variable is constructed by subtracting Clinton's scores on the 4-point "honest" and "moral" trait items from Dole's scores; the resulting character measure can take on values from −6 to +6. The *empathy* variable is created by subtracting Clinton's score on the "really cares about people like me" item from Dole's score. The *competence* variable is created by subtracting Clinton's score on "knowledgeable" from Dole's score. These measures can take on values from −3 to +3. The *leadership* variable is created by subtracting Clinton's scores on the "strong leader," "inspiring," and "get things done" items from Dole's scores. This last measure can range from −9 to +9. As expected, the mean of *integrity* is positive (1.43) while that of *empathy* is negative (−.2), indicating that while Clinton faced an "integrity gap," Dole suffered from an "empathy gap." The means for *leadership* and *competence* were fairly neutral (−.04 and −.06, respectively). A logistic regression model was estimated, as shown in equation 1 of table 3.11 (p. 68).[10] Each of these 8 variables was statistically significant, though the *competence* variable was only marginally significant. This model can correctly predict the major party votes of nearly 94 percent of the respondents.[11]

An attempt was made to analyze the effects of some of the other variables treated in this chapter. Another estimate is shown in equation 2 of table 3.11, using a host of other attitudinal variables (including abortion, women's role, affirmative action) and demographics (including gender, age, education, race, Hispanic descent, region, income, marital status, and whether the person is currently a smoker), but none of these other variables approached statistical significance.[12] There was a large gender gap in the voting (see Norrander's discussion in chapter 9), the family issue was important in the campaign (Weisberg and Kelly 1997), racial voting differences remained high in 1996, and voters of Hispanic descent voted disproportionately for Clinton (see the analysis by Stanley and Niemi in chapter 10), but these effects are apparently captured through partisanship and the other main variables in this analysis. Similarly, the bivariate analysis earlier in this chapter found that the vote decision varied with positions on abortion, women's role, and affirmative action, but multivariate analysis finds that these issue variables were not statistically significant; their effects must also be captured through the other predictor variables.

Thus, when we look at the 1996 election, we see multiple forces playing through at once. President Clinton had the expected benefit of partisanship, and, as usual, this was a potent variable, but reelection involved more than partisanship. Character had an important effect too, but the candidate qualities factor was not as unidirectional as the Republicans hoped. Integrity mattered, but so did empathy, and the analysis of the relative effects of these predictors suggests that the integrity issue was less potent than empathy, on which Clinton held the lead. Analyses of the 1996 vote that include integrity as a variable, but not empathy, miss the vital advantage that this aspect of Clinton's image gave to his reelection. It wasn't just the economy this time around, but the economy did matter. An ideological effect is also visible; Clinton held his own among conservatives, while liberals had no choice but to support him. There is also indication of a religious commitment effect for evangelical Protestants, though it was somewhat limited in importance. In contrast, such issues as abortion and affirmative action did not have independent effects on the vote, even if there were voting differences on these issues.

The result is a complicated story, but elections are complicated events. A wide variety of forces affect individual voting decisions, though at least we can find that some forces matter more than others. The Democrats had the edge on partisanship, though pure independents did not break in the candidate's favor. Clinton was advantaged by the healthy economy, though ideology worked against him. Finally, Clinton avoided being completely disadvantaged on the candidate factor, where his dominance on empathy helped overcome his weakness on the integrity dimension. Thus partisanship, issue, and candidate factors all helped Clinton win reelection, while his liabilities in each of these areas kept down the size of his victory. As a result, this was not a landslide election that conferred a strong policy mandate, even if the people chose to reelect a president.

TABLE 3.11

1996 MAJOR PARTY PRESIDENTIAL VOTE DETERMINANTS

Independent variable	Equation 1			Equation 2	
	Coefficient (Standard error)	P value	Potency[a]	Coefficient (Standard error)	P value
Constant	-2.490 (.919)	.001		-3.902 (1.650)	.018
Party ID	.494 (.088)	.000	.612	.526 (.101)	.000
Ideology	.444 (.161)	.006	.381	.432 (.196)	.027
Evangelical Protestant religious commitment	.262 (.098)	.007	.253	.292 (.119)	.014
Evaluation of the economy	-.478 (.194)	.014	.320	-.657 (.238)	.006
Integrity	.328 (.097)	.001	.595	.280 (.113)	.013
Empathy	1.126 (.215)	.000	.802	1.162 (.248)	.000
Competence	.486 (.248)	.049	.430	.320 (.280)	.255
Leadership	.231 (.086)	.007	.545	.283 (.099)	.004
Gender				-.116 (.353)	.742
Age				.007 (.011)	.548
Smoker				.099 (.124)	.424

Education	.192 (.127)	.129
White	−.155 (.704)	.826
Hispanic descent	−.966 (.730)	.185
Southern	−.299 (.382)	.433
Income	.0472 (.046)	.305
Married	−.446 (.441)	.312
Abortion	−.079 (.187)	.673
Affirmative action	.009 (.143)	.948
Women's role	.010 (.128)	.939
N	914	749
χ^2	944.911 (8 df / $p < .001$)	783.152 (20 pf / $p < .001$)
Pseudo-R^2	.75	.76
−2 log likelihood	307.906	204.059
Percentage correctly predicted	93.76	93.99
Percentage baseline prediction	56.2	56.6

SOURCE: 1996 National Election Study.

NOTE: The dependent variable is major party presidential vote, coded 0 for Clinton and 1 for Dole.

a. The difference between the probability of voting for Dole when the row variable is at its 5th percentile value and the probability of voting for Dole when it is at its 95th percentile value, with all other variables at their means.

4

The Partisan Choice: Bill Clinton or Bob Dole?

CHARLES E. SMITH JR., PETER M. RADCLIFFE,
AND JOHN H. KESSEL

FOUR PRESIDENTS—Dwight Eisenhower, Richard Nixon, Ronald Reagan, and Bill Clinton—have been reelected since 1952.[1] Although their second elections shared a number of characteristics with their first, they were not identical events. In 1952, voters thought Governor Adlai Stevenson's experience was to be preferred to General Eisenhower's, but they felt closer to the Republican Party than the Democratic. In 1956, these attitudes were reversed. In 1968, Richard Nixon was regarded as a somewhat more desirable candidate than Hubert Humphrey, and foreign policy was not significantly related to vote choice. Four years later, Nixon was viewed as much more qualified than George McGovern, and foreign policy was quite consequential in Nixon's reelection. In 1980, voters awarded the White House to Ronald Reagan because of dissatisfaction with inflation and international events (especially the Iranian seizure of American diplomats in Tehran). By 1984, inflation was under control, but foreign policy (which usually helps Republicans) actually produced a few votes for Walter Mondale. Reelection is a renewal of authority, not a replication of the original decision.

So it was with Bill Clinton's reelection. In 1992, attitudes about economics were the most potent in determining vote choice. In 1996, economics was one of several relatively potent issues, but attitudes about trust and general issues were more consequential. Also in 1996, significant issue attitudes were less pro-Democratic than they had been in 1992, but attitudes about civil liberties, social benefits, and economic management were still sufficiently Democratic to sustain President Clinton in the face of personal unpopularity. And we later see that the 1996 election had a slightly more partisan tone than the one in 1992. In short, Americans reelected the same president but for different reasons.[2]

To reach these conclusions, we drew on a series of questions that have been asked in every election year since 1952.[3] These open-ended questions simply invite voters to express their attitudes about politics without trying to structure their answers in any particular framework.[4] Questions about the parties come first:

> *Is there anything in particular that you like about the Republican Party?*
> *Is there anything in particular that you don't like about the Republican Party?*
> *Is there anything in particular that you like about the Democratic Party?*
> *Is there anything in particular that you don't like about the Democratic Party?*

A parallel series of questions about the candidates for president comes next:

> *Is there anything in particular about Mr. Clinton that might make you want to vote for him?*
> *Is there anything in particular about Mr. Clinton that might make you want to vote against him?*
> *Is there anything in particular about Mr. Dole that might make you want to vote for him?*
> *Is there anything in particular about Mr. Dole that might make you want to vote against him?*

The data generated by these questions have proven to be quite robust; they have a reasonable level of information, show that the voters are capable of differentiating between dissimilar aspects of attitudinal objects, and track well with real-world political events. Unfortunately, only half of the sample was asked the full set of these questions in 1996, but we still have ample data for analysis.

Voters responding to these questions make thousands of comments on scores of topics. In order to link these comments to vote choice, the responses must be assembled into a limited number of broad categories. Two categories—candidates and parties—are implied by the questions themselves. It turns out, though, that respondents make more remarks about issues than about candidates or parties, so as a first broad cut we explore the effects of candidates, parties, and issues. We then decompose the three categories—candidates, parties, and issues—into sixteen categories to permit a finer-grained analysis. This model has now been applied to every presidential election in this half-century. It predicted between 85 and 91 percent of individual voters' decisions in each election from 1952 through 1992. In 1996, the 3-variable model predicted 91 percent of vote choices correctly, and the 16-variable model predicted 93 percent accurately.

Elements of the Model

POSSIBLE CAUSES OF VOTE CHOICE

How one arrays the comments depends on what one is trying to explain. We have two goals. One is to isolate potential causes of choice between the two major candidates. The second is to use categories that allow comparisons across presidential elections.[5] In constructing the discrete attitude categories to decompose the broad candidate component, therefore, we wanted them to be specific enough to permit concrete statements yet inclusive enough that comments falling into each would occur over a series of elections.

The largest category of candidate references is a general category. This includes three classes of comments: those that are too general to be assigned to one of the specific categories ("He's a good [or bad] man," or "He's good [or bad] for the country"), statements on topics (such as the candidate's age) that did not occur often enough to justify the creation of separate categories, and comments that occur relatively frequently in a single campaign but are absent in other elections.

Two categories deal with attitudes about the candidates' experience. *Record and incumbency* concerns perceptions about the candidates' records. If an incumbent is running for reelection, this is likely to be a key category. *Experience* is a shortened name for more specific experience—military experience, diplomatic background, campaign ability. Sometimes the comments (e.g., "He's experienced in foreign affairs") refer directly to a presidential skill.

Two more categories are also office related. *Management* deals with executive capacity: how the candidate would be likely to run the government if elected, as well as more general references to leadership. *Intelligence* is given a broad enough definition to include comments about the candidate's education and willingness to accept new ideas as well as cognitive skill in a general sense. The other specific candidate categories relate more to judgments about the individual than to judgments about executive ability. *Trust* touches upon confidence, honesty, and any specific comments bearing on the candidate's integrity. *Personality* includes any comments about image and mannerisms, such as warmth, aloofness, and dignity.

It turned out that there were so few *party* comments in the three general categories that there was little choice in how to subdivide them.[6] As a practical matter, they could only be divided into two classes. Attitudes about *people in the party* concern all party members other than the candidate themselves: vice-presidential candidates, incumbent presidents not running for reelection, prominent senators and governors, party workers, and so on. All other party comments were categorized as *party affect*. These included trust of one party or the other, references to party factions, and the representativeness of the parties.

The subcategories for the *issues* comments were based on prior work. Six issue categories had been discerned in a content analysis of presidential State of the Union messages (Kessel 1974), and nearly identical issue areas resulted from analyses of congressional roll-call votes (Clausen 1973). Since similar results had been obtained by different methods applied to different institutional domains, and both analyses covered extended time periods, we thought these policy areas might be useful categories in voting studies.[7] This has turned out to be true. The first policy area, *international involvement*, concerns the traditional diplomacy of negotiation and the newer diplomacy of foreign aid, arms sales, information exchange, and presidential travel, as well as the military power that supports U.S. foreign policy. *Economic management* deals with attempts by the federal government to direct the national economy: the use of economic controls, adjustments in the level of federal spending, tax policy, and so forth.

The next two policy areas have usually had less impact than foreign policy and economics. *Social benefits* includes programs that help individuals: education, health care, welfare, and the like. *Civil liberties* embraces the great guarantees of individual liberty against government oppression, the protection of rights of classes of citizens by the government, and increasingly, a willingness to tolerate various lifestyles.

The final two specific categories are distinctive but rarely elicit many comments. Both may be conceptualized as special cases of other areas. The first, *natural resources*, may be thought of as a special case of economic management in which regulatory policy is used in the areas of the environment and energy. The second, *agriculture* policy, may be viewed as a special case of social benefits in which farmers are the beneficiaries.[8]

In addition to the specific issue categories, there is a *general* issue category. As with the general candidate comments, this is composed of comments too broad to fit into the specific policy areas just reviewed. These include references to liberalism or conservatism, the policy stands of the candidates or parties, and comments about "ideas" with no mention of specifics. Although this general issue category is broad, in the past it has been a sensitive barometer of electoral sentiment.

MEASUREMENT

Vote choice is the binary dependent variable (0 = Republican, 1 = Democrat). Each of the independent variables (that is, the three broad categories and the sixteen specific categories just described) was constructed from responses to the open-ended questions about the parties and candidates. Up to five responses were coded for each question.[9]

The independent variables were constructed from these responses by summing the number of comments within each category that favor either party. First, a pro-Democratic (Clinton) sum was computed by counting the number of comments that were positive toward Clinton and the Democrats or negative toward Dole and the Republicans. A parallel pro-Republican (Dole) sum was then computed. An overall score was calculated by taking the simple difference between these sums. The resulting variables thus possess both sign (reflecting a partisan advantage) and extremity (reflecting the degree to which an advantage exists). If the sign is positive, it denotes a Democratic advantage; if the sign is negative, it denotes a Republican advantage.

PROBIT ANALYSIS

To this point we have described construction of the independent variables (potential causes of voting decisions). In order to show which independent variables are related to vote choice, we need a *multivariate analysis*, one that allows analysis of multiple variables at the same time. Controls are exercised over other possible causes. For example, we can estimate the effect of issues on vote choice in the 3-component version of our model, while controlling for the effects of candidates and parties. Likewise, when we estimate for the effects of each variable in the 16-component version of our model, the effects of the other 15 independent variables are statistically controlled.[10] From the various methods that are available for multivariate analysis, we have chosen to estimate voting models using *probit*.

Probit models were first introduced in political science more than thirty years ago (Kramer 1965). They were developed to deal with dichotomous dependent variables such as vote. The basic logic underlying the probit model has since been extended to dependent variables having more than two values, but the model's capacity to handle dichotomous dependent variables makes it particularly appropriate for the analysis of choice between two candidates.[11] Another strength of the probit model is that its coefficients yield probabilistic interpretations. In our case we can predict the probability of a Democratic vote (this also reveals the probability of a Republican vote). We rely heavily on these probabilities in interpreting the results of the analysis and in speculating about the relative influence obtained by different classes of variables in determining the outcome of the election. We also utilize them in the course of interpreting the 1996 outcome in comparison to the 1992 election.

Analysis

The broad task in this section is to examine how the variables just described combined to influence vote choices in the 1996 election. Toward this end, we rely on four different sets of statistics, the nature and relevance of which warrant some preliminary comment. First, and most central, are the estimated coefficients from two probit models, one modeling vote choice as a function of the 3 summary variables (candidate comments, party comments, and issue comments), and a second that includes the full complement of 16 components. Below, we consider the general form of the models by illustrating the simpler 3-component version.

$$Vote_i^* = \alpha + \beta_1 Candidate_i + \beta_2 Party_i + \beta_3 Issue_i + \epsilon_i$$

A very simple logic underlies this equation. $Vote_i^*$ is a generalization of the binary decision—Republican versus Democrat. That is, it is a latent and continuous variable representing the propensity to vote for one of the two options. Its value is posited simply as the sum of the considerations to the right of the equal sign, with each component being weighted by a quantity (β) that reflects its contribution in the voting calculus. Given a normal distribution for the errors (ϵ_i), these βs are probit coefficients. In examining the values we estimate for them, we focus on statistical tests that reflect the likelihood of estimating a nonzero value for a coefficient when in fact its "true" value is zero. Obviously, a zero value for β implies that the associated component had no effect on voting. Conversely, a nonzero value implies that the component played a role in determining vote choice. Where our tests suggest with at least 95 percent confidence that estimated values are nonzero, we conclude that these components were statistically significant contributors to the partisan voting calculus. This is the crucial step that demonstrates which of the possible causes of vote choice are related to the result of the 1996 election.

Although it is important, the enterprise of identifying the statistical relevance of the attitude measures as predictors of voting provides us with very little detail about how the election was decided. All we know from the tests of these coefficients is whether the attitudinal variables with which they are associated played any role at all. The remaining three sets of statistics help us add the relevant information. One of these is the standard deviation for each of the attitudinal items. Standard deviations describe the dispersion of observations *around* their central tendency. The observed scores on some of the attitudinal measures vary widely, while those on others are clustered closely about their means. Those that vary the most have larger standard deviations. All else equal, the attitudes that vary the most across individual respondents are more capable of explaining variation in voting. In other words, they are more critical to the explanation of the election outcome than are those attitudes that, because they vary little, offer little in the way of explanatory power.

The next statistic we examine combines the information about the weights voters assign to various attitudes (i.e., the probit coefficients) and the dispersion of these feelings across voters (i.e., the standard deviations). These indicators are more complicated to derive than the others. Nevertheless, this particular set of statistics is perhaps the most straightforward in terms of interpretation, for the results of these calculations are, simply, differences in the probability of voting for the Democratic candidate. These differences are determined by subtracting one prediction from the probit model with a given set of conditions from that of another prediction—one that follows from a different set of conditions.[12] The probability differences that result serve as summary indicators of the potency of the individual attitude categories in the calculus of 1996 voters. The largest values for the differences are indicative of prominent roles in the determination of the election outcome for the attitudes with which they are associated. The smaller values indicate lesser importance in this respect.

The last of the four sets of statistics is something we call the "partisan valence" of each attitudinal measure. Most simply, partisan valences are measures of partisan advantage in the attitudinal areas (and their components). Where we identify statistically relevant attitudes, the valences add meaning by indicating which, among the set of significant predictors, provided Dole with the greatest advantage, and likewise for Clinton. The valences are constructed so that if one is negative, it indicates that the Republicans had an advantage in that attitude category. If, in contrast, one is positive, it suggests that Clinton had the better hand. The precise values of the valences correspond to the percentage advantage a party enjoys because of an attitude. For instance, a –.12 indicates a 12 percent advantage for the Republicans on that attitude, whereas a +.05 denotes a 5 percent advantage for the Democrats.[13]

Since the probability differences provide information about the potency of an attitude, and the partisan valences tell which party is benefited by that attitude, the most efficient way to understand the total impact of an attitude category is to look at these two statistics. Clearly, an attitude with a high probability difference and a high partisan valence would have considerable impact on the election. An attitude with a low probability difference (but whose probit coefficient is still significant) and a low partisan valence would still have some consequence but relatively less impact. And whatever the partisan valence of an attitude, if the probit coefficient is not statistically significant, that attitude will not be potent enough to affect the vote.

Tables 4.1 and 4.2 (p. 78) report results for the probit coefficients (and two measures that allow us to assess their statistical significance), standard

TABLE 4.1

RESULTS FROM THE 3-VARIABLE VOTE MODEL, 1996

Variable	Probit coefficient (Standard error)	P value	Standard devia- tion	Proba- bility difference	Partisan valence
Constant	.118 (.096)	.217	—	—	—
Candidate attitudes	.393 (.046)	.000	3.34	.45	−.08
Partisan attitudes	.551 (.132)	.000	1.06	.21	.04
Issue attitudes	.317 (.033)	.000	5.15	.54	.08

N	506
χ^2	465.01 (3 df / p < .0001)
Pseudo-R^2	.67
−2 log likelihood	231.90
Percentage correctly predicted	91.3
Percentage baseline prediction	54.7

SOURCE: 1996 National Election Study.

deviations, probability differences, and partisan valences from the 3- and 16-component solutions, respectively.[14] Focusing first on table 4.1 and the 3-variable model, we note that the coefficients associated with all three of the attitude categories are statistically significant. *Issue attitudes*, with a probability difference of .54, are this model's most potent predictor. *Candidate attitudes*, with a probability difference of .45, come next; and partisan attitudes come a long way behind with a probability difference of only .21. This pattern, with issue attitudes the most potent, candidate attitudes in second place, and party attitudes much weaker than the other two, has manifested itself in ten of the eleven preceding contests. Only in 1976 were candidate attitudes able to edge out issue attitudes as the most potent predictor.

Partisan valences also showed a familiar common pattern. *Candidate attitudes* had a partisan valence of −.08, revealing a Republican advantage. *Issue attitudes* and *partisan attitudes*, with valence scores of +.08 and +.04, respectively, showed the Democrats to be stronger in these areas. This pattern carried echoes of many past elections. Republican candidates were more attractive in ten of the eleven preceding elections; Democratic issue positions were preferred in eight of these elections.

The 16-component solution reported in table 4.2 adds considerable detail. Only 9 of the 16 variables have statistically significant coefficients, so some of the attitudinal facets did not contribute to 1996 voting. Four of 7 is-

TABLE 4.2.

RESULTS FROM THE 16-VARIABLE VOTE MODEL, 1996

Variable	Probit coefficient (Standard error)	P value	Standard deviation	Probability difference	Partisan valence
Constant	.352 (.126)	.005	—	—	—
Candidate attitudes					
General	.450 (.103)	.000	1.39	.24	.08
Record and incumbency	.249 (.170)	.142	.70	.07	−.09
Experience	.101 (.195)	.605	.51	.02	−.34
Management	.300 (.136)	.027	.95	.11	−.07
Intelligence	.062 (.205)	.763	.49	.01	.19
Trust	.836 (.134)	.000	1.10	.35	−.38
Personality	.317 (.221)	.151	.64	.08	.05
Partisan attitudes					
People in the party	.698 (.327)	.033	.48	.13	−.005
Party affect	.526 (.162)	.001	.98	.20	.05

Continued ...

sue items had statistically relevant coefficients. In descending order of importance, *general issue attitudes, civil liberties, economic management,* and *social benefits* were all consequential. *International involvement* just missed statistical significance, but it was close enough to merit some attention. Of the 7 candidate-related categories, *trust, general candidate attitudes,* and *management* played significant roles.[15] Moreover, *trust* (actually, lack thereof) stood out as the most potent predictor in the entire model. Both of the partisan attitudes, *party affect* and *people in the party,* were statistically significant.

THE BUILDING BLOCKS OF VOTE CHOICE

There was truly a jumble of attitudes in 1996. Although most issue attitudes favored Clinton, the most consequential issue category favored Dole; and although most candidate attitudes favored Dole, the second most potent candidate category favored Clinton. Further, within the categories that tipped

TABLE 4.2. — CONTINUED

Variable	Probit coefficient (Standard error)	P value	Standard devia- tion	Proba- bility difference	Partisan valence
Issue attitudes					
General	.454	.000	1.55	.27	−.10
	(.092)				
International	.039	.075	.66	.08	−.07
involvement	(.173)				
Economic	.279	.000	2.01	.22	.17
management	(.075)				
Social benefits	.239	.006	1.78	.17	.18
	(.087)				
Civil liberties	.358	.000	1.76	.25	.03
	(.092)				
Natural resources	.464	.178	.47	.09	.38
	(.344)				
Agriculture	—	—	.04	—	—

N	505
χ^2	490.36 (15 df / $p < .0001$)
Pseudo-R^2	.70
−2 log likelihood	205.34
Percentage correctly predicted	92.7
Percentage baseline prediction	54.7

SOURCE: 1996 National Election Study.

toward Clinton, we find pro-Dole comments, and within the categories that tipped toward Dole, we find pro-Clinton comments. To find the roots of electoral choice amid this clutter, we must simultaneously consider three questions: How potent were the variables? Which candidate did the variables favor? And how did the content within each category "add up" to favor one candidate or the other?

ISSUE ATTITUDES — With a probability difference of .27, *general* issues had the strongest impact of any issue category. What was surprising was the partisan valence of −.10. In every election since 1952, the nebulous attitudes in this category had produced an edge for the winner. Yet here we had a 10 percent advantage for the *losing* candidate. What happened? Most important, 1996 was a conservative season. Voters were likely to praise Senator Dole for his conservatism and criticize President Clinton as being too liberal. Similarly, Bob Dole got credit for opposing government activity, while Bill Clinton was blamed for favoring government activity. The vague "general assessments," such as "I like his ideas," were split: 5 favorable to 2 unfavorable for Clinton comments and 4 to 3 for those mentioning Dole. There were, however, more comments about Dole. All this raises another question. If 1996 was a conservative year, how did the Democrats prevail on issues? Put most simply, while many Americans agree with conservatism as an abstraction, they like specific liberal programs such as Social Security and student loans.

The most potent specific category in 1996 was *civil liberties*, with a probability difference of .25. But its partisan valence (+.03) did not bring a strong breeze to President Clinton's sails. In the 1990s, the most salient civil liberties issues revolved around lifestyle questions, and of these, abortion was the most prominent. Both candidates got more criticism than praise on this issue, and the criticism was so equally spread that neither Clinton nor Dole could claim any net advantage. The next most frequent comments dealt with public morality and gay rights. Bob Dole benefited from his advocacy of a strict morality and his opposition to gay rights. Smaller groups of respondents were concerned with the candidates' locations on a generosity-selfishness dimension, and with gun control. Bill Clinton profited from opinions on both these issues.

Economic management, with a probability difference of .22, was nearly as potent as civil liberties, but its partisan valence (+.17) brought many more voters to the Democratic banner. The surprise here was the relative lack of potency in a variable that had been the most consequential in every election since 1976. The dominance of economic voting, however, is a sometimes thing. If we go back to 1960 and 1964, we find that economic management was only the sixth most important influence. It ranked fifth in 1996.[16]

Within economics, the most frequent comments turned on whether the party was closer to the common person or big business, with Democrats overwhelmingly getting credit for speaking for the little guy and the Republicans getting equal blame for speaking for the corporate rich. Fewer comments were made about the middle class, but here, too, the Democrats were in better shape, never a good sign for the GOP. The second most common topic was tax policy. This category was better for Republicans; voters had kind words for Dole's tax-reduction plans and criticism for Clinton's actions. The last large topic was economic prosperity. Almost all these comments were pro-Clinton. It is often said that it is hard to beat an incumbent when times are good. This is true, but there were nearly three times as many comments linking Democrats to the average citizen and Republicans to big business as references to prosperity. As long as the Republicans are perceived as the party of the rich, they're going to be in trouble.

Social benefits, with a probability difference of .17, was somewhat less potent, but its partisan valence of +.18 reflected voters' support for Clinton on every topic within this rubric. Both Clinton's and Dole's stands opposing welfare programs were endorsed, though Clinton received more support than Dole. Education, the next most commented on topic, was an area in which Clinton was supported and Dole was criticized. President Clinton also won praise for health care, although Senator Dole was less criticized on this topic. The least salient topics were programs for the elderly, and feelings about poor people. These returned to the pattern seen in education, praise for Clinton and criticism for Dole. Social benefits usually produces Democratic votes, and certainly did so in 1996.

Finally, *international involvement* just missed statistical significance.[17] To the extent that foreign policy had any impact, the partisan valence of −.07 suggests it helped Senator Dole. Dole was seen as more decisive on foreign policy than Clinton and was also favored for advocating a stronger military posture. Clinton had a slight advantage in voters' overall assessments of foreign affairs and won approbation for handling trouble spots more deftly than Dole.[18]

CANDIDATE ATTITUDES — For the first time since this documentation began, *trust* was more strongly related to vote choice than any other attitude in this 16-variable model. With a probability difference of .35 and a partisan valence of −.38, trustworthiness was not only important, but also a source of considerable criticism of Bill Clinton. Just over half the comments mentioned honesty. Very large majorities stated that President Clinton was dishonest and that Senator Dole was honest. Principles and specific scandals were the other major topics. There were twice as many comments about Clinton's principles as Dole's. The Clinton responses were filled with complaints about his lack of principles, whereas those about Dole were quite supportive. Almost everyone who referred to Whitewater, the travel office, and the White House acquisition of FBI files was critical of Clinton.

Presidents have been reelected in spite of public distrust. Lyndon Johnson, Richard Nixon, and Bill Clinton were all able to draw on other strengths to overcome perceptions of duplicity. In 1964 Barry Goldwater was seen as the more trustworthy, but the partisan valence of every other significant attitude favored Lyndon Johnson. In 1972 George McGovern was regarded as the more trustworthy, but Richard Nixon was strongly favored on every other candidate attitude. In 1996, as this analysis shows, Bill Clinton was sustained by other attitudes as well. Reelection, however, does not erase public doubts. In fact, well-established skepticism about presidential integrity hobbled Johnson as he contended with Vietnam and Nixon as he was overwhelmed by Watergate. Clinton's second-term difficulties are reminiscent of the predicaments his two predecessors brought on themselves.

The *general* candidate category ranked second in impact among the candidate groupings, with a probability difference of .24. This candidate category benefited President Clinton's candidacy (partisan valence = +.08). There were two kinds of comments in this cluster, some so broad as to resist classification and others referring to specific Clinton or Dole attributes. A number of respondents said that they just liked or disliked Clinton or Dole, or thought one or the other was good or bad for the country. President Clinton did better than Senator Dole in this classification. The second set of broad comments included general references and judgments that one candidate was better than his opponent. These commendations and criticisms were equally distributed.

The largest number of specific comments concerned age. A great many people thought Dole's age was a handicap; those who mentioned Clinton's youth did so favorably. The Kansas senator was also criticized for his speaking ability and campaign tactics. A number of comments dealt with the candidates' wives. Most concerned Hillary Clinton and were critical; the smaller number of comments about Elizabeth Dole tended to be favorable. Finally, there were statements about the candidates' past encounters with sex, financial problems, or drugs. These could just as easily have been included in the trust category, and they echoed the same widespread criticism of Bill Clinton. All these diverse components added up to a pro-Clinton valence because of the many criticisms of Senator Dole's age and the smaller number of respondents who "just liked" President Clinton.

Management exerted much less potency (probability difference = .11), and with a partisan valence of −.07 gave Senator Dole some advantage. Not quite half of the comments dealt with perceptions of the candidates as good or bad administrators. The "good" code combined perceptions of a good or businesslike administration with a balanced budget and cautious spending, and the "bad" code meant the opposite.[19] In this pairing there were many more positive than negative remarks about Senator Dole. In contrast, there were a few more negative than positive comments about President Clinton. About a quarter of the responses were more general assessments of the job being done, and these were quite favorable to Clinton. A few people made reference to management in other settings or to staff quality, and these comments were anti-Clinton.[20]

In brief, two of the three candidate clusters bolstered Senator Dole's candidacy. Trust was entirely anti-Clinton, and there were enough pro-Dole comments in the management category to give him a smaller lead there. The general candidate comments aided President Clinton's chances, but the real reasons he was able to overcome questions about his integrity were to be found in attitudes about issues and the parties.

PARTY ATTITUDES — Parties have long been the least of the issue-candidate-party triumvirate, but party attitudes were a bit more potent in 1996 than in most recent elections. *Party affect*, with a probability difference of .20, was sixth overall in potency, and its partisan valence of +.05 strengthened Bill Clinton's reelection effort somewhat. Party affect was most frequently heard in candidate appraisal, "He's a good Democrat/Republican" from a supporter or "He's a typical Democrat/Republican. What can you expect?" from an opponent. Beyond this, there was a scattering of comments dealing with party matters. The Democratic advantages came in support for Clinton as a good Democrat and in perceptions of their party as more representative. Republican advantages were in being seen as more trustworthy, better organized, and more likely to be viewed in positive terms.

People in the party had less impact on vote choice. With a partisan valence of –.005, it was Republican by the barest of margins, and its probability difference of .13 was not very potent either. The few comments in this category were quite scattered. Both vice presidential candidates garnered some compliments, but beyond this there were just random comments about various party figures.

SUMMARY — President Clinton's reelection support was assembled from nine components. In descending order of potency, they were *trust* (completely anti-Clinton), *general issue* attitudes (pro-Dole), *civil liberties* (pro-Clinton), *general candidate* attitudes (pro-Clinton), *economic management* (pro-Clinton), *party affect* (pro-Clinton), *social benefits* (completely pro-Clinton), *people in the party* (barely pro-Dole), and *management* (pro-Dole). With such a melange, there was no simple reason for his reelection or any clear prediction about his remaining years in office. Among Clinton supporters, there might have been a consensus that he should pursue somewhat liberal policies regarding economics and social benefits, thus reinforcing affect for the Democratic Party. Across the electorate, however, the only agreement was that he would be returned to office for another term.

CHANGE FROM 1992 to 1996

How does this compare to Clinton's first run for the presidency? In concluding our analysis, we offer a formal comparison between two discrete points in time, 1992 and 1996, juxtaposing model results from Clinton's original election with his successful reelection effort.

At the outset, we suggested that successful reelection efforts need not be viewed as simple replications of the decisions made by voters four years earlier, but instead as renewals of authority. Here, we examine the wellsprings of voter decisions during Clinton's successful bid for renewal against those made by voters during his predecessor's failed attempt in 1992. Our comparisons are animated by the changes we observe between 1992 and 1996 in the four categories of statistics we have already described. All numbers are reported in tables 4.3 (p. 84) and 4.4 (p. 86).

In both tables, cell entries are simply the arithmetic differences between the 1992 and 1996 statistics calculated by subtracting the 1992 National

Election Study data from corresponding values from the 1996 data set. Changes in the coefficients from election to election indicate that voters assigned different weights to the attitudinal categories in these elections. Changes in the partisan valences associated with the attitude categories suggest that one party was advantaged or disadvantaged to a different degree on these items in 1992 versus 1996. Dispersion differences, as evidenced by changes in the standard deviations, imply that the electorate became either more or less polarized in how they viewed the parties' candidates in these areas.

Since the probability scores combine the information in the coefficient and standard deviation, observed changes in these numbers summarize the other shifts to some degree. As such, these changes come closer than the others to describing electoral change in summary form. For precisely the same reason, however, they can mask interesting but compensating shifts in the other measures of electoral change. Moreover, because these are summary, descriptive statistics, the statistical purchase of observed probability differences cannot be tested. By contrast, for each of the other three differenced statistics in the tables (coefficients, standard deviations, and valences), we report tests of statistical significance, attaching a star when the magnitude of a difference exceeds (with 95 percent confidence) the value we should expect from sampling error.[21] The signs of the cell entries in the coefficient, standard deviation, and probability difference columns are negative when the observed change is such that the magnitude of these statistics declined from 1992 to 1996, and positive when they increased. The entries in the valence column have negative signs when the observed change favored Bob Dole and positive signs when the change favored Bill Clinton.

Results in table 4.3 provide a summary view of changes across the two

TABLE 4.3.

CHANGES BETWEEN 1992 AND 1996:

THE 3-VARIABLE VOTE MODEL

	Change in			
Variable	Probit coefficient	Standard deviation	Probability difference[a]	Partisan valence
Candidate attitudes	.031	.43*	.08	−.07*
Partisan attitudes	.175	.03*	.07	−.04
Issue attitudes	−.007	.09*	.00	−.08*

SOURCE: 1992 and 1996 National Election Studies.

NOTE: Cell entries are arithmetic differences between results from 1996 and 1992.

a. Statistical significance tests are not applicable to these differences.

*p < .05.

84

elections. None of the probit coefficients are statistically different from election to election. In the *issue* area, there is not even an appreciable change in the probability difference score. The *candidate* and *party* results are quite different; the probability difference scores for each of these components increased from 1992 to 1996. These shifts occurred for two very different reasons. The increased potency of partisan attitudes is owed largely to the increase in the value of its coefficient from one election to the next. This coefficient change, however, is not statistically significant, so the magnitude of the corresponding shift in probability differences (.07) should be interpreted with caution.

In contrast, a similar shift in the probability difference scores on the *candidate* variable is owed almost entirely to a large and statistically relevant change in the dispersion of this item from 1992 to 1996. Voters were more polarized in their views about the candidates in 1996 than they were in 1992. As a result, the candidate dimension of voting was more important in the more recent election.

In sum, in both 1992 and 1996, issue attitudes and candidate attitudes were the two main determinants of voting (see again table 4.1, p. 77). When voting in the two years is compared, however, voting in 1996 was similarly dependent on issues, more candidate-oriented, and perhaps somewhat more partisan.

Results in table 4.4 (p. 86) add considerable detail to these inferences. Three probability difference change scores stand out—one from the candidate area and two from issues. The candidate attribute is *trust*. In the earlier section we saw that attitudes about trust stood out as the most potent predictor in the 1996 model. This was not true in 1992, and the change is borne out in every column of table 4.4. First, this is the only statistically significant change in the value of a coefficient from one election to the next. When coupled with a substantial (and also statistically relevant) standard deviation shift, the result is a probability difference change (+.21) with a magnitude more than twice that associated with any other single predictor in the model. Clearly, the 1996 election was far more dependent upon *trust* than the first Clinton victory.

How, then, did he manage to reclaim the White House? Perhaps the best answer lies in two notable and compensating changes that constitute the dominant results in the area of issues. One of these is in the area of *social benefits* (+.10); the other is *economic management* (−.10). The latter result is largely attributable to a considerable decline in this variable's standard deviation (−.49) from 1992 to 1996. By contrast, the dispersion of *social benefits* increased by a similar margin (.33). Similarly, the coefficients associated with these variables moved in opposite directions across these elections. The net result is that social issues were more important in 1996 than in 1992, while economic issues declined in importance.[22] Recalling some differ-

TABLE 4.4.

CHANGES BETWEEN 1992 AND 1996:

THE 16-VARIABLE VOTE MODEL

		Change in		
Variable	*Probit coefficient*	*Standard deviation*	*Probability difference*	*Partisan valence*
Candidate attitudes				
General	.112	.15*	.09	−.06
Record and incumbency	−.281	−.05	−.08	−.01
Experience	−.275	−.09*	−.06	.08*
Management	.041	.09*	.03	−.13*
Intelligence	−.347	−.10*	−.08	.02
Trust	.353*	.30*	.21	−.25*
Personality	.078	−.01	.02	.18*
Partisan attitudes				
People in the party	.423	−.07	.08	−.09
Party affect	.119	.19*	.09	−.03
Issue attitudes				
General	−.014	.58*	.09	−.12*
International involvement	−.053	−.43*	−.05	−.06
Economic management	−.085	−.49*	−.10	.04*
Social benefits	.111	.33*	.10	−.15
Civil liberties	−.085	−.13	−.05	−.05
Natural resources	−.001	.02*	.01	.04*
Agriculture	—	−.07	—	—

SOURCE: 1992 and 1996 National Election Studies.

NOTE: Cell entries are arithmetic differences between results from 1996 and 1992. Statistical significance tests are not applicable to the differences in probability difference change column.

*$p < .05$.

ences in the campaigns associated with the 1992 and 1996 election efforts helps fit these results into context.

During the 1992 campaign, then-Governor Clinton's campaign manager, James Carville, kept a sign posted in campaign headquarters that, in only four words, defined a whole election year: "It's the economy, stupid!" Four years later, in 1996, Bob Dole and the Republicans tried, in fits and starts, to replicate both the theme and its resonance with American voters. With low inflation and steady economic expansion, they were left with budget balancing, spending restraints, and tax cuts as primary economic messages. Meanwhile, President Clinton and the Democrats stressed the evident prosperity and emphasized the need to protect Social Security, Medicaid, Medicare, education, and the environment as the budget-balancing process went forward.

In writing about the 1992 election (Smith and Kessel 1995, 124), we characterized the text of Carville's sign as being "right on the mark," and in its day, it certainly was. In writing about the 1996 election, we are forced to conclude that, to the degree that the economy was "it" in 1992, it was not "it" in 1996. A combination of lifestyle issues, social benefits, and economics ruled the issues world by 1996. President Clinton's recognition of these changes was vital in his reelection strategies.

5

Comparing Models of the Vote:
The Answers Depend on the Questions

JOHN H. KESSEL AND HERBERT F. WEISBERG

THE ANALYSES of the 1996 NES survey in chapters 3 and 4 nicely illustrate the choices that data analysts make when deciding what questions to analyze and how to model the individual's vote decision. These chapters obtain some results that seem at odds with one another. Actually there are more places where the two analyses agree, as when both find that a partisan term is important for understanding the election outcome. Still, several differences can easily be observed. The purposes of this chapter are to discuss the similarities in results as well as the differences and to use this as an example of the contrast between closed-ended and open-ended approaches.

Closed-ended and Open-ended Questions

It is a commonplace in the field of survey research that the wording of questions affects the answers that are obtained. One can get seemingly opposite distributions of public opinion by wording a survey question in different ways. As examples, asking people whether or not they would "prohibit" an action obtains a different result from asking them whether they would "not permit" the same action, and public attitudes on abortion look very different when asked in terms of the mother's choice or protecting the unborn. While it has received less public attention, survey researchers know that question format can also affect the answers that are obtained. Two of the most common formats are closed-ended questions and open-ended questions.

CLOSED-ENDED QUESTIONS

A closed-ended question gives the respondent alternatives from which to select. For example, "Would you say that over the past year the nation's economy has gotten better, stayed the same, or gotten worse?" offers three choices. To answer, the respondent need only select one. Further, he or she does not need any concrete information such as whether the Consumer's Price Index has been increasing. Since a closed-ended question is relatively easy to answer, most people do so, and with large numbers of answers, stable estimates of opinion on the issue can be obtained. The danger of such a closed-ended question is that a person who has not thought about the economy for months can easily volunteer, "It's stayed about the same." A less-common problem is that a respondent who is well informed has no way of giving a qualified answer, such as that the national economy has improved, but there is high unemployment locally.

The success of closed-ended questions is tied directly to the adroitness of the question writers in phrasing questions so they will refer only to specific attitudes and avoiding connotations that would tap other attitudes. Question writers also have the challenge of forecasting, during the summer when the items are written, which topics will dominate the election campaign that fall. Questionnaire drafters do remarkably well, but handicapped by the bluntness of language, insufficient space, and an inability to forecast campaign developments, it would be too much to expect them to write closed-ended items that capture all of the vote-related attitudes.

Closed-ended questions are most appropriate when they rest on well-developed theories. Since the concept of party identification was first introduced in 1952, a considerable body of theory has developed around it. In this instance, the meaning of party identification is well known, and analysts can exploit sophisticated theories, so party identification is included from the outset in chapter 3. Similarly, Donald Kinder's (1986) probing of the dimensions of reactions to presidential candidates has shown the theoretical importance of including measures of candidate evaluation in voting models.

Asking everyone the same set of closed-ended questions makes a series of psychological assumptions about the process underlying survey answers. The most prevalent theory in social psychology about how individuals evaluate candidates is called an "on-line" or "impression-driven" model (Lodge, McGraw, and Stroh 1989; Hastie and Park 1986). According to this model, people incorporate events, issues, candidate traits, and the like into a running tally on each candidate. But people forget these individual bits of information once they have been incorporated into this running tally, retaining only the summary tally. When closed-ended questions ask people about events, issues, and candidate traits, they remind voters about each piece of information that went into that tally so that respondents remember how they evaluated those pieces of information.[1]

This strategy requires that the questionnaire include closed-ended questions on all the relevant considerations, which is, of course, impossible. Yet it has one crucial advantage: closed-ended questions also permit the researcher to ask about topics that might have had subconscious effects on the respondents. Indeed this may be what is happening when respondents are able to report on closed-ended questions that they feel that Clinton cares about people like them while empathy is rarely cited in those terms in open-ended responses. Empathy may have been incorporated into voters' running tallies about Clinton and yet no longer be part of their active memories.

Nonresponse can be a severe problem for closed-ended questions when large numbers of people answer "don't know" to a question. In this situation the data analysis could end up being based on a nonrepresentative part of the sample. Fortunately, this is not a serious problem for most closed-ended NES questions, with the important exception of the ideology measure used in chapter 3 for which many respondents resort to a "don't know" response. Excluding the "don't know" respondents from the analysis would bias the results toward more educated respondents who are more comfortable with abstract concepts such as ideology, so the "don't know" respondents have been assigned to the middle "moderate" category on ideology. This inevitably miscategorizes some people, however, which is likely to detract from the fit of the model.

The net result of all this is that an analyst of closed-ended questions is in the best position to develop a model when the questions are all related to strong attitudes, when the issues in a given election are captured by these attitudes, and when all are based on well-developed theories. An analyst is in the worst position when closed-ended questions tap weak or nonexistent attitudes, when questions about important election themes are not available, and when the theoretical work has not been done.

OPEN-ENDED QUESTIONS

Open-ended questions do not provide already-framed answers. They simply invite people to give their views on a topic. Asking respondents if there is anything in particular that they like or dislike about the Democratic and Republican parties provides an opportunity for respondents to state their views without hinting what those views should be. The ideas that come most speedily to mind usually provide the answers to open-ended questions. This depends on *accessibility*, which refers to the ability to recall mental constructs (i.e., attitudes, thoughts, and so forth). Other things being equal, a category that has recently been activated can be most easily activated again. Therefore, accessibility depends on *chronic accessibility*, the ability to access constructs that one uses all the time, and *temporary accessibility* that allows one to recall a particular category because it has been *primed* by use a short while before. The ability of a chess grandmaster to visualize various arrangements of pieces on a chess board would be an example of *chronic accessibility*, while *temporary accessibility* would be demonstrated by the capacity of someone uninterested in baseball to speak about the National League pennant winner because a World Series game had just been on television (Aldrich, Sullivan, and Borgida 1989, 125–26; Fazio 1986; Fiske and Taylor 1991, 257–66; Nelson and Oxley 1999).

The way that a campaign dialogue will be reflected in open-ended responses depends on what portions of it individual voters capture and what they are able to recall. If one voter were deeply interested in politics, and had reached judgments that he liked the incumbent president's economic and social policies, disapproved of his foreign policies, and thought the president was an effective leader, that voter would have chronic accessibility to settled attitudes. His responses would be little affected by the claims and counterclaims of a campaign. If a second voter were a strong partisan, she might be a *near ideologue* who can verbalize at some length, but whose views reflect those of her party (Campbell et al. 1960, 231–33). This voter would also have chronic accessibility to her attitudes, but since they were partisan, her answers would likely be filled with the positions taken by her party in the fall campaign. If there were a third voter who had little interest in politics, he would likely have temporary accessibility to a mental category that had been primed by some recent development. His brief response might reflect a campaign event the previous day or he might recall a conversation unrelated to the campaign. These three examples can only hint at the wide variety of cognitive structures in the electorate, but they do suggest the ways in which the voters' mental images of the campaign affect their responses to open-ended questions.

Open-ended questions present some well-known practical problems. When responding to "what are your thoughts about X?" a taciturn person may say very little while a garrulous person may say a great deal. In these two cases, the length of the answers will have little relation to what each person knows. Further, since individuals vary so widely in their interests, open-ended responses include a large number of topics, some of which have been mentioned by relatively few persons. Therefore, much time-consuming work is needed to classify these responses into tractable categories. The analyst using closed-ended questions, in contrast, can proceed directly to statistical analysis without having to spend time on this task.

Combining the many verbal answers to the "like and dislike" questions into a small number of response categories for data analysis poses a number of problems.[2] The open-ended analyst knows the substantive meaning of the categories because the respondents provide that information. In the trust category, for example, the overwhelming proportion of the answers mentioned three things: honesty, principles, and Whitewater or some similar incident. Hence, we know what elements are contained within the trust category. The data in table 4.2 (p. 78), however, are based on the total trust category. We can make some reasonable guesses about the impact of honesty, sincerity, and the other attitudes,[3] but coefficients giving the relation of these specific attitudes to vote cannot be calculated. In this respect, the closed-ended items about specific attitudes are better.

Another problem occurs when disparate comments are grouped together into an overall category such as the "general" categories in chapter 4. Half a dozen types of responses constituted almost all the answers in the general candidate category, but two of these were so broad that they represented nothing more than positive or negative evaluations of the candidates, two more were anti-Dole (references to age and campaign tactics), and two more were anti-Clinton (references to Hillary Clinton and damaging personal incidents). When specific topics run in opposite directions (as when age worked against Dole whereas damaging personal incidents worked against Clinton), and the two are combined into the same general candidate category, their separate effects are masked.

Nonresponse poses still another problem for the analysis of the open-ended party and candidate like and dislike questions. Take the "international involvement" item as an example. A respondent who makes no comments on any of the questions that refer to international involvement gets coded as zero on this item, just as the person who makes one comment favorable to the Democrats on that issue and one comment favorable to the Republicans (so that the person's comments cancel out to zero). These two respondents are likely to be very different, however, with the first having little reaction to international involvement while the second has enough reactions to have mixed feelings on which party is preferable on the issue. This problem is more likely to occur in the 16-variable vote model, where the reactions to the parties and candidates are divided into so many subcategories that many respondents are likely not to have made any comments on most of the 16 variables. The effects of this problem have never been systematically investigated, but it may be more difficult to find a category significant when few have volunteered comments that fall into that category.

There have been general challenges to the use of open-ended questions. Richard Nisbett and Timothy Wilson (1977) dispute the ability of people to give reasons for their behaviors, and Wendy Rahn, Jon Krosnick, and Marijke Breuning (1994) have applied this to candidate evaluations. Other social psychologists (Fiske and Taylor 1991) point to several studies critical of Nisbett and Wilson (pp. 399–402) and conclude that under the appropriate conditions people can report on the content of their thoughts (p. 270). In any case, statistical analysis of the open-ended comments is designed to obviate some of these problems. If a voter mentions a specific topic in response to a likes/dislikes question, it does not mean that the topic is necessarily related to this person's vote choice. Subsequent statistical analysis is necessary to determine which factors have a significant effect, just as is the case with closed-ended questions.

In sum, open-ended questions work best with articulate respondents who have well-developed thoughts about the subject matter. They are not appropriate if a pollster needs answers in a hurry. Neither are they suitable if an analyst needs to know the exact relationships between a large number of variables in order to develop a multistage model. Open-ended questions, however, do provide an opportunity for people who care intensely about their views on such issues as gun control to state their views. They are useful in exploring new areas of research. If a topic has not been previously studied, inductive studies of open-ended responses may be the fastest way to discern fruitful avenues of investigation. And the repeated use of well-framed open-ended questions, as in the National Election Studies, can be very rewarding because changes in the answers from one election to the next can be attributed entirely to changed political circumstances rather than variation in question wording.

Different Models

While many of the differences between the analyses are due to the use of closed-ended questions in chapter 3 and open-ended questions in chapter 4, some are caused by differences in the models used. The NES preelection survey includes about an hour's worth of questions on a wide variety of topics. While both open-ended and closed-ended questions are used, there are many more of the latter. Including hundreds of closed-ended variables in the same model would violate the standard of parsimony. Additionally, several of these predictor variables would be highly correlated, so including all of them would make it more difficult for any of them to achieve statistical significance. Therefore, analysts using closed-ended questions must decide what they wish to emphasize in a particular model and select accordingly.

The model presented in chapter 3 was developed inductively. Variables were selected if bivariate analysis showed them to be related to the 1996 vote. This guarantees a sensitivity to the topics important in that election. A second selection criterion was whether the variables were of theoretical interest to the analysts. To measure candidate attractiveness, the analysts relied on four separate dimensions that Kinder has shown to be related to candidate assessment. Party identification is included to measure the effects of partisanship. In addition to ideology (self-assessment of liberalism/conservatism), closed-ended items about the economy, abortion, affirmative action, and the role of women were used to determine the role of issues. Evangelical commitment and 7 other demographic variables were included to see if these had any effects on vote. Including variables that were important in 1996 allows this analysis to reflect new issues and other matters that affect voting (such as the newly found relevance of evangelical religious commitment), though this variable selection strategy is ad hoc and makes comparisons with models for other election years more difficult.

Less question selection was involved in the model presented in chapter 4. It was based on the likes and dislikes questions that have been repeated in every presidential election study since 1952. The model took advantage of the repetition, and was constructed so it could be applied to successive presidential elections.[4] But if the analyst could not select other data, a good deal of choice was involved in how the categories are constructed. There is no need for there to be 3 or 16 categories. Indeed, the well-known model constructed by Donald Stokes (Stokes et al. 1958) had 6 categories. Further, which attitudes are grouped into which categories has a major bearing on whether they are more or less closely related to vote choice. For example, group references (for example, being good for working people or being too close to working people) are assigned to issue categories, in the case of working people to economic management. If they had all been assembled together into a separate group category, it is likely that the group category would have been very important and the issue categories less important. This potential for increasing or decreasing the importance of categories obviously affects the correspondence between this open-ended model and any closed-ended model.

Although we pose open- and closed-ended questions as alternatives in this chapter, we recognize that both could be used at once in the same analysis. For example, the empathy variable used in chapter 3 could be added to the analysis of the open-ended responses in chapter 4, or a count of references to age in the open-ended responses could be included with the analysis of the closed-ended questions in chapter 3. Such a mixed model would be less theoretically pure than the models estimated in our chapters above, however, and could lead to interpretation problems. That is, if adding a variable from the other model caused a noticeable change, the issue would be whether it did so because of the substantive information it contained or because it was measured differently. To avoid this ambiguity, we report only pure models in our chapters.

In two important respects, the models are quite similar. Both analyze only the major-party presidential vote, so results cannot be attributed to handling the Perot alternative. Even if the researchers wanted to include the Perot vote, questions on which many of the predictors are based were not included in the 1996 NES survey on Perot. Also, chapter 3 uses logit analysis while chapter 4 uses probit analysis—techniques that are both appropriate for analyzing a dichotomous dependent variable. They make slightly different assumptions about the distribution of the underlying variable, but the two methods give very similar substantive results (Aldrich and Nelson 1984).

A very consequential difference between the two chapters is that the analysis in chapter 3 is based on the whole sample, whereas that in chapter 4 is based on only a random half-sample who were asked what they liked and disliked about both the candidates and the political parties. This complicates matters because while the best comparison between the two models should involve the same respondents, reducing the number of cases (in this instance from 1,034 voters to 506 voters) also reduces the likelihood that variables will be found to be statistically significant. In this note, therefore, we will place our prime reliance on comparisons between the closed-ended and open-ended results using the half-sample, but we will also make secondary reference to variables reported to be statistically significant in chapter 3 using the full sample.[5]

Indeterminacies

Given the differences between closed-ended and open-ended questions, and the further differences between the two models themselves, there are bound to be some variables included in one model but not in the other. In these cases, dissimilarities in the findings are indeterminate. If the first model has no data that bear on a finding in the second model, there is no way that the first model can be used to judge the accuracy of the second on this point. Nor can one conclude that one model is correct and the other is not. All that can be said is that the models are different.

What independent variables are included in one model but not in the other? To begin with, the empathy item is the independent variable most strongly related to vote in the closed-ended model, whereas only a few people gave answers mentioning caring when the likes and dislikes questions were asked. It may be that caring wasn't salient enough to come to mind when the open-ended questions were asked. It may be that the candidate trait items have a disproportionate emphasis on personal qualities as opposed to job-related qualifications, and consequently some of the open-ended comments cannot be mapped into the candidate trait items very well. We could speculate at length, but all we know is that the models cannot be compared with respect to this variable.

Coming from the other direction, the candidate trait items (and hence the closed-ended model) did not include any references to the candidates' age, which was very important in the open-ended general candidate category. A single candidate trait question, gets things done (part of the leadership variable), refers to the candidates' management capacity, so a limited comparison is possible there. Otherwise, the candidate attributes of age and management ability are indeterminate.

With respect to issues, the closed-ended analysis did not include items that correspond to social benefits, an open-ended category that included welfare, education, health care, aid to the elderly, and aid to poor people. The closed-ended analysis does have an abortion item, and abortion was frequently mentioned in the open-ended comments grouped under civil liberties. Nevertheless, the closed-ended analysis does not include variables that refer to public morality, gay rights, gun control, or generosity/selfishness, which together account for a substantial proportion of the civil liberties comments.

Finally, the full version of the closed-ended model (equation 2 in table 3.11, p. 67) includes evangelical commitment and a series of demographic variables: gender, age, smoker, education, white, income, and married. Evangelical commitment, not included in the open-ended model, was statistically significant, so this is another indeterminacy. None of the demographic variables are significant, but the effects of these factors on the attitudinal variables are controlled. There are no controls for demographic factors in the open-ended models.

To reiterate, the absence of similar variables does not mean that one model is correct and the other is not—only that comparisons cannot be made with respect to these variables.

Direct Comparisons

The abortion issue demonstrates the one major difference between the two models. Abortion is the most prominent part of the civil liberties category, which in turn was the most potent specific issue attitude in 1996 according to chapter 4. But analysis of a closed-ended abortion question in chapter 3 shows that it is not significant as a predictor of the vote when other variables are controlled. It may be that the effects of abortion are being captured by some of the controlling variables, for example, the significant effect of evangelical commitment may be picking up the abortion issue. It may also be that this difference arises because an issue such as abortion can be the most important voting issue for an intense subset of respondents who mention it spontaneously in the open-ended material and vote accordingly, though the issue matters less when attitudes are elicited from everyone. Or the difference may be due to the likes and dislikes format that leads open-ended respondents to mention abortion in relation to parties and candidates whereas the closed-ended item ascertains only the respondents' own opinions, and that the party/candidate-related responses are more likely to be related to vote choice than personal opinions. In any case, there is a consequential difference in the impact of abortion between the two analyses.

Otherwise, the analyses lead to reasonably similar conclusions. To begin with the candidate attributes, it seems clear that the closed-ended integrity variable and the open-ended trust category are measuring the same thing. Both the full-sample analysis in chapter 3 and the half-sample analysis in chapter 4 agree that this character issue hurt Clinton, though obviously not enough to cost him the election. Since the closed-ended competence variable depends on whether the candidate is seen as knowledgeable, it is tapping the same attitudes as the open-ended intelligence category. Both models show this as favoring Clinton, but at best having only marginal significance in determining the vote. It is barely significant in the full-sample reduced model in chapter 3, and is not statistically significant in chapter 4. Only a partial comparison of the closed-ended leadership variable is possible. This trait dimension rests on three stimuli: whether the candidate provides strong leadership, is inspiring, and gets things done. Inspection of the open-ended comments does not show either Clinton or Dole being seen as strong leaders or inspiring. The "gets things done" item, however, can be matched against the open-ended management category. The management element that seems to provide the best fit is a general assessment of the job the candidates had done. These open-ended comments, like the closed-ended leadership variable, favored President Clinton. On a more global level, while attitudes toward candidates were operationalized quite differently in these two models, both found them important in the 1996 vote decision.

Partisanship is measured quite differently in the closed-ended and open-ended models. In chapter 3, party identification is used; in chapter 4, party image based on the party-related attitudes is employed. Party identification and party image are related, but one's self-identification as a Republican or a Democrat is much more strongly associated with vote choice than one's perception of the two parties. Partisanship is significantly associated with vote choice in both models, but predictably party identification plays a stronger role in the models in chapter 3 than the party image in the models in chapter 4. Still, a measure of partisanship is clearly important to understanding the vote; which measure is used matters less.

Ideology, specifically one's self-placement on a liberal-conservative scale, in the closed-ended models can be easily mapped into the general issue variable in the open-ended models. This category includes both references to liberalism and conservatism and to the closely related preference for more government activity or less government activity. Both chapters agreed that ideology was statistically significant, and both agreed that ideology tended to the conservative side in 1996. Bill Clinton had to swim against the ideological tide. Finally, while both models found economic variables significant (retrospective evaluations of the national economy in the full sample in chapter 3 and economic management in chapter 4), both agreed that the economy was not the most potent factor in Clinton's reelection.

Conclusion

What kind of question is best—closed-ended or open-ended? There is no simple answer because each kind has advantages as well as limitations. Analyses based on the two types of questions can actually be compared along a number of different dimensions, as the discussion in this chapter has illustrated. What may be most intriguing are the different assumptions about the psychological processes underlying individual responses and their different implications for models of voter decisionmaking. In the end, each type provides useful information that helps complement the other.

These two chapters provide one of the rare instances in which we are able to contrast closed-ended and open-ended models for the same election. Where direct comparisons could be made, the only real substantive difference concerned abortion. The candidate attributes that could be compared had similar effects; partisanship was important in both solutions; both models reached similar conclusions about the impact of ideology and the economy. Both models correctly predicted well over 90 percent of the major-party vote choices. And in the small minority of cases where erroneous predictions were made, both models tended to overpredict the Clinton vote.

This is an impressive level of agreement. Given the very real differences between the closed-ended and open-ended approaches, and the further differences between the material included in the two models, it would not have been surprising to find that chapters 3 and 4 reached substantially different conclusions. Yet this is not what happened. There are instances when one model could cast light on a topic that the other model could not address, but the answers are usually the same when both models can address the same topics. The precise answers depend on the questions, but the thrust of the answers is the same regardless of the questions.

6

The Impact of the Economy
on the 1996 Election:
The Invisible Foot

Dean Lacy and J. Tobin Grant

"It's the economy, stupid" emerged as the unofficial slogan of Bill Clinton's 1992 presidential campaign. It was a stinging reminder to incumbent George Bush that the economy had stagnated since the early years of his term. Even though the economy had improved somewhat during the final months of the 1992 campaign, voter perceptions of the economy lagged. The 1992 National Election Study (NES) asked voters, "How about the economy in the country as a whole? Would you say that over the past year the nation's economy has gotten better, stayed about the same, or gotten worse?" Seventy-five percent of respondents answered that economic conditions had worsened over the previous year; 22 percent believed conditions had remained the same; only 3 percent believed the economy had improved. George Bush lost the election, in large part, because of what was perceived as a poor economy (Alvarez and Nagler 1995).

Clinton's arrival at the White House did little to reverse the economic conditions that had aided him in the 1992 election. Economic growth was lower in 1993 than in 1992. It appeared that Clinton's unofficial slogan would become fodder for his opponents as they prepared to stop his quest for reelection. Such fears (or hopes) were premature. After the president suffered a disastrous 1994 loss of his party's seats in Congress, economic conditions became the best in decades. By 1995, and continuing through 1996, the unemployment rate fell below 5.5 percent, and the inflation rate fell below 3 percent. The stock market rocketed to record highs, and public sentiment reflected economic confidence. In the 1996 NES postelection interviews, only 11 percent of respondents believed that economic conditions had worsened during the past year; 62 percent believed the economy had remained the same; and 27 percent believed the economy had improved.

Public evaluations of the economy in 1996 were among the most positive ever recorded by the NES. In each election year since 1980, the NES has asked respondents to rate national economic conditions over the past year. Table 6.1 shows the distribution of public perceptions of the economy from 1980 to 1996. The percentage of the American public who had a negative evaluation of the economy was smaller in 1996 than in any previous year on record. Since the NES began recording perceptions of the national economy, Presidents Reagan (1984) and Clinton (1996) have won reelection when the economy appeared healthy. Presidents Carter (1980) and Bush (1992) lost their reelection bids, and in both years more than half of NES respondents believed the economy had declined during the preceding year. In every year, 35 percent or less of voters who perceived a declining economy voted for the incumbent party (see table 6.2). These figures alone suggest that economic conditions—or at least public perceptions of economic conditions—exert a powerful influence on voting behavior and election outcomes.

TABLE 6.1

RETROSPECTIVE EVALUATION OF NATIONAL ECONOMY
(IN PERCENTAGES)

	Better	*Same*	*Worse*
1980	3.7	13.0	83.3
1984	42.8	33.5	23.7
1988	18.8	50.0	31.2
1992	4.6	23.1	72.3
1996	27.5	62.2	10.3

SOURCE: 1980–96 National Election Studies.

TABLE 6.2

VOTE FOR INCUMBENT'S PARTY BY RETROSPECTIVE EVALUA-
TION OF NATIONAL ECONOMY (IN PERCENTAGES)

	Better	*Same*	*Worse*
1980	48.7	63.7	35.2
1984	79.2	52.0	20.3
1988	76.2	52.3	34.0
1992	71.1	51.2	25.9
1996	72.8	47.2	27.5

SOURCE: 1980–96 National Election Studies.

The economy wields an invisible foot in American presidential elections, able to kick incumbent presidents out of office when economic conditions turn poor. Few political scientists would argue against the proposition that incumbent presidents tend to win when the economy is stable or improving. Similarly, few political scientists would argue against the claim that voter perceptions of the economy exert a significant influence—both statistically and substantively—on voters' choice of candidates. In this chapter we provide evidence supporting both propositions. First, we estimate a multivariate model of the 1996 vote, showing that perceptions of the economy prove statistically and substantively significant as a predictor of vote choice. Second, we demonstrate that had perceptions of the economy been as bad in 1996 as they were in 1992, Bill Clinton would have lost his bid for reelection. We also add a new twist to the literature on economics and elections by demonstrating that economic perceptions influence voter turnout. Voters who perceive a declining economy disapprove of incumbents in one of two ways: by voting against them or by not voting.

The Electoral Impact of Economic Conditions

The link between the economy and voting was established some forty years ago. Since Anthony Downs (1957) first presented his economic theory of voting, analysis of the connection between the economy and electoral politics has become one of the more overtilled areas of research in American political science (Arnold 1982, 93). One the earliest findings in the literature on economic voting is that citizens vote retrospectively (Key 1966). According to this theory, voters punish the incumbent party if their personal economic situations are poor. Morris Fiorina (1981) argues that voters base evaluations of a candidate's future performance in office on the past performance of the candidate's party. Voters punish incumbents for a poor economy by revising downward their opinion of the incumbent's prospects for managing the economy in the future.

Donald Kinder and D. Roderick Kiewiet (1981) find that voters' retrospective evaluations of the economy are not tied to the voters' personal economic conditions, however. A voter is less likely to ask candidates, "What have you done for me lately?" than "What have you done for the country lately?" (Kinder and Kiewiet 1981; Kinder and Mebane 1983; Kramer 1983; Markus 1988). Instead of reacting to their own economic conditions, voters employ a sociotropic, or group-based, evaluation of the economy when choosing for whom to vote. Americans place the moral responsibility of individual economic conditions on the shoulders of the individual, but they place the moral responsibility of national economic conditions on our elected leaders, particularly the president (McCloskey and Zaller 1984).

Exactly what voters look for when evaluating the economy is not clear. Studies of the link between economics and elections focus on various economic indicators, such as unemployment, inflation, growth rates, or the "misery index," which combines inflation and unemployment rates. It is clear, however, that perception becomes reality. Measures of voter perceptions of economic conditions tend to perform remarkably well as an explanation for vote choice in presidential elections but less well as an explanation in congressional elections.

An implicit assumption throughout the literature on the economy and vote choice is that the economic perceptions influence a voter's choice of candidates, not a voter's choice of whether to vote. When the time comes to vote in a competitive election, every potential voter has at least three choices: vote for the incumbent party, vote for a challenger, or abstain. In the past two American presidential elections, voters have had a choice of at least two challengers, leaving four or more options for voters on election day.

Because the economy has such a strong effect on those deciding for whom to vote, it seems reasonable that it would also affect voter turnout. Unlike the exhaustive literature on vote choice, research on the economy and voter turnout remains largely untouched. This research offers three hypotheses on the economy's effect on voter turnout (cf. Rosenstone 1982). On the one hand, poor economic conditions may serve to mobilize potential voters, particularly those facing economic hardships, to seek retribution on the incumbent responsible for their plight (see Schlozman and Verba 1979). On the other hand, a bad economy may suppress voter turnout because potential voters facing personal adversity will focus less attention on politics (Rosenstone 1982; Wolfinger and Rosenstone 1980). Finally, there is also the possibility that economic conditions have no effect on voter turnout (Fiorina 1978 documents this in congressional elections).

In a cross-national analysis, Benjamin Radcliff (1992) finds that the effect of the economy on turnout is mitigated by government spending on social programs. In countries where social spending is either very limited or very extensive, citizens respond to a poor economy by going to the polls. In countries such as the United States, however, with only moderate levels of government spending on social programs, a poor economy leads to a withdrawal from the political process. Steven Rosenstone (1982) finds that for every 10 percent of potential voters who are personally worse off, there is a 1 percent decrease in voter turnout.

The research on turnout and perceptions of the economy leads to a conundrum. From the research on vote choice, we know that people who think the economy is declining are more likely to punish incumbents. But these very same people may be less likely to vote. While the literature on the economy and voting suggests there is a link between perceptions of the economy and turnout, the research to date has not examined the link directly due to two omissions. First, like early work on the economy and vote choice, the research on turnout assumes that only personal economic conditions matter to voters. Rosenstone (1982) uses a person's subjective judgment of his or her own financial situation in a model of turnout. If voters choose between candidates based on sociotropic rather than personal judgments of the economy, then one might expect that evaluations of the national economy will affect turnout. No research to date has examined the influence of perceptions of the national economy on turnout. A second omission from the literature linking economic conditions to vote choice is that the decision to vote is modeled as a dichotomous choice—to vote or not to vote. While researchers assume that voters who go to the polls in response to a poor economy also punish the incumbent party, this has not been tested empirically. As with the vote-choice literature, work on the economy and turnout does not include all of the options available to citizens. By integrating an individual-level analysis of the decision to vote with the decision of whom to vote for, we are able to clarify the link between economic conditions, voter turnout, and vote choice.

To understand properly the role of the economy on voting, we must begin by recognizing that the economy is not the only factor in a person's vote calculus. In the 1996 election, as in previous elections, voters rely on their party identification, issue preferences, and evaluations of the candidates. While there are numerous variations of this vote model, from all of them we draw one certain conclusion—the economy is important, but it is not all-important.

Still the Economy?

To assess the impact of economic perceptions on the 1996 election, we estimate a model of vote choice. Our model includes a four-category dependent variable: vote for Clinton, vote for Dole, vote for Perot, and abstain. The dependent variable in our model presumes that the decision not to vote is politically meaningful. We include abstention as a choice, recognizing, as John Aldrich (1997, 422) does, "Whether one votes, therefore, depends on consideration of whom or what one would support, once in the booth, and cannot . . . be understood except in relation to candidate choice."[1]

Since the choice is unordered, we must estimate the model using a multinomial discrete choice estimation technique such as multinomial logit (MNL) or multinomial probit (MNP).[2] The independent variables include two evaluations of the economy: one measure taps perceptions of the national economy, the other measures the change in a person's own financial situation over the previous year (see table 6.3, p. 104, for question wording). We also include in the model various control variables to separate the effect

TABLE 6.3

VARIABLE CONSTRUCTION

Age categories	Age categories: 18 to 29, 30 to 44, and 45 to 59.
African American	African American = 1; not African American = 0.
Democrat	Democrat (includes independent leaners) = 1; others = 0.
Education	Number of years in school from 0 to 18.
Female	Female = 1; male = 0.
Ideology	Extremely liberal = 1; extremely conservative = 7. "We hear a lot of talk these days about liberals and conservatives. Please think of a 7-point scale on which the political views that people might hold are arranged from extremely liberal to extremely conservative. On this scale, a measurement of 1 means extremely liberal political views, and a measurement of 7 means extremely conservative political views. Moderate or middle-of-the-road views are at point 4, and of course there are points in between at 2, 3, 5, and 6. Where would you place yourself on this scale, or haven't you thought much about this?"
Nation's economy worsened	"How about the economy in the country as a whole? Would you say that over the past year the nation's economy has gotten better, stayed about the same, or gotten worse?" Follow-up: "Would you say much better/worse or somewhat better/worse?" Scores range from 1 (much better) to 5 (much worse).
Personal finances worsened	"We are interested in how people are getting along financially these days. Would you say that you (and your family living here) are better off or worse off financially than you were a year ago?" Follow-up: "Is that much better/worse off or somewhat better/worse off?" Scores range from 1 (much better off) to 5 (much worse off).
Republican	Republican (including independent leaners) = 1; others = 0.

of economic perceptions from partisanship, ideology, and demographic variables.[3] To measure partisanship, we include a dummy variable if the respondent is a Democrat or Republican. Pure independents are the base category.[4] We include a voter's self-placement on a 7-point left-right scale as a measure of ideology. We also include gender, race, education level, income, and age. We estimate the model using multinomial logit with Clinton as the base category. Results appear in table 6.4.

Retrospective evaluations of the national economy prove statistically significant as an explanation of voter choice. Since high values on the national economic evaluation indicate that the respondent believed the economy declined, we expect that the coefficient on the national economy variable should be positive for each choice (Dole, Perot, and absention). The

TABLE 6.4

DETERMINANTS OF VOTE CHOICE

IN THE 1996 PRESIDENTIAL ELECTION

Coefficients for Clinton are normalized to zero

| | Coefficient (Standard error) for | | |
Independent variable	Dole	Perot	Abstain
Constant	−4.911*	−2.741*	2.142*
	(.893)	(1.146)	(.612)
Personal finance worsened	.110	.125	.029
	(.095)	(.128)	(.073)
National economy worsened	.711*	.709*	.464*
	(.121)	(.161)	(.089)
Democrat	−2.490*	−1.478*	−1.831*
	(.404)	(.450)	(.297)
Republican	1.258*	−.425	−.457
	(.374)	(.478)	(.322)
Ideology	.369*	.086	.092*
	(.063)	(.072)	(.038)
Female	−.234	−.641*	−.250*
	(.190)	(.267)	(.146)
Income	.017	−.055	−.052*
	(.020)	(.028)	(.013)
Education	.102*	−.048	−.182*
	(.044)	(.061)	(.033)
Age: 18–29	−.317	.660	1.765*
	(.340)	(.503)	(.284)
Age: 30–44	−.049	1.077*	1.252*
	(.263)	(.407)	(.220)
Age: 45–59	−.534*	.064	.562*
	(.284)	(.468)	(.234)
African American	−3.124*	−2.587*	−.286
	(.977)	(.972)	(.203)

N   1517
Likelihood ratio   1103.53

SOURCE: 1996 National Election Study.

*$p < .05$, one-tailed.

results indicate that people who believe the national economy worsened are more likely to vote for Dole or Perot or to abstain than they are to vote for Clinton. The coefficients across choices are directly comparable: negative evaluations of the national economy appear to have an equal effect (.71) on the likelihood of voting for Dole or Perot. The effect on not voting is lower (.46) but still statistically significant. The coefficients must be transformed into predicted probabilities of choosing each alternative in order to demonstrate the full effect of national economic evaluations. Table 6.5 shows the probability that the average voter in the sample will choose each of the alternatives given the belief that the economy grew much better, stayed the same, and grew much worse.[5]

TABLE 6.5

ESTIMATED 1996 VOTE PROBABILITY BY RETROSPECTIVE
EVALUATION OF NATIONAL ECONOMY

	Much better	*Remained the same*	*Much worse*
Clinton	.60	.35	.15
Dole	.05	.13	.23
Perot	.02	.06	.10
Abstain	.32	.47	.51

SOURCE: Based on table 6.3.

The "average voter" who believed the economy greatly improved had a .60 probability of voting for Clinton in 1996, .32 probability of abstaining, and a slim probability (.05 or less) of voting for either Dole or Perot. The average voter who believed the economy grew much worse was most likely to abstain, but if he or she voted, the most likely choice was Dole. The average voter who perceived a severe economic downturn was still more likely to vote for Bill Clinton than for Ross Perot.

A person's evaluation of his or her own economic situation has little impact on the vote. Retrospective personal evaluations do not reach conventional levels of statistical significance for any of the alternatives. Substantively, the effect of one's personal economic condition is weak. The average voter in the sample will most likely vote for Clinton regardless of his or her perception of changes in his or her own economic condition.

Other independent variables in the model have predictable effects on the vote decision. Democrats are more likely to vote for Clinton than to choose Dole, Perot, or abstention (indicated by the negative sign on the coefficient). Republicans are more likely to vote for Dole than Clinton, but they are more likely to vote for Clinton than Perot. Republican Party identification is not a statistically significant predictor of the choice between Clinton and abstention. The effect of ideology is also generally predictable. Persons who place themselves farther to the right are more likely to vote for Dole or to abstain. There is no effect for Ross Perot: a voter's ideological position does not do much to explain the choice between Perot and Clinton.

Some surprising effects emerge among the sociodemographic variables. People with higher family incomes are more likely to vote for Clinton than to abstain, but there is no effect for Dole or Perot. Family income does not appear to separate the Dole and Perot voters from Clinton voters.[6] Women are more likely to vote for Clinton than to vote for Perot or to abstain, but there is no gender gap in the support of Bob Dole and Bill Clinton, contrary to popular accounts that Dole lost the votes of "soccer moms." This result is easily explained: The gender gap appears in party identification, not in vote choice. Women tend to vote for Democratic candidates because women are more often Democrats. Voters with higher levels of education are more likely to vote for Clinton than they are to vote for Dole or to abstain, but there is no relationship between education level and vote for Ross Perot. African American voters are more likely to choose Clinton than to vote for Dole or Perot, but African Americans are not more likely than other Americans to abstain, controlling for other factors (Wolfinger and Rosenstone 1980).

We code age as a set of dummy variables, with people 60 and over as the base category, since age is nonlinearly related to vote choice (Alvarez and Nagler 1995). Compared to voters 60 and older, voters between the ages of 45 and 59 are much more likely to vote for Clinton than for Dole, while voters in the other cohorts (18–29 and 30–44) are as likely as senior citizens to vote for Clinton. The 30–44-year-olds are more likely than senior citizens to vote for Perot. The other age groups (18–29 and 44–59) are no different from senior citizens in levels of support for Perot. The most striking effect of age is on voter turnout. All age cohorts are more likely than senior citizens to abstain. The coefficients on the age cohorts for abstention indicate that each successively younger cohort is more likely not to vote than to vote for Clinton.

The model performs well at explaining the vote. In the sample of 1517 respondents used to estimate the coefficients, 35.7 percent voted for Clinton, 25.7 percent for Dole, 4.7 percent for Perot, and 33.8 percent claim not to have voted.[7] Our model predicts that 35.6 percent of the sample voted for Clinton, 25.7 percent for Dole, 4.2 percent for Perot, with 34.4 percent abstaining. This translates into a predicted three-way vote of 54.3 percent for Clinton, 39.1 percent for Dole, and 6.4 percent for Perot. The deviation from the election's actual results (49 percent for Clinton, 41 percent for Dole, and 9 percent for Perot) is due to the NES sample, not to the model. The model is a significant improvement over a null model without the explanatory variables, as indicated by the likelihood ratio test.

While the effects of the demographic variables are interesting, they serve primarily as control variables. Our focus is on the economy. Even controlling for partisanship, ideology, and demographic factors, a voter's evaluation of the national economy is a crucial explanation not only of a choice among the competing candidates but also of a decision to vote. The full electoral effect of evaluations of the economy emerges from a simulation of what the 1996 vote would have been under 1992 perceptions of the economy (table 6.6, p. 108). By taking the average voter evaluation of the economy in 1992 (the economy grew worse, or 4.1 on the NES scale) and substituting it for voter evaluations of the economy in 1996, we can estimate what the presidential vote would have been under 1992 conditions, assuming all else equal. Under 1992 economic conditions, Bill Clinton would have been supported by 24.4 percent of the sample, Bob Dole by 30.1 percent, and Ross Perot by 6.3 percent. Thirty-nine percent of the sample would have abstained.[8] In a three-way race, Dole would have garnered 49 percent of the votes, with Clinton getting only 40 percent of the votes and Perot receiving 10 percent. In a failing economy, Bill Clinton would have suffered the same fate as George Bush did in 1992.

TABLE 6.6

ESTIMATED 1996 PRESIDENTIAL VOTE UNDER 1996
AND 1992 ECONOMIC PERCEPTIONS
(IN PERCENTAGES)

	Predicted outcome (includes abstention)	Predicted vote share (excludes abstention)	Predicted vote share without Perot
1996 perceptions			
Clinton	35.6	54.3	58.2
Dole	25.7	39.1	41.8
Perot	4.2	6.4	—
Abstain	34.4	—	—
1992 perceptions			
Clinton	24.4	40.0	44.0
Dole	30.1	49.0	56.0
Perot	6.3	10.0	—
Abstain	39.1	—	—

SOURCE: Based on table 6.4.

Personal economic conditions carry much less weight in elections. If the average voter's perception of his or her personal economic situation had been the same as the average voter's perception in 1992, vote shares would have been 35.4 percent for Clinton, 25.8 percent Dole, 4.3 percent for Perot, and 34.5 percent abstention. Again, it is the national economy, not personal economic conditions, for which voters punish incumbents.

The model allows us to evaluate the impact of Ross Perot on the 1996 election. By dividing each voter's predicted probability of voting for Clinton, voting for Dole, or abstaining by one minus his or her predicted probability of voting for Perot, we obtain the likely vote outcome had Perot not entered the race. With Perot out of the 1996 race, Bill Clinton would have polled

37.1 percent of the sample, Bob Dole 26.7 percent, and 36.2 percent would have abstained. This translates into a two-party vote of 58.2 percent for Clinton and 41.8 percent for Dole. Perot's presence in the election lowered Clinton's vote share by more than it lowered Dole's. Our results also enable us to calculate the difference in abstention with Perot in the race and out of the race: voter turnout would have decreased by 2.2 percentage points with Perot out of the race (see Lacy and Burden 1999 for similar calculations for the 1992 election).

In a two-way race between Clinton and Dole, the effect of the economy appears even more pronounced. Under 1992 economic conditions, Clinton would have received only 44 percent of the vote, with Dole earning the remaining majority in a landslide.

The results from the model and simulations clearly document the tremendous kick of the economy's invisible foot in presidential elections. What we do not know, however, is how far back voters look when evaluating the economic performance of presidents, and whether they evaluate only the direction of the economy rather than its overall health. The NES questions ask respondents to rate whether economic conditions improved or declined over the previous year. But what if an incumbent presided over three years of a dismal economy and one year of improvement? Presumably, given the questions from the NES, the incumbent would benefit from the improvement. What if the incumbent led the country into depression, only to improve the economy gradually during the final year of his term? Despite the volumes of research on economic performance and the presidential vote, we still know little about the length of voters' memories and their willingness to let improvements in the economy overshadow the depths of economic downturns.

Another field of research worth cultivating is the determinants of perceptions of the national economy. Economic perceptions may be endogenous to vote choice. That is, voters who decide to support Bill Clinton in 1996 may decide that the economy is doing well, rather than vice versa. A panel study of voter perceptions of the economy and their preference (or approval) of candidates may clarify the direction of the causal arrow: do perceptions of the economy influence vote choice, or does vote choice determine perceptions of the economy? Our analysis has assumed that perceptions of the national economy are primarily exogenous, or determined by things other than one's choice of candidates.

Conclusion

The economy has the ability to kick incumbent presidents out of office, as it did George Bush in 1992. Bill Clinton would have suffered Bush's fate in 1996 were it not for the economic turnaround of 1993 and 1994. In every election since 1980, when the NES first incorporated retrospective evaluations of the national economy into its battery of questions, the incumbent party has won reelection during good times and lost during bad.

Our estimation of the economy's influence on the election confirmed several theories on the economy and elections. As in previous elections, evaluations of the economy were critical to vote choice. People who believe the economy is stable or performing well tend to support the incumbent; people who believe the economy is performing poorly tend to vote for a challenger or stay at home. Sociotropic concerns influence the vote decision more than personal concerns. While voters hold the president accountable for national economic conditions, they do not blame the president for their personal economic condition.

Our findings do more than merely confirm current theories of economics and voting. We add to current theory by including abstention as a choice that is also influenced by perceptions of the economy. Economic conditions affect turnout. A better economy appears to yield higher turnout, and a failing economy depresses turnout. Incumbents may lose election during economic downturns in part as a result of the decline in turnout among their supporters.

Our results establish the relationship between economic perceptions and voter turnout for one election. More work is needed to chart this relationship through time and space. Our results also suggest that studies of turnout may need to include voter perceptions of the economy as a control variable in two respects. First, some groups that appear to turn out at lower rates may do so because their perceptions of the economy differ from the perceptions of other groups with higher turnout rates. Second, temporal changes in turnout may be the result of changing economic conditions. Despite perceptions that economic conditions and elections are an overtilled area of research in political science, we see much ground barely broken.

7

Hillary Clinton and
the President's Reelection

ANTHONY MUGHAN AND BARRY C. BURDEN

PRESIDENTIAL ELECTION campaign strategies and vote choice have tended to be seen as revolving solely around the Democratic and Republican presidential candidates. In the 1990s, however, this characterization of the personality dynamics of presidential election campaigns appears to have become less accurate as new actors have emerged center stage: the wives of the major-party candidates. The 1992 contest was the first in which party strategists deliberately made the "traditional" Barbara Bush and the "modern" Hillary Rodham Clinton into campaign issues in the anticipation that, having distinctive qualities, opinions, and lifestyles, each would bring her husband votes he would not otherwise have won. The evidence suggested that this strategy was more effective for the Democrats than it was for the Republicans, with Mrs. Clinton having a more substantial impact on the two-party presidential vote than Mrs. Bush (Mughan and Burden 1995). The longer-term importance of the 1992 precedent, though, is that the mold may have been set for future contests. Wives had become potentially important influences in their husbands' campaigns and could not be allowed to remain in obscurity. Their qualifications to be in the White House became subject to public scrutiny. Thus, in the run-up to the 1996 campaign, the cover of *Time* magazine (1 July 1996) asked momentously, "Hillary vs. Liddy: Who Would Be the Better First Lady?" and then devoted seventeen pages to discussing the competing candidates for the position of first lady. CNN broadcast a television special on the major candidates' wives, and an Ohio newspaper, the *Toledo Blade*, even offered to host a debate between them. Elizabeth Dole declined the offer.

Clearly the Democratic and Republican candidates' wives attracted unprecedented media attention in the presidential election campaigns of the 1990s.[1] But whether, and under what conditions, they had an impact on the voting public's choice of president is a separate question altogether. It is not simply a function of personal popularity, since Barbara Bush enjoyed a much higher public standing than did Hillary Clinton in 1992, but Mrs. Bush's personality did not have the same electoral impact (Mughan and Burden 1995). This chapter examines the electoral impact of the candidates' wives mostly in the context of the 1996 presidential election, which differed from its immediate predecessor insofar as the Democratic and Republican candidates' wives were far more similar to one another than they had been in 1992. Both Hillary Clinton and Elizabeth Dole were educated career women who had built substantial reputations in their chosen fields independently of their husbands. Mrs. Clinton, of course, had become more visible, and more controversial, during her husband's first term, and public opinion toward her, particularly in the form of a sharp decline in popularity, was surely taken into account by the Clinton campaign strategists (Burrell 1997).

The Background

The great political prominence of presidential candidates' wives in the 1990s is not altogether a surprise. The role of women in American society has changed greatly in the past decade or two. More women are in the workforce; more women have achieved positions of economic, social, and political leadership; and, generally, the relationship between men and women is more nearly equal than it ever was in the past. This "quiet revolution" has had a number of consequences. One is that the image of the wife and her role has changed radically. The contemporary conception of marriage is one of a partnership in which husband and wife share responsibilities, set goals, and discuss the means of achieving those goals. These societal changes have brought into the open what has always been quietly recognized in U.S. political life, which is that presidential wives have privileged access to the country's chief executive and can be potent influences on his thought and actions (Caroli 1987; O'Connor et al. 1996). Moreover, this recognition of privileged access has brought increased media scrutiny and public attention.

There are also strategic reasons why this new style of wife should have come to the fore in the presidential contests of the 1990s. One consequence of women's changed role in society is that women make distinctive demands of government and show distinctive patterns of political behavior (Cook et al. 1994; chapter 9 of this book). Candidates' wives are one way of appealing to this large and distinctive electoral constituency, if only by the implication that the woman's voice will be clearly heard in the White House if her husband is elected. A candidate's wife may serve the purposes of campaign strategists in another way as well. Her image and personality can be conveyed to voters in such a way as to suggest that she complements the president and is not simply a reflection of him. A candidate may adopt a strong stance on a controversial policy issue, while the suggestion is made to voters who think differently that the last word has not been said on the matter because his wife does not altogether share his convictions. In 1992, for example, when George Bush took a strong antiabortion position, his wife voiced more moderate views. In the same vein, the presidential candidate can appeal to one wing of his party and his wife to another. As candidate and president, for example, Bill Clinton has carefully cultivated the centrist appeal that he deemed necessary for election and reelection in America in the 1990s, whereas his wife has served throughout as his "administration's official, oratorical liberal ... overwhelmingly popular among the core Democratic constituencies that Mr. Clinton wants to rally for the fall" (Bumiller 1996; see also Brock 1996; Burrell 1997; Nelson 1993).

At first, Hillary Clinton's public standing did not obviously suffer for her open partisanship. In 1992, public admiration for her was lower than that for the well-regarded Barbara Bush, but about the same as that for the two presidential candidates (Mughan and Burden 1995, 139). But after the election, popular regard for the president's wife started to fall as she bore much of the blame for the failure of one of her husband's major policy proposals, health-care reform. She also became embroiled in a series of scandals, beginning with the Whitewater affair, a failed land deal in Arkansas that occurred while her husband was governor of the state. Mrs. Clinton was later accused of covering up her involvement in that deal while she was in the White House, and these charges resulted, in January 1996, in her being the only first lady ever to be called to testify before a federal grand jury. Then came "Travelgate," a scandal in which Mrs. Clinton was accused of being a key figure in the unfair dismissal of the White House Travel Office to make way for Arkansas cronies.

In contrast, Bob Dole's wife, Elizabeth, did not carry scandalous baggage with her into the 1996 campaign. Though she had been involved in Washington politics for years, she was relatively unknown to the American public. The image she presented during the 1996 campaign was one of a congenial, loyal, and apolitical wife—in short, "the supportive spouse of Bob Dole" (Bystrom et al. 1998, 23). Her lively personality contrasted sharply with that of a husband who came across in general to voters as aged, dour, and saturnine. She walked into the audience at the Republican National Convention to deliver a charming, talk-show-like speech lauding her husband's personal virtues and presidential credentials, and she made a nationally televised campaign commercial for him. Presented to the American public in this way, she was thought to have enough popular appeal to "encourage people (and especially women voters) to take a second, third, or fourth look at" her husband as a viable presidential candidate (Bumiller 1996). Moreover, perhaps not wishing to have her equated in the public mind with that other career woman, Hillary Clinton, Republican campaign strategists chose to play down, even ignore, her substantial career achievements and political track record. She had served as a cabinet secretary under two different Republican presidents—she was the first woman to do so—and had left government to become director of the American Red Cross. Perhaps again to distinguish herself from the Democratic first lady, Mrs. Dole made it clear that she intended to return to this job should her husband win the election, thus implying that the American public could rest assured that she would not fall into a career of political intrigue, scandal, and "behind-the-scenes" influence in the White House.

As in 1992, then, the wives were by a mixture of design and default prominent actors in the presidential campaign. But what was their contribution, if any, to the outcome of the election? Our answer to this question is divided into three parts. First, since for wives to matter they must minimally have their own identities, Hillary Clinton and Elizabeth Dole are shown not simply to be extensions of their husbands in the eyes of the American voting public. Second, we turn to the question whether their independent identities had implications for individuals' voting decisions. Despite the first lady's fall in public esteem, we find that she again had a substantial effect on vote choice. The more popular Elizabeth Dole also had an electoral impact, but it was not as strong as Hillary Clinton's. Third, we consider how Mrs. Clinton's continued electoral impact despite declining popularity is to be interpreted. Does it represent a "wives' effect" or a "Hillary effect"? Moreover, if the latter, should the 1990s be seen less as a sea change in the dynamics of presidential election outcomes than as a break from a pattern that will resume once the current, controversial first lady leaves the White House at the end of her husband's second term?

Husbands and Wives in the Public Eye

The minimal precondition of wives having an independent electoral impact is that they not simply be extensions of their husbands in the public eye. This was certainly the case in 1992 and the continuation of media scrutiny suggests that it should have continued to be the case in 1996.[2] What may have changed, however, is the pattern of support for them and their husbands and, with it, the electoral implications of their public standing. The decline in approval that Hillary Clinton experienced during her initial term as first lady, for example, could conceivably have wiped out the independent electoral impact she enjoyed in 1992.

We operationalize evaluations of the wives using the 1996 National Election Study (NES) preelection survey "feeling thermometer" questions. These questions ask respondents to place each of a series of national political figures on a thermometer scale scored from 0 to 100, where 100 represents warmest feelings, 0 is coldest, and 50 is neutral. Table 7.1 presents the means and standard deviations of thermometer ratings for the Clintons, Bushes, and Doles. These statistics apply only to respondents who report voting for the Democratic or Republican presidential candidates. Ross Perot, a significant third-party candidate for the second time running, is not included in part because his wife, Margot, played no role at all in his campaign. Serving as a first look at the public's reaction to the wives relative to their husbands, it provides little reason to conclude that husband and wife, either Democratic or Republican, are indistinguishable from each other for voters. There is continuity across the two elections in that the Republican wives have the highest score in both contests. Their husbands were relatively unpopular, with George Bush having the lowest score in 1992 and Bob Dole the second lowest in 1996.

TABLE 7.1

FEELING THERMOMETER DESCRIPTIVE STATISTICS

	1992			*1996*		
	Mean	*Standard deviation*	N	Mean	*Standard deviation*	N
Bill Clinton	57.7	25.7	1341	58.7	31.3	1029
Hillary Clinton	55.7	23.2	1296	52.3	31.5	1024
George Bush/Bob Dole	52.6	28.4	1350	54.6	24.1	1027
Barbara Bush/Elizabeth Dole	69.0	23.0	1339	62.8	22.1	975

SOURCE: 1992 and 1996 American National Election Studies.

NOTE: Thermometer scores range from 0 to 100. Sample includes major-party voters only.

There is also change, however, and it involves the Clintons. On the one hand, the president's rating increases marginally in 1996, but that of his wife drops substantially, making her the least popular of all four actors in this contest.[3] On the other hand, the standard deviation of the scores for both Clintons, and especially Mrs. Clinton, increases appreciably in magnitude. This suggests a polarization of reactions to them between 1992 and 1996, with some groups of voters giving them relatively higher scores in the latter election and others giving them relatively lower ones.

The decline in the first lady's public standing would seem to be one of the stories of the Clinton presidency. Not only is it of interest in its own right, but her diminished standing with voters as a whole might be expected to have made her less of an electoral asset to her husband than she was in

1992. It is also possible that Elizabeth Dole suffered the same fate, since she was substantially less popular than her 1992 predecessor, Barbara Bush. But insofar as she was still the most popular of all four actors in 1996, the possibility remains that Republican strategists' hopes were realized and that part of her popularity was transferred to her husband.

The prospect of a differential effect for the two wives gets that much stronger when the four spouses are treated not as individuals but as husband-and-wife pairs. The purpose of looking at them from this perspective is to allow for the possibility that spouses may have different mean thermometer scores, but that this difference is more or less uniform across all groups of voters. In other words, much the same mean difference is repeated among partisans, independents, ideologues, moderates, men, women, blacks, whites, and so on. This being the case, the correlations between spousal thermometer ratings would approach unity and, statistically speaking, any separate effects would be impossible to isolate.

The 1992 and 1996 correlations between all four thermometer scores are presented in table 7.2. At one level, the results are not surprising, as they have a strong partisan element. In both 1992 and 1996, Democratic and Republican scores of wives or husbands are always negatively related, while evaluations of husband and wife of the same party are always positively related. What does change, however, is the closeness of the relationship; there is greater overlap between the two pairs of husband and wife scores in 1996, especially for Bill and Hillary Clinton. The correlations go from .634 to .653 for the Republican pair and from .733 to .863 for the Democratic Clintons.[4] Thus, it would seem that, especially for Hillary Clinton, the wife's appeal

TABLE 7.2

CORRELATIONS BETWEEN FEELING THERMOMETERS

		Bill Clinton	Hillary Clinton	Bob Dole	Barbara Bush
1996					
	Hillary Clinton	.863	—		
	Bob Dole	−.575	−.503	—	
	Elizabeth Dole	−.468	−.393	.653	—
1992					
	Hillary Clinton	.733	—		
	Barbara Bush	−.397	−.228	—	
	George Bush	−.540	−.409	—	.634

SOURCE: 1992 and 1996 American National Election Studies.

NOTE: Entries are pairwise correlations. Sample includes major-party voters only. Ns range from 973 to 1339.

narrowed to become more concentrated than before in those partisan groups giving disproportionate support to her husband. But it also raises the possibility that the wives' greater indistinguishability from their husbands in 1996 threatens any status they may have as independent influences on the presidential vote. Media prominence notwithstanding, did the reaction of voters to the two women matter for how their husbands fared in the 1996 presidential contest?

We address this question by estimating standard vote equations to explain the two-party vote decision in 1992 and 1996 separately. Presented in table 7.3 (p. 118) are two logit models of the presidential vote that estimate the separate effects of husbands and wives after controlling for a range of other potential influences on the vote.[5] Evaluations of the Clintons and Doles are again operationalized using feeling thermometer responses.[6] Other influences fall into a number of categories, the first of which is political-ideological. The variables in this category are scores on the 7-point party identification scale ranging from strong Republican to strong Democrat and on the 7-point liberal-conservative political ideology scale. The second category contains a number of sociodemographic variables commonly associated with voting preference. Dichotomized, they are race (white or black), gender (male or female), education (college educated or less), and union membership (household member or not). We have also included age, given the "generation gap" between Clinton and his Republican opponent. Next are two "women's issues," abortion and health care, for which the wives might be acting as surrogates; controlling on these issues, in other words, might eliminate any independent effect the wives have on the presidential vote. The fourth category comprises two questions pertaining to the candidates' character traits. Respondents were asked to evaluate on 4-point scales whether "moral" and "cares about people like me" apply to the candidates. We subtracted the Bush and Dole scores from Clinton's to create indicators of the "morality gap" and the "empathy gap" (see chapter 3 in this volume). Finally, there is a performance question relating to respondents' retrospective perceptions of recent national (sociotropic) economic fortunes. The dependent variable is coded so that positive coefficients reflect a higher likelihood of voting Democratic.

The logit results are detailed in table 7.3. For our purposes, the two most important findings involve the candidates' wives, specifically Hillary Clinton. First, she had a greater impact on the vote than either Barbara Bush or Elizabeth Dole despite attracting lower average thermometer ratings than either of them. Second, Mrs. Clinton's impact on the vote held steady in 1996, going from .050 to .052, at the same time that her mean thermometer rating decreased from 55.7 to 52.3 (see table 7.1, p. 115). Personal popularity, in other words, is not the same as electoral impact; the relationship between the two is more complex.

TABLE 7.3
1992 AND 1996 VOTE EQUATIONS

Independent variable	1992		1996	
	Coefficient (Standard error)	P value	Coefficient (Standard error)	P value
Constant	2.896 (2.209)	.095	1.848 (2.237)	.205
Personal evaluations				
Hillary Clinton	.050 (.015)	<.001	.052 (.013)	<.001
Barbara Bush/Elizabeth Dole	−.003 (.016)	.422	−.025 (.014)	.040
Bill Clinton	.074 (.017)	<.001	.064 (.016)	<.001
George Bush/Bob Dole	−.085 (.016)	<.001	−.073 (.016)	<.001
Political orientations				
Partisanship	−.486 (.140)	<.001	−.311 (.122)	.006
Ideology	−.660 (.217)	.001	.042 (.213)	.421
Sociodemographic elements				
Race	−1.037 (.994)	.129	−2.081 (1.26)	.050
Gender	.026 (.476)	.428	.978 (.420)	.010
Age	.009 (.014)	.266	−.006 (.012)	.317
College education	−.378 (.469)	.211	−.272 (.478)	.239
Union membership	−.638 (.559)	.127	.417 (.474)	.190

Continued ...

The other results are in some ways predictable. Partisanship was highly important in 1996, just as it was in 1992, as were the husbands' thermometer ratings. Yet the coefficients on these three variables, especially ideology, all decreased in 1996, meaning that other factors likely increased in importance. Indeed, we find the emergence in 1996 of a "gender gap" and a "race gap" that was not present four years earlier. Note, however, that the "character" issue receded in the 1996 contest. Clinton may in 1992 have drawn some advantage from his empathetic image and at the same time suffered for perceived moral lapses, but neither factor mattered at all for his vote share

TABLE 7.3 — CONTINUED

Independent variable	1992		1996	
	Coefficient (Standard error)	P value	Coefficient (Standard error)	P value
Issues				
National economy	−.115 (.225)	.304	−.020 (.164)	.453
Abortion	.407 (231)	.035	.344 (.219)	.054
Health care	.105 (.139)	.226	−.176 (.118)	.068
Character traits				
Empathy gap	−.351 (.258)	.087	−.128 (.254)	.358
Morality gap	−.581 (.262)	.014	.044 (.235)	.426
N	776		700	
χ^2 (16)	893.47		781.06	
Pseudo-R^2	.849		.805	
−2 log likelihood	−79.34		−94.64	
Percentage correctly predicted	96.0		95.4	
Percentage baseline prediction	58.9		51.3	

SOURCE: 1992 and 1996 American National Election Studies.

NOTE: *P* values are based on one-tailed *z* tests.

in 1996. It could be, however, that their lack of influence is more apparent than real, being an artifact of respondents' thermometer rating of the incumbent president encompassing assessments of more specific elements of his character.[7]

Again, our most important conclusion is that, even when controlling for other proven predictors of the presidential vote, including partisanship, ideology, and evaluations of the candidates, Hillary Clinton and, to a substantially lesser extent, Elizabeth Dole, still independently influence the vote for their husbands. It is possible to gain a more intuitive grasp of the relative impact of the two wives by predicting the probability that an individual will vote for one candidate rather than the other given that individual's evaluation of each of the wives. Table 7.4 (p. 120) reports the probability of choosing Bill Clinton when evaluations of the wives are most negative, most positive, and neutral, holding all other independent variables in the equation in table 7.3 constant at their modal values.[8] These values are reasonable because some respondents fell in each of the nine cells. Immediately striking is that the likelihood of voting for Clinton given combinations of reactions to the two candidates' wives ranges across almost the whole gamut from 0 to 1, which represents a large potential effect for the wives. For example, the probability of a pro-Clinton vote goes from a meager 3 percent for the person giving Elizabeth Dole a thermometer score of 100 and Hillary Clinton one of 0 to an almost perfect 99 percent for the individual with the reverse pattern of scores. But perhaps the most striking feature of table 7.4 is just how asymmetric the impact of the two women is. Across the board, regard for the president's wife is more closely associated with voting for her husband than is affect for Elizabeth Dole with voting for her husband. Take those scoring each wife 0, generally Republicans in the case of Mrs. Clinton and Democrats in the case of Mrs. Dole. Those scoring the Democratic

TABLE 7.4

PREDICTED VOTE PROBABILITIES

	Elizabeth Dole evaluation			
	Coldest (0)	Neutral (50)	Warmest (100)	Maximum change
Hillary Clinton evaluation				
Coldest (0)	.299	.108	.033	.266
Neutral (50)	.849	.615	.312	.537
Warmest (100)	.987	.955	.857	.130
Maximum change	.688	.847	.824	

SOURCE: Based on table 7.3.

NOTE: Entries are estimated probabilities of voting for Clinton over Dole holding all variables except the wives' thermometer ratings at their modal values.

candidate's wife 0 show no more than a .266 change in the probability of not voting for Clinton as their affect for Elizabeth Dole increases from 0 to 100. By contrast, those scoring Mrs. Dole zero show a .688 increase in the probability of a pro-Clinton vote as their evaluation of the Democratic candidate's wife goes from the minimum to the maximum. This difference is open to a number of explanations. One is that Hillary Clinton was simply somehow better at translating personal affect into Democratic Party support, perhaps because of her greater electioneering experience or because of her being clearly identified with liberal causes. Another is that Democrats, perhaps more accepting of the changed role of women in American society, are readier to allow their assessment of a woman to influence their voting decision.[9] In addition, more people had opinions about Hillary Clinton than about Elizabeth Dole, so evaluations of Mrs. Clinton may have played a larger role in the election outcome because of familiarity differences alone.

A great paradox of the 1996 election, then, is that Hillary Clinton remained a potent influence on its outcome at the same time that her personal public standing dipped amid scandal and controversy. It is a paradox, however, that is not difficult to resolve. The key to its resolution lies in table 7.1, which pointed to a greater polarization in the voting public's reaction to her and her husband. Those who liked them in 1992 liked them more in 1996, and those who disliked them in 1992 disliked them more in 1996. In the president's case, the positive and negative movements in popular evaluations of him tended to cancel each other out overall, whereas for her the negative movement exceeded the positive and lowered her net score.

This dynamic is readily apparent in table 7.5, which details how each of Bill and Hillary Clinton's mean thermometer scores changed between the

TABLE 7.5

POLARIZATION OF THERMOMETER SCORES

	Bill Clinton		Hillary Clinton	
	1992	*1996*	*1992*	*1996*
Group				
Democrats[a,b]	73.5	81.7	67.4	73.0
Independents[b]	56.3	56.4	54.0	51.1
Republicans[a,b]	36.3	31.5	41.1	27.3
Liberals[a,b]	69.8	79.0	65.8	71.9
Moderates[a,b]	59.2	69.9	56.2	63.7
Conservatives[a,b]	48.1	45.6	48.1	39.9
Men[a,b]	55.1	53.4	53.8	45.7
Women[b]	59.8	63.1	57.3	57.8
Blacks[a,b]	74.0	85.5	66.5	78.6
Whites[a,b]	55.2	55.6	54.1	49.3

SOURCE: 1992 and 1996 American National Election Studies.

NOTE: Sample includes major-party voters only.

a. Bill Clinton differences significant at $p < .05$, one-tailed test.

b. Hillary Clinton differences significant at $p < .05$, one-tailed test.

two elections in a number of core Democratic support groups. The standing of the president and his wife improved sharply in the eyes of Democratic identifiers, liberals, and blacks. At the same time, they dipped more or less equally sharply among Republicans and conservatives. As for the first lady specifically, her support may have dropped sharply among men, but it remained constant among women, who were significantly more likely to vote for Bill Clinton in 1996 than were males (see table 7.3, p. 118). The same asymmetry characterizes the racial reaction to her. Whites liked her less in 1996 than in 1992, but her standing among blacks went up even more sharply than did her husband's; of course, blacks were far more likely to vote Democratic in both contests than were whites. Hillary Clinton's popularity, in other words, tended to strengthen among the same core Democratic clienteles where her husband's did.[10] At the same time, though, her fortunes did not move strictly in tandem with his. She retained a distinct personality in the eyes of these groups, and her attractiveness to them above and beyond that of her husband seems to have translated into extra votes that contributed to the success of his reelection bid.

Wives' Effect or Hillary Effect?

How does one account for the different vote-delivering performances of Barbara Bush and Elizabeth Dole on the one hand and Hillary Clinton on the other? A number of possible explanations can be dismissed at the outset. The most obvious, and most easily discounted, is the "incumbency hypothesis," which holds that the current president's wife is more influential than his challenger's since the former is more visible and has greater name recognition after four years as first lady because of all the publicity and media exposure she has received. The weakness of this hypothesis is that Barbara Bush was the incumbent first lady when, despite the best efforts of Republican strategists, she failed to match the influence of Hillary Clinton in 1992.

A second potential explanation is the "professional woman hypothesis," which explains wives' effects by their appeal to the new breed of professional, career women eager for public recognition and political representation. Hillary Clinton of course fits this mold, but it is also the case that few presidential candidates' wives have enjoyed more successful careers in and out of politics than Elizabeth Dole. Mrs. Dole in turn may have had more influence in the electoral arena than her immediate Republican predecessor, the more traditional Barbara Bush, but she had a small impact relative to that of Hillary Clinton.

A related explanation is what might be called the "women's issues hypothesis," which begins with the recognition that a number of issues have emerged on the political agenda in recent years that are of special concern to women and that lead to an electoral bonus for presidential candidates whose wives are taken to be sympathetic on these issues. It is noticeable, however, that Hillary Clinton was more circumspect on such issues in 1996 after the failure of health-care reform, yet she was at least as influential in shaping the outcome of the presidential election. Though she had attended the controversial United Nations women's conference in Beijing before the election and had written a book about the welfare of children, she kept a low profile during the campaign on issues such as abortion, equal rights, family-leave policies, child care, and breast cancer. Again, therefore, closer inspection discounts this "women's issues hypothesis."

More plausible given the evidence presented in this chapter is the explanation of Hillary Clinton's electoral influence as a "party effect" rooted in the greater readiness of Democrats, compared to Republicans, to accept women's changed role in society and to allow their attitudes and behaviors to be swayed by their assessments of relevant women. The problem, however, is that it is difficult to separate this "party effect" from a more particularistic "Hillary effect," since there is no comparable evidence on any Democratic presidential candidate's wife other than Hillary Clinton. Indeed, we will not be in a position to know whether it is a "Hillary effect" until this highly controversial woman leaves the political stage in the year 2000 to make way for another Democratic wife, assuming, of course, that the Democratic candidate is male and married.

Good cases can be made for the permanence or transience of Mrs. Clinton's effect. On the one hand, she does seem to have transformed expectations of American government by making an activist first lady acceptable to a large part of the electorate. In a December 1996 CBS News/*New York Times* poll, for example, 54.4 percent of respondents believed that the president's wife had "about the right amount" (49.2 percent) or "too little" (5.2 percent) influence "on the decisions Bill Clinton made as president."[11] The remaining 45.6 percent thought she had too much influence. More to the point, though, the first lady's influence was not seen as an aberration that would pass with her departure from the White House and a return to normality. Fully 66.6 percent of respondents to the same survey thought that her influence was "about the same as other first ladies', only just more visible." Moreover, this view was reasonably evenly distributed over the electorate as a whole. Just over two-thirds of independents and 71.1 percent of moderates believed that Mrs. Clinton had about the same level of influence as earlier first ladies.[12]

The point is that there is widespread public acceptance of an influential role for the first lady in presidential decisions. Republican strategists chose to adhere to a relatively traditional, politically deferential image of the first lady when they presented both Barbara Bush and Elizabeth Dole as individuals who were above the partisan fray and without their own political agendas. Presumably this strategy was based on a number of considerations, including (1) the fear of alienating supporters with more traditional views of the proper role of women in American society; (2) the view that an America disturbed by its experience with Hillary Clinton would reject a politicized first lady in the White House; and (3) the conviction that being as widely popular as possible was the best way for Mrs. Bush and Mrs. Dole to expand their husbands' support beyond the traditional Republican base. This analysis suggests they could not have been more wrong. Some Americans may balk at an unelected figure directly influencing presidential decisions, but many of them have no problem accepting the legitimacy of a second politician in the White House. Hillary Clinton's electoral influence is ample testimony to the fallacy of the assumption that first ladies are there to be seen and not heard. This was the Republicans' first mistake.

Their second mistake in what might be called their "wives strategy" has been to lose sight of a long-standing and basic truism of electoral politics, which is that campaigns are waged to reinforce partisan loyalties and mobilize traditional supporters rather than to convert other parties' supporters. This is the clear lesson of the "Hillary factor" in 1992 and 1996. Barbara Bush and Elizabeth Dole were broadly popular, but theirs was a diffuse popularity that tended neither to reinforce Republican partisan loyalties nor to weaken Democratic ones. Hillary Clinton stood in sharp contrast to them in that she was an unabashed liberal Democrat who left the courting of moderates to her husband. In bashing Mrs. Clinton for her public liberalism in 1992 (and somewhat less so in 1996), the Republicans appear to have made her more popular in the liberal wing of the Democratic Party and to have reinforced its support for a husband who had jeopardized it by moving to the center. Ironically, Mrs. Clinton's stewardship of the Clinton administration's unsuccessful health-care proposals and her continued courting of the liberal wing of the party during her husband's first administration cost her support among Americans as a whole, but this was outweighed by her increased standing among core Democratic groups. The result in 1996 was that she was even more effective in bolstering support for her more centrist husband among this core clientele than she had been in 1992.[13]

The lesson would seem to be that public popularity is not a sufficient condition for candidates' wives to add to their husbands' vote shares. Instead, they become electoral forces in their own right when they are presented as the partisan political actors that most Americans believe it legitimate for them to be. The trick is not to have a candidate's wife appeal outside her husband's partisan fold but to have her shore up loyal support within it. Voters committed to the support of a party may not object to an unelected wife having the ear of the president, but they do seem to want to be reassured that she is whispering the right things into it, especially should they doubt her husband's partisan instincts. If this diagnosis of Hillary Clinton's electoral impact is valid, then she may indeed have been one of a kind, and candidates' wives (or husbands) in the future may continue to enjoy high levels of media exposure but have no automatic electoral impact. Much will depend on the individuals themselves.

8

The Media and the 1996 Presidential Campaign

HERBERT B. ASHER AND ANDREW R. TOMLINSON

PRIOR TO THE 1992 presidential contest, many political observers marveled at the skillful presidential campaigns run by Republican operatives in 1980, 1984, and 1988. The Republican Party seemed to have a lock not only on the Electoral College but also on savvy campaign practitioners adept at campaign strategy, media messaging, and political polling. In contrast, the Democratic campaigns were seen as uninspired, ineffective, and reactive, especially in 1988. Then the experience of 1992 shook up the conventional wisdom. An incumbent Republican president with a very experienced campaign team was embarrassed by a Democratic effort that was far superior in defining the campaign issues and generating the appropriate messages in a timely and effective fashion.

The 1996 campaign was in many ways a repeat of the 1992 situation. The Clinton reelection effort was more skillful than the Dole campaign at setting the agenda, defining the campaign, staying on message, and, when necessary, anticipating and responding to the challenges posed by the opposition.

The Media Environment in 1996

The 1992 presidential campaign was characterized by dramatic innovations in the candidates' communication with the voters. Advertisements targeted to specific audiences became more common on cable television. The candidates routinely circumvented the national media by utilizing satellite technology to communicate with local television stations, where they could anticipate receiving more extensive and more positive coverage. The candidates also appeared on daytime and evening television talk shows and late-night entertainment programs, as well as radio interview and talk shows. In 1992, the Internet became a visible place for presidential campaigning for the first time.

⌐ There were fewer innovations in the 1996 campaign, no great expansion or major new breakthroughs. For example, the candidates all had websites, but there was no great surge in their use as a source for campaign information. About 29 percent of Americans had access to the Internet or the World Wide Web and only about one-fourth of those with access (or about 7 percent overall) had seen any campaign information on the net (1996 NES item). Talk radio, especially conservative talk radio, was seen by some as a noteworthy factor in the GOP's capture of Congress in 1994. But in 1996 Dole ignored talk radio until the outcry from conservatives led him to change his stance.

Certainly, one important characteristic of the media environment in 1996 was the decrease in media coverage given to the campaign. There was less coverage and less citizen involvement in the campaign as measured by the size of the audience watching the presidential debates or by citizens' own statements of how interested they were in the campaign. One reason for the lesser attention was that the presidential contest was never a real horserace; throughout the campaign, the electoral arithmetic had Clinton solidly ahead. This perception, reinforced by extensive media coverage of the polls, may have dampened voter interest. For Dole, the most consistent and negative media message was how poorly he was running; for Clinton, the dominant negative media theme was his character deficiencies. Also dampening enthusiasm in 1996 was the lessened credibility of the Perot campaign as a meaningful alternative. Undoubtedly Perot's own actions since 1992 and his exclusion from the presidential debates in 1996 helped undermine his strength as a presidential candidate.

⌐ One major development in 1996 was the increased importance of local television as a vehicle for campaign advertising. Rather than spend scarce campaign dollars on national ads, the campaigns targeted key electoral vote states and regions within these states to air their commercials. Goldstein (1997) states that 163,760 presidential campaign ads were broadcast on local television in the country's top 75 media markets (which include 80 percent of the American population). The Clinton/Gore campaign and the Democratic National Committee ran only 12 spots on network television and 214 spots on national cable networks, while the Dole/Kemp campaign and the Republican National Committee ran 102 and 1,622 spots on network television and the national cable networks respectively. Even though the national ads obviously had a much larger audience than the local spots, they still constituted a small part of the campaigns' advertising budgets.

The dramatic nature of this shift to local spots is highlighted by Patrick Devlin (1995), who notes that prior to the 1992 presidential campaign, the normal practice was to spend about two-thirds of the media budget on national ads. The 1992 Clinton/Gore campaign reversed the traditional pattern, spending 75 percent of its advertising budget on local buys, a pattern that became more pronounced in 1996. In 1992 the Bush campaign did not follow this move to local advertising, but in 1996 the Dole campaign emulated the local thrust of the Clinton media strategy. This local focus of the paid media will likely continue in the future, particularly when the Electoral College arithmetic yields a subset of potentially competitive states that comprise the election battleground.

Two other developments in 1996 may shape future media campaigns. The first was the effort by the Free Media for Straight Talk Coalition to pressure the television networks to provide the presidential candidates with some free airtime to present their views without the intervention of reporters and commentators. The coalition enjoyed some modest success in 1996, but this effort is unlikely to change the media environment very much unless the candidates receive substantially more time.

The other important development was a pair of federal court decisions that will facilitate the flow of money from multiple sources into future media campaigns. One decision (*FEC v. Christian Action Network*) dealt with the Christian Action Network, which in the weeks before the 1992 presidential election had run a television ad and two newspaper ads sharply criticizing candidate Bill Clinton's position on homosexual issues. The Court of Appeals for the Fourth Circuit summarily affirmed a district court ruling that these communications and how they were paid for were outside the jurisdiction of the Federal Election Commission because they did not expressly advocate the election or defeat of Bill Clinton. The courts did not view these ads as campaign ads but as issue advocacy, which they were unwilling to limit.

A Supreme Court decision (*FEC v. Colorado Republican Federal Campaign Committee*) upheld the ability of the Colorado Republican Party to make unlimited independent expenditures in federal elections. Indeed, judicial rulings in recent years have allowed unlimited expenditures on issue advocacy ads and mailings by interest groups, labor unions, corporations, and political parties. As long as the expenditures advocate a position on an issue but do not call for the election or defeat of a candidate, these expenditures are protected as free speech and hence cannot be limited. Obviously, this is a major loophole through which huge amounts of money can flow for the purchase of ads and mailings, which can affect campaign outcomes even if they do not directly advocate voting for or against any particular candidate.

Even before these federal court decisions, the Clinton/Gore campaign designed a plan by which the Democratic National Committee (DNC) transferred about $32 million to various state Democratic parties in 1995 to support a massive advertising campaign that at least indirectly helped the Clinton/Gore campaign (Abramson and Wayne 1997). The state parties in key states such as California, Pennsylvania, Florida, Ohio, and Michigan all received millions of dollars from the DNC and in turn spent similar amounts on ads favorable to Clinton, even if the ads did not directly call for Clinton's reelection. Much of the money raised to support this effort was "soft money," not subject to contribution limits and other federal laws and regulations that govern direct contributions to candidate campaigns. Indeed, one of the issues addressed in the campaign finance hearings of 1997 was whether the DNC and the Clinton/Gore campaign knowingly raised and used soft money for inappropriate or illegal purposes. Although these dollars were transferred to the state parties, the decision of how to spend them was made at the national level. And that decision was to spend them on issue advocacy ads. But as Jill Abramson and Leslie Wayne (1997) note, the distinction between an issue ad and a candidate ad can be blurred. Although the issue ads never called for a Clinton vote, they featured the president and his policies. One ad that attacked the GOP agenda stated: "Reform welfare. Cut taxes. Protect Medicare. President Clinton says get it done. Meet our challenges. Protect our values." It is clear that without changes in court rulings and our campaign finance laws, issue ads as a means to circumvent contribution and expenditure limits, as well as reporting requirements, will be a prominent feature of campaigns in the future.

The Primary Season

From the beginning, Bill Clinton enjoyed a huge advantage over Bob Dole —Clinton did not face any challenges to his nomination from Jesse Jackson or any other prominent Democrat on his left. This enabled Clinton to run as the "new Democrat" that he claimed to be in the 1992 campaign. Moreover, after besting the GOP congressional leadership in the 1995 budget and legislative wars, Clinton could portray himself as a moderate protecting programs from right-wing radicals who would go so far as to shut down government. Clinton also benefited by a media campaign in late 1995, sponsored in part by the DNC, that spent almost $18 million highlighting the president's accomplishments and negatively defining the Republican opposition. Kenneth Goldstein (1997) notes that, overall, the Democratic National Committee paid for 31,847 Clinton ads (about 34 percent of all Clinton commercials), with the greatest DNC involvement occurring very early in the campaign. Because Clinton was unopposed for renomination in 1996, he was able to use his public and private dollars in the primary season to define further his presidency and the Republican opposition.

In contrast, Bob Dole faced a very crowded field in the GOP primaries. Much of this field was to his right, as was the Republican primary electorate in many states; hence Dole had to appeal first to a primary electorate more conservative than the general election voters. Moreover, as the acknowledged Republican front-runner, Dole was the target of attacks by his fellow candidates and of extensive media emphasis on his poll and primary performances. When Dole's performance in some of the early primaries and caucuses did not meet expectations, the media criticized the candidate and his campaign. After winning the critical South Carolina primary in early March, Dole had an easy path to the nomination. Because he had faced so many opponents in a primary and caucus system that was so heavily front-loaded in 1996, however, Dole's campaign effectively ran out of money in mid-spring of 1996. Had the Republican National Committee (RNC) not purchased ads for Dole after he had clinched the nomination, he would have been off television until the GOP convention, when he would receive general election public funding of $62 million upon formally receiving the Republican presidential nomination. Overall, the RNC paid for 36 percent of all Dole spots, the bulk of them airing in the summer of 1996 (Goldstein 1997, 7).

Even as Dole wrapped up the nomination, his general election prospects seemed gloomy according to the polls. Something dramatic had to happen, and that something became Dole's May announcement of his resignation from the U.S. Senate. While it created a short-lived media stir, however, this move failed to change the dynamics of the campaign. Indeed, after Dole left the Senate, the president and the Republican-controlled Congress had a productive legislative session that enabled Clinton to conduct a mini Rose Garden strategy in August as he held a number of bill-signing ceremonies.

The National Conventions

The major function of the national nominating convention today is to serve as a springboard to a successful general election campaign. To that end, conventions are pure media events, totally scripted for television.

GOP strategists believed that their party needed to soften its harsh image and appeal more strongly to women and minorities. Thus, their convention featured moderate Republican female officeholders such as U.S. Representative Susan Molinari and New Jersey Governor Christine Todd Whitman along with a keynote address by retired General Colin Powell. All three were pro-choice Republicans at a convention dominated by antiabortion delegates. Pat Buchanan, the most significant challenger to Dole's nomination, was not given a meaningful opportunity for prime-time participation because convention managers were afraid he would repeat the 1992 Houston convention performance in which he excoriated all those who did not agree with his very conservative agenda. The politically unpopular Newt Gingrich was also kept out of prime time, and the Contract with America was barely mentioned. The fact that Bob Dole had been in Washington, D.C., for thirty years was conveniently forgotten, and Republican National Chairman Haley Barbour and candidate Dole immediately dismissed the conservative Republican platform as simply a piece of paper that no one reads. Elizabeth Dole's nomination speech on behalf of her spouse was one of the media highlights of the convention. But the greatest excitement was generated by the unexpected selection of Jack Kemp as Dole's running mate, although the media were quick to point out the long-standing differences between Dole and Kemp on such issues as supply-side economics and affirmative action. By the end of the convention, Dole had become a supply sider by endorsing a 15-percent tax cut, and Kemp had changed his position on affirmative action. Both changes were noted with skepticism by political observers. More important, while Dole got a short-lived bump from the GOP convention, the basic dynamics of the presidential contest did not change. Indeed, many polls showed that Americans were dubious about tax cuts, preferring to move more quickly toward a balanced budget or to provide support for desired programs.

The Democratic convention was equally contrived for the media—featured speakers included actor Christopher Reeve and former Reagan press secretary James Brady. The Democrats were determined to present a middle-of-the-road, responsible portrait to the American electorate. The platform was drafted early, out of the media spotlight, and all controversy was squeezed out of the convention deliberations. By and large, party liberals were not prominent at the convention. The first lady's role was to focus on the safe issues of family and family values. Both at the convention and throughout the campaign, Clinton himself proposed initiatives that many observers did not view as being of presidential caliber, such as school uniforms and V-chips. These issues, along with Clinton's support for more research on breast cancer, expansion of the Brady (gun control) law, and tax breaks for education, allowed him to run as the centrist, family-friendly incumbent.

Thus, both parties' conventions were political makeovers, designed to portray the party and the nominees as moderate and centrist. Both parties recognized that controversy over issues would be treated by the media not as honest and open airing of differences but as an indicator that a political party did not have its own house in order, which could hurt its candidates in the general election. Hence both parties produced conventions contrived only to get their postconvention bounces in the polls. Many of the media felt that they had been used; the television networks, upset at covering what to them were nonevents, threatened to decrease convention coverage substantially in 2000 below the already reduced 1996 levels. A Gallup poll conducted in late August 1996 showed that two-thirds of Americans favored one-hour evening coverage of the conventions by the television networks, with only 26 percent preferring full convention coverage during prime time.

Dissecting the Dole Campaign

During the general election, the media devoted much attention to the mechanics and strategy of the Dole campaign, in part because the Dole operatives engaged in highly public discussion and critique of how their campaign was going. The mechanics of the Clinton campaign received little media attention because most political observers viewed the Clinton campaign as a smoothly run operation.

Two specific incidents in the Dole campaign stand out. The first involved the Electoral College arithmetic. It became clear very quickly that Clinton had a huge lead in the Electoral College and that Dole's chance for victory required that every key state break for him, a very unlikely occurrence. To change those odds, the Dole campaign decided to challenge Clinton in California and put its fifty-four electoral votes in play. Unfortunately, the public discussion about shifting resources from other states to California generated media stories that Dole was downplaying Ohio and other states, which also were absolutely critical to his campaign.

Yet another blunder was the open debate within the Dole organization about whether to go negative against Clinton. This also became a topic of extensive media coverage and served to underline the perception that Dole was mean-spirited. Ironically, the Clinton campaign had been running negative ads about "Dole/Gingrich" and the Republicans for months, yet it was the Dole campaign that was seen by voters as negative. In terms of overall views of the respective campaigns, an October 1996 Gallup poll showed that voters, by an overwhelming 70 percent to 16 percent margin, thought Clinton had the better political campaign.

The Debates

The debates were certainly the major media events of the campaign, headlined by controversy about who would be allowed to participate. The Presidential Debate Commission ultimately decided that Ross Perot would not be invited to participate for a number of reasons including his poor standing in the polls, while the Republican and Democratic candidates were automatically included. Despite Perot's presence on the ballot in all fifty states and the District of Columbia in 1996, his receipt of $23 million in public funds in 1996 based on his performance four years earlier, and a poll standing that was not much lower than his standing at the comparable time in the 1992 campaign when he ultimately got 19 percent, the debate commission concluded that Perot had little chance to win and therefore should not be included in the debates. Of course, this became a self-fulfilling prophecy; without the opportunity to participate in debates, the Perot candidacy lost credibility. (Perot also experienced difficulty with the television networks that refused to sell him the longer blocks of airtime needed for his half-hour "infomercials.")

Much of the media coverage of the debates focused on the horserace—who won the debate, who lost, did Dole gain ground, did Clinton accomplish what he needed to in order to maintain his lead. A slew of polls generally showed Clinton to be the winner of the debates, and Al Gore was seen as the victor in the vice-presidential debate. According to Gallup poll figures, Clinton won the first debate by a 51–32-percent margin over Dole and the second debate by 59–29 percent, an advantage much greater than his lead in voter preferences at that time.

Throughout the debates, the media speculated widely about whether Dole would take the gloves off and harshly attack Clinton. In the first debate, however, Dole declined to answer a question posed to him about the Clintons' ethics, and during the vice-presidential debate, Jack Kemp promised that Dole would not attack Clinton. And when Dole was more aggressive and critical of Clinton in the second debate, it only reinforced the perception that Dole was running a negative campaign. A Gallup poll conducted after the second debate found that 58 percent of the respondents thought that Dole "was more unfair in criticizing his opponent"; only 18 percent of the respondents attributed that to Clinton.

The timing of the debates was very much determined by the Clinton campaign team. Because Dole was so far behind, he wanted a one-on-one shot at Clinton in the debates without Perot to muddy the waters, and the Clinton negotiators agreed to this in exchange for their choice of times and format. When asked why the debates occurred several weeks before the election when citizen attention to the campaign was at a low level, former Clinton aide George Stephanopolous responded, "Because we didn't want them to pay attention ... the debates were a metaphor for the campaign. We wanted the debates to be a nonevent" (Broder 1997).

Citizens, Campaigns, and the Media

Given that a recurring theme of media coverage was the tone and tenor of the Dole campaign, a theme fostered by the campaign's too-public discussions of whether to go negative, it is interesting to see how citizens reacted to the campaigns.

Obviously, a campaign has many facets, involving paid advertising as well as earned media attention. One can focus on the candidates' public statements, but one can also examine the words of campaign surrogates. Unfortunately, the data available to us do not capture all the aspects of the campaign. The information we do have generally shows that Americans saw the Dole campaign as negative. For example, a CBS News/*New York Times* poll conducted 10–13 October 1996 asked the following questions about the candidates: Has Bill Clinton been spending more time explaining what he would do in a second term as president or attacking Bob Dole? Has Bob Dole been spending more time explaining what he would do as president or attacking Bill Clinton? Sixty-eight percent of the respondents said Clinton was spending more time explaining; only 19 percent responded attacking. In contrast, 50 percent of the respondents believed that Dole was attacking, while 40 percent believed he was explaining his ideas.

A number of polls queried Americans about the candidates' campaign commercials, trying to ascertain how many Americans had seen or heard the commercials and whether they were positive or negative in content. For example, a CBS News/*New York Times* poll conducted between 17 and 20 October 1996 asked the following questions: Have you seen or heard any Dole or Clinton campaign commercials on television or radio in the last week? [If so] Do you think any of the Dole [Clinton] campaign commercials have made unfair charges against Bill Clinton [Bob Dole], or not? Overall, 63 percent of the registered voters recalled hearing or seeing a Clinton or Dole commercial; 55 percent remembered a Dole ad, while 49 percent recalled a Clinton commercial. Respondents split 45 percent to 45 percent as to whether any of the Dole campaign commercials made unfair charges against Clinton. In contrast, respondents strongly rejected, by 58 percent to 30 percent, that Clinton's campaign commercials made unfair charges against Dole. What is intriguing about these figures is that the Clinton campaign had been running ads critical of Dole much longer than the Dole campaign had been running ads critical of Clinton, yet Clinton's ads were seen as less negative and unfair. Part of the explanation for this is that the typical Clinton ad criticizing Dole (or Dole/Gingrich) usually included positive information about what the president had accomplished on the issues discussed in the ad. Thus, the Clinton ads tended to be comparative in content, not simply attacking Dole, and they were not seen as so negative as the Dole ads (Prior 1997).

The NES 1996 election survey includes more extensive questions about media usage and attentiveness to campaign advertisements. With respect to campaign commercials, respondents were first asked if they could recall seeing any ads for political candidates on television during the fall. Those who did see the ads were asked if they could remember which candidate sponsored the "ad they remembered best" and were then asked if they could remember anything the ad "said or showed." Up to five different mentions were recorded for each respondent, coded by candidate and by content.

Thus, it is possible to examine not only whether respondents saw political ads but also what they saw and who sponsored them. Note that the NES questions differ from the CBS News/*New York Times* items mentioned above by referring only to television, by referring to all candidates in general, and by referring to the fall rather than the past week. Despite these differences in the question wording, the NES survey, like the CBS News/*New York Times* poll, shows that more respondents recall seeing a Dole ad (54.3 percent) than seeing a Clinton ad (36.8 percent).

Overall, 47.8 percent of the NES respondents recalled seeing ads sponsored by a presidential candidate in the fall of 1996. Prior to the fall campaign, many observers had expected the South and the West (except for California) to be solid Republican territory, the Northeast to be a strong Clinton area, and the North Central states to be the campaign battleground. These expectations proved incorrect, as Dole had to struggle to secure and solidify the GOP base throughout the country. Thus, there were few regional differences in recall of presidential campaign ads, as Dole was forced to advertise in what were thought to be his strong areas, and Clinton attempted to win some of these GOP-leaning states (see table 8.1). In three of the four regions, fewer than half could recall a presidential ad; only in the West did a majority (59.6 percent) of citizens report remembering an ad. Part of the

TABLE 8.1

BEST-REMEMBERED 1996 PRESIDENTIAL CAMPAIGN AD,
BY REGION (IN PERCENTAGES)

	Northeast	North Central	South	West
No candidate's ad recalled	57.3	52.1	56.6	40.4
Clinton ad	14.8	19.5	15.3	21.6
Dole ad	24.6	24.2	23.0	34.0
Perot ad	3.3	4.2	5.2	4.0
Total	100.0	100.0	100.0	100.0
(N)	(337)	(405)	(601)	(371)

SOURCE: 1996 National Election Study.

high recall in the West reflects the decision of the Dole campaign to contest California. The California respondents constitute 50 percent of the western sample and had an overall recall rate of 67 percent. Thus, without the California respondents, the West looks more like the rest of the country. One other noteworthy point in table 8.1 is the greater recall of Dole commercials than of Clinton commercials in all four regions. This seems to run counter to data indicating that slightly more Clinton spots than Dole ads were aired after Labor Day and many more Clinton spots prior to Labor Day (Goldstein 1997, 34).

Table 8.2 presents the distribution of ad recall by citizens' candidate preferences. Note that no matter their vote choice, citizens were more likely to recall a Dole ad. The Perot voters are intriguing because they were more likely to remember a presidential ad than were the Clinton and Dole supporters; indeed, they were the group most likely to recall a Dole or a Perot ad and least likely to remember a Clinton commercial.

TABLE 8.2

1996 PRESIDENTIAL CAMPAIGN AD RECALL,

BY CANDIDATE CHOICE

(IN PERCENTAGES)

	Clinton voters	Dole voters	Perot voters
No candidate's ad recalled	52.9	49.7	36.9
Clinton ad	18.0	19.6	15.5
Dole ad	24.9	27.0	34.5
Perot ad	4.2	3.8	13.1
Total	100.0	100.0	100.0
(N)	(590)	(445)	(84)

SOURCE: 1996 National Election Study.

Asked how they perceived the Clinton or Dole or Perot ad they remembered best, respondents provided results similar to those of the CBS News/ *New York Times* poll cited earlier. Americans were much more likely to see the Clinton commercials as positive and the Dole commercials as negative and attacking (see table 8.3, p. 136). Perot ads were recalled as being overwhelmingly positive, while 45.5 percent of the reactions to the Clinton ads described them as positive, 37.7 percent as attacking, and only 6 percent as negative. For Dole ads, the perceptions were quite different. Less than a fifth of the responses described the ads as positive, 47.9 percent as attacking, and 27.6 percent as negative.[1]

Table 8.4 (p. 136) presents citizens' perceptions of Clinton and Dole ads controlling for the citizens' own candidate preference. (Similar results are obtained if one controls for party identification rather than candidate preference.) On some ad characteristics, Clinton and Dole supporters agreed. For example, both Clinton and Dole voters were more likely to describe Dole ads as attacking; 47.3 percent of the Clinton voters saw Dole ads as attacking, while only 34.1 percent described Clinton's ads that way. Likewise, 54.3 of the Dole supporters described Dole's ads as attacking, compared to 45.9 percent making the same evaluation about Clinton's ads.

TABLE 8.3

CONTENT OF 1996 PRESIDENTIAL CAMPAIGN AD RECALL,
BY AD SPONSOR (IN PERCENTAGES)

	Clinton ad	Dole ad	Perot ad
Negative	6.0	27.6	5.2
Attacking	37.7	47.9	0
Positive	45.5	18.5	94.8
Other	10.8	6.0	0
Total	100.0	100.0	100.0
(N)	(299)	(382)	(24)

SOURCE: 1996 National Election Study.

TABLE 8.4

CONTENT OF 1996 PRESIDENTIAL CAMPAIGN AD RECALL,
FOR CLINTON AND DOLE VOTERS ONLY
(IN PERCENTAGES)

	Clinton voters		Dole voters	
	Clinton ad	Dole ad	Clinton ad	Dole ad
Negative	2.6	29.3	10.5	11.7
Misleading/dishonest	2.3	1.8	8.8	0
Positive	59.5	15.6	24.9	31.6
Attacking	34.1	47.3	45.9	54.3
Other	1.5	6.1	9.8	2.4
Total	100.0	100.0	100.0	100.0
(N)	(109)	(88)	(144)	(100)

SOURCE: 1996 National Election Study.

With respect to whether the ads were seen as positive or negative, there were sharp differences between supporters of Dole and Clinton. Almost 60 percent of the Clinton supporters described his ads as positive; only about 16 percent said the same about Dole's ads. Among Dole voters, the pattern was reversed; they were somewhat more likely to see Dole's ads as positive. In terms of negativity, Dole supporters saw little difference between Dole and Clinton commercials, while Clinton backers were much more likely to say that Dole's ads were negative. These results suggest that certain characteristics of political ads must be regarded as conceptually distinct. In particular, an ad can be seen as attacking without being considered negative. But the characteristics of being "positive" or "negative" seem to have more overtones of good and bad. In any event, supporters of a candidate were more likely to attribute positive qualities to their preferred candidate's commercials.

It is noteworthy that citizens' perceptions of the commercial content they remembered best closely mirrored an objective analysis of the actual content of the ad. Examining all the ads aired on television, Goldstein (1997) found that 70 percent of the Dole ads were negative, 15 percent were positive, and 15 percent offered a contrast between Dole and Clinton. The pattern for Clinton ads was very different. Six percent were positive, 28 percent were negative, and 66 percent compared Clinton and Dole. And, as mentioned earlier, Clinton's contrast ads often went after Dole (or Dole/Gingrich), but they also included positive information about the president's accomplishments. This blending of negative and positive information helps explain why relatively few citizens perceived Clinton's ads to be negative.

Goldstein (1997) has conducted one of the few systematic analyses of the impact of advertising on the 1996 presidential contest. In particular, he focused on whether advertising tone—positive versus negative—affected turnout and whether campaign advertising affected vote choice. With respect to the first topic, Goldstein found no definitive evidence that negative advertising demobilized the electorate and reduced turnout. Earlier research, often based on experimental methodology (e.g., Ansolabehere and Iyengar 1995; Ansolabehere et al. 1994), had argued that negative advertising depressed turnout. But Goldstein, using procedures that assessed the tone, volume, and content of real campaign commercials in the actual election setting, found no individual-level effects of negative advertising on citizen turnout or efficacy. Goldstein's findings are also supported by the work of Steven Finkel and John Geer (1998), although this was based on elections other than 1996.

With respect to vote choice, Goldstein found that campaign advertising affected voters' decisions, although not to the same extent as other factors such as partisanship and issue preferences. Nevertheless, Goldstein pointed out, a good advertising campaign can net a candidate a few more percentage points of the vote, and in a close race in a key state, this gain can be critical to the election outcome. Thus, we can expect that targeted advertising in key states and key areas within states will continue to be the norm in future presidential contests.

Citizens' Use of the Media

The 1996 presidential campaign gave citizens many sources of political information, ranging from the traditional print and electronic media to the newer Internet and websites. As discussed earlier, few citizens availed themselves of the information superhighway. Even more significant was that many citizens claimed not to use the more traditional media outlets for their campaign information. Table 8.5 shows the frequency of use of five media—network television news, local television news, newspapers, magazines, and radio—as assessed by the NES 1996 survey. The survey generally used two questions to determine how much citizens relied on a particular medium for campaign information. For example, with respect to national television news, respondents were first asked how many days in the past week they had watched the national news on television. If they replied at least one day, they were then asked, "How much attention did you pay to news on national news shows about the campaign for president—a great deal, quite a bit, some, very little, or none?" Respondents who did not watch the national news at all and those who watched the national news but paid no attention to the presidential campaign were both classified as not using the national news as a source of campaign information.

Table 8.5 shows that relatively few respondents claim to rely on any of the media a great deal, with national television news cited most often at 12.5 percent. With respect to the two print media, sizable majorities said they did not rely on newspapers or magazines at all. These patterns are a function of both a citizenry for whom politics is generally not a very salient or positive feature and a campaign that did not excite voters as much as the 1992 contest had. Table 8.6 (p. 140) shows the comparable data for media usage in the 1992 campaign.

While the percentage of Americans who cared about who won the election was similar in 1992 and 1996, the level of interest in the presidential campaign was down substantially in 1996 from 1992. In 1992, 51.3 percent of Americans said they were very interested in the campaign, 39.2 percent were somewhat interested, and only 9.5 percent were not much interested. But in 1996, only 27.5 percent were very interested, 49.9 percent moderately interested, and 22.5 percent not much interested.

This lower interest is also reflected in the time at which citizens made their presidential vote choice in 1992 and 1996. In 1992, 26.3 percent of Americans had decided their choice before the conventions, compared to 33.7 percent in 1996. Likewise, fully 25 percent of citizens made up their minds in October and the last week before the election in 1992, compared to only 17.6 percent in 1996. Obviously, the electoral environment was quite different in 1992 than in 1996. Clinton was a newcomer to the national scene in 1992, as was Perot. The polls showed a closer race in 1992. And Perot's reentry into the presidential contest in October 1992 provided additional excitement in a contest that was already more competitive than the 1996 race. For many citizens, the 1996 outcome was a foregone conclusion, fed in part by the media's heavy emphasis on the poor prospects of the Dole campaign.

TABLE 8.5. ATTENTION PAID TO VARIOUS MEDIA DURING THE 1996 ELECTION CAMPAIGN
(IN PERCENTAGES)

	Network TV news	Local TV news	Newspaper articles	Magazine articles	Radio news[a]
No attention paid or medium not used[b]	23.2	18.6	56.1	65.4	58.9
Very little	13.0	18.9	6.7	8.2	18.7
Some	28.1	33.6	20.4	16.8	14.8
Quite a bit	23.1	21.1	11.0	6.6	7.6
A great deal	12.5	7.8	5.8	3.0	—
Total	100.0	100.0	100.0	100.0	100.0
(N)	(1712)	(1712)	(1714)	(1516)	(1516)

SOURCE: 1996 National Election Study.

a. Categories for radio speeches and discussions listened to are as follows: None, just one or two, several, a good many.

b. Includes voter respondents who did not use this medium and those who did but paid no attention to campaign news.

TABLE 8.6. ATTENTION PAID TO VARIOUS MEDIA DURING THE 1992 ELECTION CAMPAIGN
(IN PERCENTAGES)

	Television news	Newspaper articles	Magazine articles	Radio news[a]
No attention paid or medium not used[b]	13.8	54.3	77.4	63.5
Very little	10.5	5.9	2.6	17.5
Some ˙	27.8	18.1	9.4	11.6
Quite a bit	28.6	13.8	7.2	7.3
A great deal	19.4	7.9	3.4	—
Total	100.0	100.0	100.0	100.0
(N)	(2299)	(1740)	(2305)	(2303)

SOURCE: 1992 National Election Study.

a. Categories for radio speeches and discussions listened to are as follows: None, just one or two, several, a good many.

b. Includes voter respondents who did not use this medium and those who did but paid no attention to campaign news.

As one would intuitively expect, citizens who used the media heavily for campaign information were more likely to vote, more likely to be interested in the campaign, and more likely to recall a campaign ad. And citizens who were more interested in the campaign and more likely to recall a campaign ad were more likely to be heavier media users.

Perot supporters in 1996 differed in their media attentiveness from Clinton and Dole supporters in that Perot supporters were less likely than Clinton and Dole voters to use the media for campaign news. For example, about 16 and 18 percent of Clinton and Dole voters respectively paid a great deal of attention to national news coverage of the campaign compared to only 9.4 percent of the Perot voters. About 31 percent of Perot voters did not rely on national news coverage at all compared to only 17 and 16 percent of Clinton and Dole voters. Similar patterns emerge with local television news and newspapers. A simple count of the number of media that citizens used shows lower media usage on the part of Perot supporters. The explanation for this may be very simple and based in the reality of campaign coverage: Perot received less media coverage than the major-party candidates and was certainly treated as a less viable and credible candidate by the media in 1996 than in 1992.

Conclusion

The media lessons of 1996 were obvious. First, avoid public, intraparty conflict. Both parties accomplished this goal at their national conventions, but only the Democrats were able to avoid a divisive struggle for the nomination. Second, start the media campaign early to inoculate oneself against subsequent charges by the opposition and to set the campaign agenda. Because his campaign had early money and because he had no primary opposition, Clinton was able to define himself and the Republican opposition in the latter part of 1995 and the first part of 1996. And the need for Dole to appeal to the conservative wing of the GOP in order to secure the nomination increased the effectiveness of the Clinton campaign's media strategy of positioning Clinton as the last defense against the radical Republican conservatives. Third, keep internal debates and disputes about one's campaign out of the media limelight. The frequency and openness with which Dole operatives talked with reporters about the campaign's problems served to reinforce the perception that Dole was destined to lose. Moreover, it gave the opposition to chance to go on the offensive even before the Dole campaign had committed itself to such decisions as contesting California or going negative. Finally, target your media dollars to where the key votes are. As has often been written, a presidential election is not simply a national election, but a series of fifty state elections in which the ultimate objective is to win a majority of the Electoral College votes. The Clinton campaign targeted not only specific states but also particular cities and regions within states. In both 1992 and 1996, that strategy brought great success to the Democratic ticket, and with the Republican campaign moving toward local advertising in 1996, one can expect that future presidential elections will follow this path.

PART II

Group Voting in 1996

9

Is the Gender Gap Growing?

Barbara Norrander

IN THE PAST TWO DECADES, scholars and journalists have paid increasing attention to the political differences between men and women. Journalists labeled the election of 1992 the "Year of the Woman," 1994 the "Year of the Angry White Male," and 1996 the "Year of the Soccer Mom." Scholars also have spent more time analyzing gender gaps in electoral choices, partisanship, and political issues (Andersen 1997). As a result, we now know more about the political differences between men and women. Yet, in the recent past, these gender differences often were small, just meeting levels of statistical significance. Gender differences were dwarfed by distinctions between blacks and whites, rich and poor, and those with different levels of education. By 1992 and 1996, however, the size of the partisan and electoral gaps had grown significantly. A gender gap of 10 percentage points brought Clinton to the presidency in 1992, and a gap of 15 percentage points kept him in office in 1996. Whether this increase in gender voting patterns represents a permanent augmentation of the gender gap obviously cannot be known until future elections have come to pass. Nevertheless, a closer inspection of the development of the current gender gap in partisanship, issues, and presidential choices might shed light on the possibility of gender differences in future elections.

In exploring why the gender gap has grown, four topics are to be covered. First, the growth of a gender gap in party identification is tied into a realignment toward the Republican Party. Second, stages in which gender divisions on issues became apparent are illustrated with survey data from 1952 to 1996. Third, occurrences of gender gaps in presidential voting are delineated over the past forty years. Finally, this chapter tests the influence of gender on perceptions of Bill Clinton as a challenger, as a midterm president, and as an incumbent president seeking reelection. As these topics are explored, we discover that the gender gap developed as the changing preferences of men led them to desert the Democratic Party for the Republicans. Women's preferences have remained more stable over time, and as a result they now outnumber men in the Democratic Party.

The Evolution of the Gender Gap in Partisan Preferences

Most of the original attention given to the gender gap centered on women's support of the Democratic Party during the 1980 election. Women, it was argued, found Ronald Reagan less attractive than men did and so voted for Jimmy Carter. Initial speculation centered on Reagan's opposition to abortion rights and the change in the Republican Party's platform to a pro-life stance. Reagan's opposition to the Equal Rights Amendment also was viewed as a reason women would be less likely than men to support him. Explanations centered on such "women's issues" proved false, however, since men and women divided similarly on their abortion positions and issues of gender equality in politics (Cook, Jelen, and Wilcox 1992; Mansbridge 1985).

Attention next turned to differences between men's and women's political attitudes on other issues. Women are less supportive than men are of using force to solve political problems (Conover and Sapiro 1993; Fite, Genest, and Wilcox 1990; Shapiro and Mahajan 1986; Smith 1984). Men give greater support than women to capital punishment and military interventions and less support to gun control. In a second issue arena, women express greater support than men for "compassion issues." Thus, women are slightly more likely than men to approve of using the government to alleviate economic inequality ("Women and Men" 1982). Reagan's strong anticommunist position, his call for a significant tax cut, and his desire for a smaller government providing fewer services appeared to be more attractive to men than to women. The final explanation for divergence between men's and women's votes centered on economics. Women earn less than men, are more likely to receive welfare benefits, and are more likely to be employed in social welfare occupations that rely on government funding (Erie and Rein 1988). These issue and situational differences supposedly moved women to support Democratic candidates more often than men did.

Overlooked in many of these arguments is that actual changes in partisan preferences over the past thirty years have occurred primarily among men (Kenski 1988; Miller 1991; Wirls 1986). Men left the Democratic Party and moved into the Republican Party. Women's political preferences changed less or not at all. Men also have been more likely to declare themselves political independents, while women are more likely to consider themselves partisans (Norrander 1997a). This tendency meant that for most of the 1970s and 1980s, women outnumbered men in both parties. To measure partisan differences between men and women fully, it becomes necessary to collapse leaning independents in with the appropriate partisan category. Figure 9.1 (p. 148) uses this expanded definition of partisans to trace the decline in support for the Democratic Party among men, which, in fact, created the gender gap.

Prior to 1964, women were slightly more likely than men to be Republicans, not Democrats. In figure 9.1, this pro-Republican gap among women is statistically significant in 1954 ($p < .10$) and 1956 ($p < .05$). The few scholars who noted this Republican bias among women attributed it to age differences between the sexes. Women, since they tended to outlive men, were more likely to include those whose partisanship dated back to the Republican era before the New Deal realignment (Campbell et al. 1960). Yet the group with the most distinguishing partisan characteristic in the 1950s was southern males. During this time period, the Democratic gender gap in the South stood at 9 percentage points, with 69 percent of men and 60 percent of women professing a Democratic preference. The gap among Republican preferences was only 3 percentage points in both the North and the South. After 1964, male support for the Democratic Party began to drop in the nation as a whole, but especially in the South. By the mid-1980s, southern male preferences for the Democratic Party had dropped to 51 percent, while southern women's preferences fell to 58 percent. Southerners, who had their own tradition of a conservative Democratic Party, left the national party as it increasingly took liberal stands on social welfare and civil rights issues. By the late 1980s, southern men were moving into the Republican Party at a faster rate than southern women.

The exodus of southern males from the Democratic Party began to affect nationwide totals in the early 1970s to the extent that women began to outnumber men in the Democratic Party. In figure 9.1, the current gender gap alignment, with women more likely than men to be Democratic, first reaches statistical significance in 1972 ($p < .01$) and 1974 ($p < .10$). The gender gap collapses in 1976 as men temporarily returned to support Democrat Jimmy Carter after the Watergate scandal and President Gerald Ford's inability to revive a stagnant economy. But by 1980, greater numbers of men than women had again begun to show their disapproval of the Democratic Party. This gender gap remains statistically significant thereafter ($p < .05$ except in 1990 when $p < .10$).

During the 1970s and 1980s the gender gap tended to collapse in off-year congressional elections as southern males returned to the Democratic Party (Norrander 1997b). The more conservative southern Democratic Party survived to some extent into the 1980s, allowing for greater male support of state and local Democratic candidates. Southerners may even have held dual partisan identities during this period, when they saw themselves as Republicans at the national level and as Democrats at the state level (Jewell and Ol-

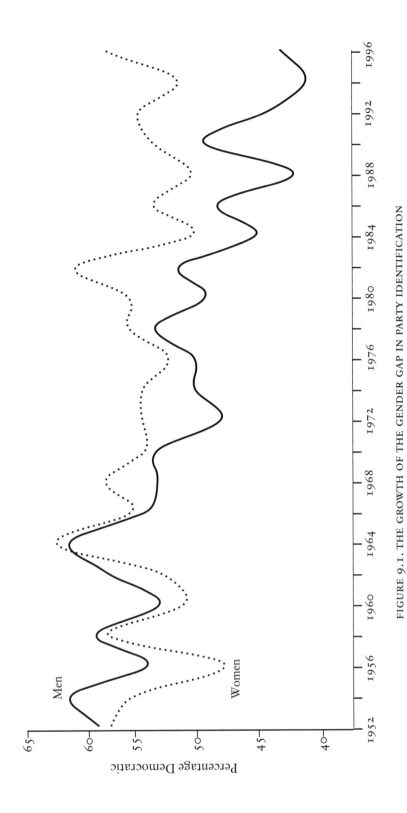

FIGURE 9.1. THE GROWTH OF THE GENDER GAP IN PARTY IDENTIFICATION

SOURCE: 1952–94 National Election Studies cumulative file, 1996. Democratic category includes leaners.

son 1988). This phenomenon apparently was stronger among southern men than women. Gradually the Republican realignment took hold in the South as the Republican Party began to field better candidates for a variety of elective offices. As a result, conservative southerners could support the Republican Party for both presidential and congressional offices. The 1994 midterm elections may have signaled the finalization of the Republican realignment in the South, since the gender gap did not collapse in that off-year election.

A gender gap also emerged in the North as the result of the exit of males from the Democratic Party. Northern male preferences fell from an average of 50 percent in the 1950s to 44 percent by the late 1980s. Women's partisan preferences outside the South have not changed significantly over the past forty years. In the North, the gender gap in the 1970s and 1980s tended to collapse in presidential election years as women became slightly more Republican during these elections (Norrander 1997b). Republican presidential candidates actually had considerable success in attracting support from both men and women in the 1980s. As in the South, these fluctuations disappeared after the 1992 election, and the gender gap grew wider and more stable.

By the mid-1990s, a significant, stable gender gap characterized political partisanship in America. This gender gap emerged from a realignment of voters away from the Democratic and toward the Republican Party (see also Kaufmann and Petrocik 1997). Men participated in this realignment much more fully than women. As a result, by the early 1970s women outnumbered men in the Democratic Party. In 1992 the gender gap among Democratic identifiers rose to 10 percentage points, and by 1996 this gap had risen to 14 percentage points.

The Gender Gap in Issue Positions

Tracing the growth of the gender gap on political issues is more difficult than doing so for party identification because few issue questions have been asked in identical formats over an extended period of time. The content of surveys changed as the issue agenda changed. Wars ended, the economy rebounded, and scandals passed into memory. New movements brought questions of civil rights and environmentalism to the forefront. Policy changes also made some survey questions obsolete. It hardly makes sense today to ask whether birth-control devices should be legal. This question, however, could be asked until the mid-1960s when the Supreme Court struck down bans on birth control as violating a person's right to privacy. Improvements in the art of asking survey questions also mean that issue questions are rarely asked in the same format today as they were in the early days of survey research. In 1964 the National Election Study (NES) improved its issue questions by switching to a double-sided format, rather than the single-sided agree/disagree form. This improvement, however, makes it difficult to assess changes in aggregate opinion over time. Still, some tentative judgements can be made about longitudinal patterns between gender and issue positions.

During the earliest periods of public opinion polling, in the 1940s through the 1960s, only two areas revealed different patterns for men and women ("Women and Men" 1982). Women were slightly less supportive than men of using force to solve political problems, particularly in the international arena. Gender differences also tended to arise in issues of domestic use of force such as gun control and capital punishment.

The second area of early gender differences was political interest and information, with women being less concerned with politics than men. In the 1950s women lagged behind men in turnout rates by 10 percentage points nationally, with larger differences in the South and among the less educated (Campbell et al. 1960). The gap was widest among those over fifty, since women in this group had been socialized prior to the passage of the Nineteenth Amendment in 1920. By the 1970s, the surviving members of this older group of women constituted a smaller portion of the electorate, and gender differences in turnout diminished to 2 percentage points (Wolfinger and Rosenstone 1980). By the 1980 election, women were voting at higher rates than men, though this pattern did not reach statistical significance in most surveys until later in the decade (Kenski 1988).

Gender differences on compassion issues emerged in the 1970s. Women gave greater support than men to using the government to aid individuals in economic difficulties ("Women and Men" 1982). Men preferred self-reliance in obtaining jobs. Women demonstrated slightly greater acceptance of using government to redistribute income and for financial support for the elderly. Yet these differences tended to be smaller than those found for use-of-force issues. For compassion issues, gender differences averaged only 3 percentage points (Shapiro and Mahajan 1986). Women also began giving greater support for government regulatory policies in areas of risk, such as consumer safety and environmental protection. Thus, women expressed greater opposition to nuclear power plants, more support for car safety issues such as speed limits and mandatory seatbelt usage, and more support for regulation of tobacco products.

Scattered gender differences occurred in other issue areas. On moral issues, such as pornography, use of drugs, birth control, and school prayer, women tended to be slightly more conservative than men. On civil rights issues, few consistent patterns existed. In the area of civil liberties, women were less tolerant than men of allowing political expression by communists (Shapiro and Mahajan 1986). On women's issues, such as abortion and the ERA, however, no consistent differences were found between men's and women's opinions. In the earliest polls, women were more supportive than men of an expanded role for women in politics and business, but these differences disappeared by the 1960s (Erskine 1971; Simon and Landis 1989). Generally, opinions on abortion revealed no gender gap, though in some instances men have been slightly more likely than women to support abortion under a wider range of circumstances (Cook, Jelen, and Wilcox 1992; Shapiro and Mahajan 1986).

A few issue questions in the 1996 NES survey can be compared to responses in earlier NES polls. For this analysis, issues are coded so that higher values indicate more conservative and greater internationalist preferences. Gender is coded so that women have higher scores. Thus, negative coefficients indicate men hold more conservative positions than women. Tau$_c$ is an appropriate bivariate statistic to measure the strength of these relationships, since it is designed for ordinal-level data with an unequal number of categories between the two variables. Table 9.1 (p. 152) shows that in the three use-of-force issues a fairly consistent gender gap occurred over the years. The two international issues produced a gender gap two-thirds of the time. Somewhat perplexing, the two measures diverge in 1996 as the defense spending issue sees a gender gap reemerging while the gap for interventionist sentiment disappears. The gender gap on defense spending vanished in the early 1990s as support for such expenditures dropped among both men and women. In 1996, support for defense spending grew among both sexes, but more dramatically so for men than women. Thus, by 1996, patterns in men's and women's support for defense spending had returned to those of the late 1980s. The gender gap disappeared on interventionism sentiment in 1996 as women's support grew to match more closely that of men. Gender differences on using force to solve domestic unrest always appear statistically significant in the NES surveys, though the question was last asked in 1992. With a fairly stable pattern in use-of-force issues over the past forty years, such issues are unlikely to explain an increasing gender gap in partisan preferences in the 1990s.

On compassion issues, gender gaps emerged or widened in the 1970s or 1980s and showed little movement in the 1990s. Opinions on government-provided health insurance divided along gender lines in the mid-1980s, and Clinton's espousal of a universal insurance plan after the 1992 election did not widen this gap to any extent. Gender differences appeared on the role of government in guaranteeing jobs in the earliest NES surveys, with the gap becoming larger and more consistent after the mid-1970s. On providing aid to African Americans, the gender gap that existed in the early 1970s reemerged in the late 1980s. A gender gap has always appeared for the government services question asked since the early 1980s. Thus, compassion issues also do not seem likely candidates for explaining an expansion in the partisan and electoral gender gap.

On women's issues asked in the NES surveys, the gender gap is erratic and often in the direction of males assuming a more liberal stance. On abor-

TABLE 9.1. THE GENDER GAP ON ISSUES

| | Use-of-force issues | | | Compassion issues | | | | Women's issues | | |
	Interven-tionism	Defense spending	Urban unrest	Health	Jobs	Minority aid	Level of services	Abortion	Women's role	Ideology
1956	-.03	—	—	.00	-.04	—	—	—	—	—
1958	-.09**	—	—	—	-.08**	—	—	—	—	—
1960	-.09**	—	—	-.08**	-.06**	—	—	—	—	—
1962	—	—	—	.01	—	—	—	—	—	—
1964	—	—	—	-.03	-.03	—	—	—	—	—
1966	—	—	—	—	—	—	—	—	—	—
1968	-.06*	—	-.16**	.01	-.06*	—	—	—	—	—
1970	—	—	-.15**	-.05	—	-.06	—	—	—	—
1972	-.03	—	-.10**	.02	-.06*	-.01	—	.05*	.03	-.01
1974	—	—	-.10**	—	-.16**	-.08**	—	—	.04*	-.07**

Year									
1976	−.05*	−.19**	−.02	−.11**	−.06*	—	.06**	.06**	−.01
1978	—	—	−.03	−.10**	−.06**	—	.00	.06**	−.04
1980	−.11**	—	—	−.07*	−.04	—	−.01	−.01	−.05
1982	−.14**	—	−.08*	−.14**	−.04	−.14**	.00	.00	−.11**
1984	−.07**	—	—	−.11**	−.04	−.12**	.05*	.06**	−.05
1986	−.12**	—	—	−.09**	−.04	−.12**	.00	—	−.08**
1988	−.06*	—	−.08**	−.08**	−.07**	−.11**	.04	.00	−.03
1990	.03	—	—	−.13**	−.09**	−.14**	.03	.07*	−.04
1992	−.08**	−.10**	−.08**	−.12**	−.08**	−.14**	.02	.00	−.08**
1994	−.07**	—	−.10**	−.15**	−.07**	−.19**	.00	.05*	−.13**
1996	−.11**	—	−.09**	−.13**	−.10**	−.14**	−.04	.00	−.18**

SOURCE: 1952–96 National Election Studies, cumulative file, 1996.

NOTE: Entries are tau$_c$. The health question changed in 1968, the jobs question in 1972, the abortion question in 1984. All questions are coded so that higher response categories indicate conservative positions or interventionism. Gender is coded so that women have the higher code. Thus a positive coefficient indicates men are more liberal and a negative coefficient indicates women are more liberal.

*$p < .05$; **$p < .01$.

tion, a gender gap emerges only one-fourth of the time, and no gap has existed since 1986. On women's role in society, a gender gap occurred in half the years, with men being more supportive of an equal role for women in society and women slightly more in favor of a traditional role. No trend exists in the occurrence of this gender gap, and in 1996 three-fourths of the population supported an equal role for women while 10 percent favored a traditional role. Thus, no apparent trend is available to explain the expanding gender gap in electoral politics.

An expanding gender gap is apparent, however, in ideological identification. One form of the ideology question, based on differences in thermometer ratings of liberals and conservatives, indicates a lack of a gender gap extending back to 1964. The question format presented in table 9.1, which is the simple question of self-identification, first revealed a gender gap in ideology in the 1974 election, but this disappeared until the 1982 election, collapsed again in 1984, reemerged in 1986, and then disappeared until 1992. Since 1992, the gap in ideological identification has held steady and appears to be gaining in strength. In general, the ideological gender gap has grown as men have become increasingly conservative over the past two decades, while no trend exists in women's ideological self-identification. By 1996, half the men in American considered themselves to be conservatives, compared to one-third of women. The divergence of the two sexes on issue positions in the 1970s and 1980s laid the groundwork for a divergence on ideology in the 1990s. Changes in the 1990s centered on self-characterizations, with a widening gender gap in both ideological and partisan identities.

The Gender Gap in Presidential Elections

As mentioned earlier, the first use of "gender gap" in connection with presidential voting occurred for the 1980 election pitting Democratic president Jimmy Carter against Republican challenger Ronald Reagan. National Organization for Women (NOW) leaders, seeing the gender pattern in media polls, coined the term gender gap in hopes of convincing Democratic Party leaders that a stronger effort to pass the ERA in state legislatures would pay off with greater voting loyalty by women in future elections. The efforts by NOW to use the gender gap to convince Democratic leaders to support a woman vice-presidential candidate in 1984 proved more successful (Bonk 1988; Mueller 1988). Feminists began using the term in their dealings with the media. As a result, the media increasingly employed the theme of a gender gap in reporting presidential preferences between 1980 and 1984. The news media portrayed women as another voting bloc, similar to union members or African Americans, who could affect the outcome of elections (Borquez, Goldenberg, and Kahn 1988).

Gender differences in presidential voting, however, predate the 1980 election. Figures in table 9.2 (p. 156) subtract the percentage of women supporting a candidate from the percentage of men doing so. (A difference-in-proportions test is used to tap the significance of the gender gap for each party's presidential vote since 1952.) Besides the national results, figures are given for both the South and the North, since rates of partisan change differ between the two regions. But the number of cases for the South averages only 169 for men and 196 for women, making statistical significance difficult to achieve. It is in the South that the reverse gender gap of the 1950s and the 1960 elections is strongest. During that time, men rather than women were more likely to vote Democratically.

Just as was true for changes in gender patterns in party identification, changes in presidential voting patterns began in the 1960s. In 1968, a gender gap occurred outside the South as George Wallace pulled more men than women away from both Richard Nixon and Hubert Humphrey. A gender gap in presidential voting has remained statistically significant in every election since 1968 with the sole exception of 1976, when Carter was able to attract the support of northern males. Generally, between 1968 and 1980 the gender gap was more likely to be statistically significant in the North than in the South, but this may simply reflect the smaller sample sizes in the South, making statistical significance more difficult to achieve. Patterns began to change slightly in 1984, when the gender gap opened up in the South, exceeding 10 percentage points in all subsequent elections. The gender gap in the North did not reach these proportions until the 1990s.

More often than not, a gender gap characterized voting in presidential elections since the 1950s. Up until 1964, men, especially southern men, supported Democratic candidates at a higher rate than women. The gender gap switched directions in the mid-1960s. Men became more supportive than women of Republican candidates in all subsequent elections except 1976, when they returned to the Democratic fold, and 1992, when they gave greater support to Ross Perot. As a result, women have been dominant among the supporters of Democratic candidates in every election since 1972, except 1976. Gender preferences in presidential voting were firmly in place by the 1990s. With Perot attracting fewer supporters in 1996, gender preferences between the two parties became more distinct, enlarging the gender gap nationwide by 5 percentage points on the Democratic side and 10 percentage points on the Republican front.

The Gender Gap in the 1996 Election

By the 1990s, a gender gap had existed on issues involving use of force and compassion and been present in presidential elections for twenty years. Still,

TABLE 9.2. THE GENDER GAP IN PRESIDENTIAL ELECTIONS (IN PERCENTAGES)

	Democratic candidate			Republican candidate			Other candidates[a]		
	National	South	North	National	South	North	National	South	North
1952	2	11	0	-2	-11	1	—	—	—
1956	7**	9	4	-7**	-9	-4	—	—	—
1960	5*	8	4	-5*	-8	-4	—	—	—
1964	-3	-1	-5	4	1	5	—	—	—
1968	-5	-7	-3	-1	4	-2	6***	3	6***
1972	-7***	-5	-7**	7***	5	6**	—	—	—
1976	0	-7	2	0	7	-2	—	—	—
1980	-6*	-3	-9**	7*	5	9**	-1	-3	0
1984	-7***	-14***	-5	8***	14***	5	—	—	—
1988	-6**	-14***	-4	7**	15***	4	—	—	—
1992	-10***	-11**	-9***	2	7	0	8***	3	11***
1996	-15***	-13**	-16***	12***	8	13***	3*	5*	2

SOURCE: 1952–94 National Election Studies, cumulative file, 1996.

NOTE: Entries are tau$_c$. Positive gap numbers indicate more males; negative gap numbers indicate more females. Statistical significance is determined by a difference-in-proportions test.

a. Other candidates were Wallace in 1968, Anderson in 1980, and Perot in 1992 and 1996.

*$p < .10$; **$p < .05$; ***$p < .01$.

between 1992 and 1996 the gender gap widened. To analyze changes in men's and women's evaluations of Clinton over time, a common indicator of support is needed. Thus, thermometer ratings (a scale from 0 to 100) of Clinton will be used as the dependent variable. Such thermometer ratings are normally closely related to the actual vote. Table 9.3 reveals how the gender gap in ratings of Clinton grew over the four-year period. On average, only 3 thermometer points separated women's from men's opinions of Clinton in 1992. Both men and women rated Clinton lower in 1994 than in 1992, but men's ratings dropped an average of 9 thermometer points while women's fell an average of 7 points. By 1996 Clinton had regained his original popularity with women but had recaptured only one-third of the rating points he had previously lost among men. Thus, by 1996 the gender gap in Clinton's evaluations had risen to nearly 9 thermometer points.

TABLE 9.3

MEAN THERMOMETER RATINGS OF CLINTON, 1992–96

	1992	*1994*	*1996*
Men	60.9	51.6	55.1
Women	63.9	56.9	63.7
Difference	−2.9*	−5.3*	−8.9*
t-ratio	−2.84	−3.99	−5.97

SOURCE: 1992, 1994, 1996 National Election Studies.

*$p < .01$.

Table 9.4 (p. 158) presents the influence of gender and issue positions on evaluations of Clinton in 1992, 1994, and 1996. Eleven issue questions were asked in all three surveys. In addition, opinions on gays in the military were asked in 1992 and 1996, but not in 1994. Approximately one-third of the 1994 survey respondents participated in the 1992 survey, and their 1992 answers were used in the 1994 analysis. For the remaining cases on this variable, and for cases with missing answers on the other issue questions, the sample's mean values were substituted for missing data. This substitution process retains a more representative sample for the analysis. In addition to the issue questions, evaluations of the national economy and one's own personal financial situation were included. Previous studies found that women tend to be more negative about the state of the economy, causing them to vote against the incumbent. In addition, women were more likely than men to cast their ballots solely on the basis of their evaluations of the national economy, while men gave weight to their own financial conditions as well (Welch and Hibbing 1992). Finally, indicators of party identification and ideology are included.

Three aspects of change are apparent in table 9.4. First, people's evalua-

TABLE 9.4. THE GENDER GAP IN EVALUATIONS OF CLINTON, 1992–96

	1992			1994			1996		
	Coefficient (Stand. err.)	P value	B	Coefficient (Stand. err.)	P value	B	Coefficient (Stand. err.)	P value	B
Constant	94.540 (4.119)	.000	—	117.574 (4.199)	.000	—	121.924 (4.046)	.000	—
Gender	-1.969 (.892)	.027	-.040*	1.056 (1.029)	.305	.019	2.394 (1.018)	.019	.042*
Party identification	-4.926 (.252)	.000	-.405**	-5.986 (.287)	.000	-.441**	-5.887 (.297)	.000	-.440**
Ideology	-.863 (.305)	.005	-.057**	-1.060 (.382)	.006	-.057**	-1.068 (.366)	.004	-.061**
Personal economy	.514 (.413)	.213	.023	-2.098 (.476)	.000	-.078**	-.794 (.492)	.107	-.030
National economy	1.940 (.521)	.000	.070**	-4.161 (.539)	.000	-.144**	-4.528 (.610)	.000	-.142**
Interventionism	.496 (.252)	.049	.035*	.605 (.285)	.034	.038*	-.154 (.298)	.605	-.009
Defense spending	-.262 (.347)	.450	-.014	-.163 (.379)	.666	-.008	.716 (.403)	.076	.034
Capital punishment	-.093 (.331)	.780	-.005	-.487 (.389)	.211	-.023	.563 (.377)	.135	.028
Level of services	-.439 (.335)	.190	-.026	-.949 (.382)	.013	-.050*	-2.772 (.407)	.000	-.139**

	Coefficient			Coefficient			Coefficient		
Jobs	−.535 (.301)	.075	−.037	−1.632 (.352)	.000	−.100**	−1.521 (.308)	.000	−.089**
Health	−.296 (.268)	.270	−.021	−1.756 (.305)	.000	−.120**	−1.161 (.321)	.000	−.073**
Minority aid	−.758 (.297)	.011	−.051*	−.911 (.362)	.012	−.053*	−.024 (.391)	.952	−.001
Affirmative action	−1.774 (.337)	.000	−.099**	−1.060 (.459)	.021	−.045*	−2.129 (.419)	.000	−.099**
Abortion	−.690 (.445)	.121	−.030	−.914 (.514)	.076	−.035	−1.263 (.514)	.014	−.048*
Women's role	−.022 (.283)	.939	−.001	.389 (.327)	.234	.023	.498 (.333)	.135	.028
School prayer	−.293 (.573)	.609	−.009	1.517 (.654)	.021	.042*	.703 (.653)	.282	.020
Gays in military	−1.677 (.293)	.000	−.114**	−.098 (.499)	.844	−.004	−1.723 (.346)	.000	−.098**
N	2226			1787			1515		
R^2	.339			.466			.555		

SOURCE: 1992, 1994, 1996 National Election Studies.

NOTE: Issues are coded with higher values indicating conservatism, internationalism, or negative evaluation of the economy. Gender is coded with women having the higher value. All equations taken together are statistically significant at the .01 level.

$*p < .05; **p < .01$.

tions of Clinton became more grounded in the issues as he became more familiar to the public as a sitting president. While this set of issues could explain only about one-third of the variation in evaluations of Clinton as a
candidate in 1992, by the time of his reelection these issues explained over
half of the variation in evaluations of Clinton. Second, the relationship between gender and evaluations of Clinton changed directions over the years
after controls for issue positions are imposed. In 1992, after controlling for
issue positions, men rather than women actually gave Clinton higher evaluations. Thus, women rated Clinton more highly than men in 1992 only because of their more liberal positions on a host of issues. Men rated Clinton
lower because of their more conservative positions, but they also gave him
the benefit of the doubt, raising their overall evaluations of him slightly. By
1994, issue positions alone were enough to explain men's and women's evaluations of Clinton. By 1996, women rated Clinton even higher than expected, given their issue positions, while men rated him lower than expected.
As Clinton became better known, he became less popular with men and
more popular with women.

The third change in evaluations of Clinton over the four-year period is
in the changing impact of several issues. Based on a statistical significance
test for differences in regression coefficients across equations (Cohen and
Cohen 1982, 111), opinions on the government's role in providing jobs and
health insurance had significantly greater effects in 1994 and 1996 than in
1992. By 1996, opinions on the general level of government services also became more strongly linked to evaluations of Clinton. Thus, as Clinton pro-
ceeded through his presidency, his evaluations became more closely linked to
traditional social welfare issues. On these compassion issues, women are
slightly more liberal and men are slightly more conservative. As a result, the
two sexes diverged in their evaluations of Clinton as time passed.

Evaluations of the state of the economy affected evaluations of Clinton
differently as he progressed from presidential candidate to incumbent president. In 1992 Clinton benefited from those with negative evaluations of the
national economy. By 1994 those with negative evaluations of the economy
and their own financial state rated Clinton lower. Only negative evaluations
of the economy and not personal finances had an impact on Clinton's popularity in 1996. A check for an interaction effect between gender, evaluations
of the economy, and ratings of Clinton revealed that in 1992 women were
more likely to be sociotropic voters. Women's, rather than men's, opinions
of the national economy influenced their ratings of Clinton. In 1994, ratings
of the economy and personal finances had similar effects for men and
women. By 1996, however, men showed a greater tendency to be sociotropic
voters. Both men and women used their evaluations of the national economy
to judge President Clinton, but men weighed these evaluations more heavily.

Conclusion

Of the three gender related themes that journalists ascribed to recent elections, the one that best explains the gender gap is 1994's focus on "The Angry White Male." Women candidates did well in 1992's "Year of the Woman," but mostly because well-qualified women candidates were poised to take advantage of an unusually large number of open-seat contests for the House of Representatives (Cook, Thomas, and Wilcox 1994). The concentration in 1996 on the movement of suburban, Republican "soccer moms" into the Democratic camp is less accurate. The gender group that increased its preference for Clinton the most was Democratic women, who widened their support over Democratic men from 3 percentage points in 1992 to 7 percentage points in 1996. Republican women increased their support of Clinton, but at a rate identical to that of Republican men (Kaufmann and Petrocik 1997). In part, this reflects the Democratic Party's strategy to counteract the normally pro-Republican vote among married couples with children by stressing family values in the campaign (Weisberg 1987; Weisberg and Kelly 1997).

Men created the gender gap by moving away from the Democratic Party at a faster pace than women. Whether this movement was fueled by anger still needs to be documented, but the analysis in this chapter confirms that men increasingly view themselves as political conservatives, and these conservative identities are reflected in increasing Republican identifications. The underlying trends that produced the gender gap occurred during the late 1960s and the 1970s, when the two sexes began to diverge in their issue positions, partisan preferences, and voting patterns. The electoral gender gap widened in 1996 as evaluations of Clinton became more closely tied to the issues that divide men and women, most notably the compassion issues of jobs, guaranteed incomes, and government services.

The future of the gender gap is intertwined with the fates of the two parties. The Republican realignment may stall if the party is unable to convince women voters to join men in switching their loyalties to "The Grand Old Party." On the other side, the Democratic Party needs to retain its edge among women voters to remain competitive, and it needs to recapture the support of men to regain the numerical advantage it held in the 1960s. The size of the gender gap in future elections will depend on a subtle and complicated mixture of party and candidate strategies, issue agendas, and partisan identification.

10

Party Coalitions in Transition: Partisanship and Group Support, 1952–96

HAROLD W. STANLEY AND
RICHARD G. NIEMI

GROUP SUPPORT for the political parties is of perennial concern to politicians and political scientists alike. Indeed, we often define parties and their ideological positions in terms of the groups of individuals that are said to support the party or to benefit from its positions on major issues. Thus, for example, we say in shorthand form that the Democrats are the party of the poor or that the Republicans are better for business interests, that the Democrats (for nearly a century after the Civil War) were strongest in the South, and that Cuban Americans are highly supportive of the Republicans.

In recent years, there has been a weakening of long-time patterns of party support to the point that one can speak of a breakdown of the old system. The so-called New Deal coalition, which took shape in the 1930s, involved broad support of the Democrats by native white southerners, labor union and working-class households, African Americans, Jews, and, to a lesser extent, Catholics. During the 1950s, breaks in this coalition began to appear, as native southern whites supported Republican candidates for the presidency; yet the coalition remained largely intact, as even these southern whites continued to think of themselves as Democratic partisans. Further weakening occurred in the ensuing years, so much so that we wrote after the 1992 election that "it is time to declare the New Deal [Democratic] coalition dead" (Stanley and Niemi 1995, 237).

The obituary for the New Deal coalition can be found in the 1994 and 1996 elections, in which the Republicans captured majority control of the House and Senate for the first time since 1952. Yet no sooner is one coalition gone than we want to know the shape of that to follow. Is there a pattern of group support in 1994 and 1996 that outlines what is to come?

More specifically, do changing patterns of party support suggest the beginning of a new, long-lasting form of coalitional behavior that will support continued Republican domination, or do they at least indicate competitive elections in which the majority in a series of elections shifts back and forth between the parties? Was President Clinton able to win reelection by reinvigorating a coalitional base that had existed in 1992?

We approach these questions by examining expressed loyalty to the political parties—that is, self-reported partisanship—over time, which essentially updates our earlier analyses of group support. We are concerned with continuity from past to present, but we are especially interested in the potential for a new system of group support that may signal the start of yet another fundamental change in voter's relations with the parties—that is, the rise of another new party system. Thus, while presenting group partisanship figures for all presidential elections since the 1950s, we concentrate our analysis on the changing patterns found in the late 1980s and in the first half of the 1990s.

Analyzing Group Support

Group support can mean a number of different, though related, things. In the past, we have looked primarily at what is called party identification —that is, which party people say they "generally support" (Stanley and Niemi 1995). Political scientists and pollsters use self-reports of this sort in an effort to assess "enduring" or long-term support for the parties, in contrast to the more short-term support gathered by specific candidates.[1] It is now well known that self-reports of party support are not entirely free of which way the political winds are blowing in response to particular campaigns, partisan scandals, and so on (see, for example, MacKuen, Erikson, and Stimson 1989; Weisberg and Smith 1991). Nevertheless, party identification, or partisanship, is less transient than individuals' voting behavior. This is especially true when one thinks of presidential voting; the presidential election is so visible that all but the most isolated individuals (who are not likely to vote in any event) have heard or read about and probably exchanged thoughts about both candidates. Hence, presidential preferences fluctuate to a degree that partisanship does not. Therefore, it is useful to consider party support in this "generic" sense.

There remains the question of how, statistically, we should assess the support of each group for a party or candidate. We could simply show the partisanship of each group—that is, how many native southern whites, urban residents, blacks, white Protestant fundamentalists, and so on, say they generally support Democrats versus Republicans. For some purposes, this approach is exactly what one wants. A problem is that such simple accounts are misleading because the groups are overlapping. For example, blacks tend to reside in urban areas. Thus, if one finds that blacks and urban residents tend to support Democrats, one is talking largely about the same people. Do both characteristics tend to make people Democratic? Trying to answer such questions raises several problems, but one is certainly aided by the use of multivariate statistical procedures (i.e., procedures that incorporate multiple variables "all at once" rather than one at a time). In this chapter we use multivariate logit analysis.[2] While this technique is complicated, a careful reading of our tables and of the explanations we provide for them should make the results understandable.

The Models

We begin by describing the multivariate models that form the basis of our analysis. In this presentation, we draw on National Election Study (NES) data from presidential elections since 1952. We define three models of party support that collectively cover the 1952–96 period.[3] For comparisons over the entire period, it is important to consider all three models, and we have previously done so (Stanley and Niemi 1991, 1992). For the present analysis, we emphasize the latest model, which can be estimated virtually without change since 1980. That model incorporates the New Deal elements, gender, church attendance, income, white Protestant fundamentalists, Hispanic origin, 1943–58 birth cohort (baby boomers), and 1959–1978 birth cohort (so-called Generation X).[4] The primary dependent variables to be explained are Democratic identification and Republican identification.[5]

For several reasons, we use separate models for Democratic and Republican identification. First, to the extent that the New Deal coalition has broken up—a thesis we developed four years ago (Stanley and Niemi 1995) —we want to be certain of that judgment, and a model of Democratic identification is most appropriate for that test. More significantly, we want to see the extent to which formerly Democratic groups have moved over to supporting the Republican Party (as opposed to becoming independent), so a model for each party is necessary. Finally, for newer groups, we want to see whether hypothesized connections to the Republicans have taken hold. As noted earlier, our focus here is on the continuing nature of the changes as reflected in the late 1980s and in the 1990s.

Results

The groups of interest are of two kinds. First are the core groups of the so-called New Deal coalition—blacks, Jews, Catholics, members of union households, and native white southerners. These are groups that gave strong support to the Democratic Party and Democratic candidates in the 1930s and for decades thereafter. Second are "newer" groups that have become more visible in the past decade or so and, in addition to the traditional groups, are the sets of individuals for whose support the parties are vying. The newer groups include women, Hispanics, churchgoers in general and Christian fundamentalists in particular, and groups defined by age or "generation."

We look at support for each party separately; while support that does not go to one party most often goes to the other, voters are more independent than they were before the 1960s, so one sometimes finds that neither party receives a boost from a particular group. The top half of table 10.1 (p. 166) presents the mean predicted probability (based on the results from the logit analysis) that a group member claims Democratic identification in each presidential election year since 1952 and the two most recent congressional elections. Essentially, these numbers are the proportions of Democrats in each group before imposing any controls for other group memberships. Note that Democratic partisanship declined for every group in 1994 except for those born between 1959 and 1970. The changes are often small; but recall that partisanship is generally quite stable in the force of temporary partisan tides. Thus, the force of the Republican tide in 1994 is demonstrated by the fact that virtually all groups were affected. In the case of many of the New Deal groups, this represented the continuation of a change that had been taking place for many years. Note, for example, the continued slide of native white southerners, Catholics, and members of union households. The same was true of support from Christian fundamentalists. In other instances, however, the decline in 1994 represented a reversal of recent patterns of support; note, especially, Hispanics, where support dropped in both 1992 and 1994, and baby boomers (born between 1943 and 1958), where support dropped precipitously in 1994.

That the uniform and sometimes sudden move toward the Republicans in 1994 was temporary is demonstrated by the equally uniform shift in group support back to the Democrats in 1996. Though the Democrats failed to win control of Congress, they won back virtually all their losses in partisanship in 1994. This helped make it possible for President Clinton to win reelection despite the midterm losses to his party. Perhaps even more important from a long-run perspective, the notion of a new partisan era launched by Newt Gingrich and the Contract with America in 1994 appears to be undermined by the fact that professed support for the Democrats returned to its pre-Contract level among all groups. If there is to be a new (continuous)

TABLE 10.1. MEAN AND INCREMENTAL PROBABILITIES OF DEMOCRATIC IDENTIFICATION
FOR MEMBERS OF EACH GROUP

	1952	1956	1960	1964	1968	1972	1976	1980	1984	1988	1990	1992	1994	1996
Mean probabilities[a]														
Black	.53	.51	.45	.74	.85	.67	.74	.74	.62	.65	.64	.64	.62	.65
Catholic	.56	.52	.64	.59	.53	.50	.50	.43	.43	.37	.45	.41	.38	.43
Jewish	.73	.62	.52	.57	.50	.52	.58	.81	.60	.36	.62	.63	.48	.63
Female	.48	.42	.49	.53	.48	.43	.42	.44	.40	.40	.43	.39	.35	.44
Native southern white	.77	.71	.72	.72	.53	.52	.52	.49	.41	.40	.38	.33	.31	.36
Union household member	.54	.51	.57	.64	.50	.46	.47	.47	.47	.42	.51	.47	.41	.43
Regular churchgoer	.50	.46	.49	.53	.47	.44	.43	.40	.37	.39	.43	.36	.35	.36
Income: top third	.43	.40	.43	.42	.39	.34	.32	.35	.32	.28	.35	.29	.19	.30
White Protestant fundamentalist	—	—	—	—	—	.46	.43	.56	.41	.37	.34	.31	.23	.34
Hispanic, non-Cuban	—	—	—	—	—	—	—	.55	.48	.52	.51	.44	.43	.52
Born 1959–70	—	—	—	—	—	—	—	.33	.31	.27	.30	.29	.31	.36
Born 1943–58	—	—	—	—	—	—	—	.39	.34	.34	.43	.37	.26	.38

Incremental probabilities[b]

Black	.17	.20	.11	.31	.50	.37	.45	.47	.34	.40	.31	.38	.37	.32
Catholic	.21	.20	.31	.18	.18	.20	.22	.14	.13	.09	.12	.15	.14	.11
Jewish	.39	.32	.18	.20	.19	.27	.36	.55	.34	.17	.33	.39	.27	.31
Female	.01	−.05	.05	.01	.04	.05	.03	.08	.05	.08	.03	.05	.04	.08
Native southern white	.45	.42	.41	.33	.20	.18	.22	.13	.07	.11	.04	.06	.05	.01
Union household member	.14	.12	.15	.18	.07	.09	.11	.11	.13	.11	.15	.15	.09	.07
Regular churchgoer	.00	−.02	−.03	−.02	−.01	.03	.03	−.04	−.04	.02	.01	−.03	.04	−.07
Income: top third	.07	−.04	−.07	−.15	−.07	−.07	−.11	−.07	−.07	−.07	−.09	−.10	−.17	−.08
White Protestant fundamentalist	—	—	—	—	—	.08	.05	.25	.10	.07	.01	.04	−.04	.03
Hispanic, non-Cuban	—	—	—	—	—	—	—	.18	.07	.16	.13	.08	.06	.11
Born 1959–70	—	—	—	—	—	—	—	−.16	−.16	−.19	−.19	−.15	−.11	−.07
Born 1943–58	—	—	—	—	—	—	—	−.09	−.11	−.09	−.05	−.05	−.09	−.02

SOURCE: 1952–96 National Election Studies.

NOTE: The three models containing the different variables were evaluated through 1996. However, presentation is greatly simplified by showing only the following: 1952–68 values are based on the model with eight variables; 1972–76 values are based on the model with nine variables; 1980–96 entries are based on the model with twelve variables. Values that can be estimated with more than one model seldom differ by more than .01 from one model to another.

a. Cells are the mean of the predicted probabilities of Democratic identification for all group members in each year.

b. Cells are the average of the difference, for each group member, between the individual's predicted probability of Democratic identification (based on all of the other characteristics in the multivariate model) and what the individual's probability would have been without the effect of the group membership.

Republican majority, it is not clear in these figures where it will find its base.[6]

Although the number of Democratic supporters declined in each group in 1994, the incremental impact of membership in a particular group, shown in the bottom half of table 10.1, gives us a different view of group effects. These numbers show how much more likely an individual is to be a Democratic identifier because of membership in a specific group; that is, the numbers consider all the other group ties of each individual and how likely those ties are to make the person Democratic. Their movements sometimes diverge considerably from the overall support levels in the top half of the table. Notably, they show that *incremental* support for the Democratic Party barely slipped at all for a number of groups in 1994, thus reinforcing the interpretation of that year as a temporary departure from longer-term movements. The long-term trends are still evident. The one that stands out especially vividly involves native white southerners; in the 1950s such individuals were at least 40 percent more likely to support the Democratic Party, taking into account their other characteristics. That figure declined steadily until finally, as of 1996, it stood virtually at ground zero, and native white southerners were no more likely to be Democrats than anyone else with the same characteristics.

Among the newer groups, one of the most significant results is that the gender gap appears to be alive and well as of the mid-1990s.[7] Even though other characteristics pushed them in a Republican direction, so that overall fewer women in 1994 said they supported the Democrats, the marginal impact of being female remained in the Democratic direction in 1994 and then tied for its highest value ever in 1996, helping Clinton win reelection and stemming the tide that occurred in 1994. Among another new group, regular churchgoers, the incremental impact of group membership was actually more pro-Democratic in 1994 than it had been two years earlier.

What does all this mean for the Republican Party? With respect to the older groups, the Republicans can be heartened by the fact that they were able to attract higher proportions of all the groups except blacks in 1994 (see table 10.2, top half, p. 170). But they were able to retain that level of support only among frequent churchgoers. Moreover, the incremental probabilities (see table 10.2, bottom half) suggest that things were far from rosy even in 1994, and they left a very mixed picture in 1996. Republicans were able to retain control of Congress, but support in terms of underlying partisanship enabled a popular president to win reelection quite handily and congressional Democrats to hold their own.

Groups that were moving away from the Democrats were not wildly embracing the Republicans. Jews, who leaned less toward the Democrats in 1994 than in 1992, leaned even farther away from the Republicans in the same year (see table 10.2, bottom half).[8] Native southern whites are increasingly Republican supporters (table 10.2, top half), and someday there may be a "multiplicative" effect that propels additional white southerners toward the Republican Party because many around them are Republican.[9] At present, however, the tendency among native southern whites toward the Republican Party is due largely to their other attributes; when these are taken into account, the latest reading shows them with no incremental likelihood of being Republican (table 10.2, lower half). Over the years, Catholics and members of union households have become less pro-Democratic, but the marginal push from these characteristics is still away from the Republicans; among Catholics, the (negative) incremental probability was as large in 1994 as it had been at any time in the past twenty years; among union households, it was as large as most other years since 1952. What sympathy the Democrats have lost among a number of their former supporting groups has gone toward identification as an independent, not to the Republicans.

The news is marginally better for the Republicans when we consider the newer groups, where there is a vague outline of a coalition that could provide the Republicans with the hope of continued majorities in Congress. After receiving the support of between 24 and 30 percent of regular churchgoers for several decades, that proportion jumped to an estimated 36 percent in both 1994 and 1996 (table 10.2, top half). The overlapping group of white Protestant fundamentalists also increased their support of the Republicans, as did baby boomers, Generation X, and those in the top third of the income distribution.

The Republican hold on these groups is somewhat tenuous, however, because they have not developed specific group appeals that bind any of these groups to the Republican Party. Regular churchgoers perhaps provide the most likely target. Republicans have consistently had an advantage among this group, and that advantage was greater in 1992 and 1996 than in most of the preceding years. Those in the top third of the income distribution provide another likely target, as they have also been marginally more supportive of Republicans since at least 1972, with this support, too, reaching new heights in two of the last three election years. Yet just how tough the task is for Republicans comes from observing their incremental appeal to white Protestant fundamentalists. In the 1970s and well into the 1980s, the tendency of this group was away from the Republicans and toward the Democrats. Probably as a result of strong support for moral and so-called family values by Presidents Reagan and Bush, this tendency has been neutralized. But note that it has been *neutralized,* not reversed.

The prospects of a generational appeal—either to boomers or to the subsequent generation—do not find much support here either. As we noted in an earlier analysis, the incremental push of being young (or now, middle-aged, as the boomers move through the life cycle) is better described as an anti-Democratic force than as a pro-Republican force. Both of the age

TABLE 10.2. MEAN AND INCREMENTAL PROBABILITIES OF REPUBLICAN IDENTIFICATION
FOR MEMBERS OF EACH GROUP

	1952	1956	1960	1964	1968	1972	1976	1980	1984	1988	1990	1992	1994	1996
Mean probabilities[a]														
Black	.13	.19	.17	.07	.02	.08	.05	.04	.04	.06	.05	.04	.03	.03
Catholic	.18	.21	.15	.17	.15	.14	.16	.19	.20	.27	.23	.19	.25	.24
Jewish	.00	.11	.08	.06	.05	.09	.08	.00	.10	.12	.10	.05	.13	.03
Female	.29	.32	.31	.25	.23	.24	.27	.23	.27	.28	.23	.24	.30	.23
Native southern white	.09	.12	.11	.09	.09	.15	.16	.18	.22	.21	.20	.26	.40	.29
Union household member	.22	.21	.17	.14	.20	.16	.14	.13	.20	.21	.20	.15	.24	.17
Regular churchgoer	.28	.29	.30	.26	.24	.26	.28	.28	.32	.32	.28	.31	.36	.36
Income: top third	.31	.34	.31	.32	.28	.30	.30	.30	.35	.35	.33	.34	.43	.35
White Protestant fundamentalist	—	—	—	—	—	.21	.21	.16	.22	.26	.28	.32	.42	.34
Hispanic, non-Cuban	—	—	—	—	—	—	—	.13	.09	.05	.12	.15	.19	.11
Born 1959–70	—	—	—	—	—	—	—	.14	.25	.28	.27	.23	.31	.26
Born 1943–58	—	—	—	—	—	—	—	.21	.28	.27	.24	.27	.36	.29

Incremental probabilities[b]

Black	−.27	−.21	−.27	−.28	−.35	−.25	−.27	−.26	−.35	−.34	−.29	−.30	−.37	−.30
Catholic	−.24	−.20	−.29	−.22	−.23	−.19	−.18	−.12	−.16	−.08	−.11	−.17	−.17	−.09
Jewish	−.41	−.30	−.32	−.33	−.33	−.29	−.28	−.33	−.33	−.31	−.26	−.34	−.28	−.27
Female	.03	.07	.02	.00	−.02	.01	.05	−.02	.00	−.00	−.04	−.04	−.05	−.03
Native southern white	−.35	−.32	−.35	−.31	−.30	−.17	−.16	−.09	−.08	−.14	−.14	−.10	.02	−.03
Union household member	−.09	−.12	−.17	−.16	−.08	−.12	−.14	−.14	−.11	−.13	−.11	−.15	−.08	−.14
Regular churchgoer	.05	.05	.06	.05	.04	.05	.06	.08	.08	.06	.06	.09	.05	.15
Income: top third	.05	.06	.02	.10	.03	.08	.08	.09	.09	.06	.09	.11	.14	.07
White Protestant fundamentalist	—	—	—	—	—	−.06	−.06	−.12	−.14	−.06	−.01	−.02	.00	−.01
Hispanic, non-Cuban	—	—	—	—	—	—	—	−.05	−.12	−.21	−.11	−.06	−.11	−.15
Born 1959–70	—	—	—	—	—	—	—	−.06	.02	.02	.04	.00	.06	.01
Born 1943–58	—	—	—	—	—	—	—	−.01	.03	−.02	−.02	.00	.04	.00

SOURCE: 1952–96 National Election Studies.

a. Cells are the mean of the predicted probabilities of Republican identification for all group members in each year.

b. Cells are the average of the difference, for each group member, between the individual's predicted probability of Republican identification (based on all of the other characteristics in the multivariate model) and what the individual's probability would have been without the effect of the group membership.

groups in tables 10.1 and 10.2 have consistently high increments in favor of independence (not shown), a reflection of the dealigning forces that have characterized American politics since the mid-1960s.

Finally, Republicans appear not to be making any headway in appealing to the growing bloc of Hispanics. Of all the changes in party support between 1994 and 1996, this is perhaps the least surprising and the most obviously connected to recent party ideology and behavior. Throughout 1995 and 1996, including just months before the election, Republicans in Congress supported anti-immigrant legislation while Democrats opposed it. In the House, for example, a majority of Democrats voted against (76–117) while Republicans were nearly unanimous in voting for (229–5)[10] a bill that would have denied illegal immigrants certain welfare benefits and would have made it harder for the government to prove job discrimination against Hispanics. In the Senate, Democrats were almost unanimous in support (41–5) and Republicans were almost unanimous in opposition (5–47) to a bill that would allow certain legal immigrants to continue to receive welfare benefits.[11] If this pattern of voting continues (as it did during 1997), it should not be surprising if Hispanics turn even more sharply away from the Republicans and toward the Democrats.

Changes in group support, if viewed over the entire period for which we have data—now stretching to more than four decades—have been dramatic enough for us four years ago to write of the demise of the New Deal coalition. But if one's interest is in the past few years, looking to interpret the 1996 Clinton reelection as well as to see whether 1994 was the start of a new period of Republican parity or dominance, the changes are far less certain. The Republicans were clearly able to draw temporary support virtually across the board in 1994. Republicans might have been especially encouraged by the fact that this support was apparent in self-identified partisan leanings, as shown here, not in the vote alone. But the 1994 and 1996 figures show how fragile that support was. The Republicans have still not been able to find a set of group attachments that seem capable of propelling them into long-term majority status. The future, viewed in terms of group support, appears to have potential for fluidity and possibly even major realignments (inasmuch as group ties are generally weaker than decades ago), but it is not yet clear that group attachments will swing heavily in one direction or the other, except possibly in one election at a time. And if the Republicans do maintain their majority in Congress, it is not yet clear that one or two groups alone will provide the foundation of the support coalition.

Group Support and the Party Coalitions

Now our attention turns to the party coalitions. In the first two sections of tables 10.3 and 10.4 (p. 175–78) we show the mean predicted probability of Democratic or Republican identification in the United States and, below that, the percentage of each coalition with a given group characteristic. This breakdown of the coalitions is in terms of overlapping groups. The percentages describing the party coalitions thus add to more than 100, as, for example, a black female churchgoer is counted in each of three categories.

Several changes are notable, and their impact on the party system is now becoming more apparent. Perhaps the most striking change is the declining proportion of women in the Republican coalition.[12] In the 1980s, "gender gap" was used to describe the greater support of women, compared with men, for the Democrats. That meant, coincidentally, that a greater proportion of the Democratic coalition was female—from 3 to 6 percentage points more than in the Republican coalition (tables 10.3 and 10.4).[13] Beginning in 1988 the gap widened, first because of a jump in the proportion of women among Democrats and then because of a substantial drop in the proportion of women among Republicans. In 1992, for the first time since at least 1952, men outnumbered women in one of the party coalitions. Despite a temporary reversal in 1994, the dominance of men in the Republican Party increased to a still higher level in the 1996 presidential election. At the same time, women have become three-fifths or even more of the Democratic coalition. In short, at the time of the second Clinton election, the two parties differed to a greater extent than ever in their relative proportions of female supporters.

Another change began quietly and, for a time, appeared to affect the two parties in the same way. Beginning with a rise in the mid-1980s among Democrats, and then with more steady increases in both parties in the early 1990s, the proportion of Hispanics began to take on some significance. While always a higher proportion of Democratic supporters, the percentages were small and therefore the partisan difference was not great. By 1996, however, it appeared that Hispanics would remain a very small proportion of the Republican coalition while becoming a more substantial force among Democrats. While still "only" about 12 percent of the Democratic coalition, Hispanics had become as large a percentage of party supporters as blacks were prior to 1964. The contrast with African Americans is telling in another way as well. From 1984 through 1992, the proportion of blacks among Democratic supporters was from two-and-a-half to more than three times that of Hispanics. In 1994 and 1996, that proportion fell substantially. Even if it fluctuates over the next several election cycles, it appears that Hispanics are becoming a more dominant force within the party at the expense of African Americans. Also on the Democratic side, the proportion of identifiers in union households continued a downward slide from about a third of the coalition in 1960 to a fifth in 1996.[14]

On the Republican side, native southern whites have become a substantial part of the Republican coalition by virtue of their increasing tilt toward that party. As late as 1990, this group was a larger fraction of the Democratic than of the Republican coalition. In the past three elections, however, this has been reversed, in a very small way at first but by a large margin in 1994. Figures for 1996 suggest that this reversal may be here to stay. Along with the large fraction of fundamentalists in the party, we may be seeing the outlines of a new and more durable Republican coalition, heavily weighted in the South and with a minority but substantial contingent of fundamentalist white Protestants.

What would happen to the coalitions if they were to lose the partisan tendency due to each group characteristic? Here we show results only for the Democratic coalition (table 10.3, second panel).[15] These results show just how resilient the Democratic coalition is. In the early 1990s, it appeared that increasing numbers of black, Jewish, and union supporters would desert the Democrats if the party did not appeal specifically to their groups. But by 1996, support from most groups turned upward again. Republicans have not been able to make a sustained appeal to these groups; were Democrats to reduce their group-specific appeals, most would still continue to support the party.

This point is made more dramatically in the final panel in table 10.3. It shows the effect on the size of the Democratic coalition of removing each group characteristic. Right up through 1996, the party benefits from a combination of overlapping characteristics. Only blacks (and women in 1996) dip as low as 90 percent, suggesting that the party would remain close to its current size even if it lost its specific appeal to any one group. This may be partly a result of President Clinton's studied effort to appeal to a broad range of groups and to avoid being "captured" by any one. Ironically, a broad-based appeal may have made the Democrats simultaneously more appealing to members of each specific group.

Conclusion

From the perspective of President Clinton's reelection, 1996 can be viewed as a year in which partisan support rebounded from what proved to be a temporary movement toward the Republicans in 1994. (That rebound may ultimately prove temporary as well.) The rebound did not occur in all groups, but it was apparent in both what we have called old and new groups. Especially noteworthy is the fact that among two groups, one large (women) and one small but growing (Hispanics), support for Democrats actually surpassed its 1992 level.

With a longer time frame in mind, the early 1990s can also be viewed as a continuation of processes that have been under way for several decades.

TABLE 10.3. SIZE AND COMPOSITION OF THE DEMOCRATIC COALITION

	1952	1956	1960	1964	1968	1972	1976	1980	1984	1988	1990	1992	1994	1996
Democratic identification in the United States[a]														
predicted probability	48	44	47	52	45	41	40	42	38	36	41	36	33	39
Percentage of Democratic coalition with a given group characteristic[b]														
Black	10	10	8	14	18	16	18	20	18	25	23	25	23	21
Catholic	27	25	30	26	26	31	33	27	32	27	32	30	32	28
Jewish	5	5	4	3	3	3	4	6	4	2	3	4	3	3
Female	55	53	59	57	59	60	61	62	60	65	58	58	60	64
Native southern white	26	27	28	21	20	21	21	22	20	23	18	17	19	17
Union household member	32	32	33	30	28	30	28	29	27	24	23	23	23	20
Regular churchgoer	42	45	51	45	41	42	44	38	38	42	44	42	47	36
Income: top third	37	28	39	29	27	27	29	25	27	26	30	29	17	26
White Protestant fundamentalist	—	—	—	—	—	17	15	20	16	20	16	15	14	14
Hispanic, non-Cuban	—	—	—	—	—	—	—	4	7	8	7	9	11	12
Born 1959–70	—	—	—	—	—	—	—	5	13	16	22	24	27	25
Born 1943–58	—	—	—	—	—	—	34	34	34	35	34	34	25	31

a. These estimates, derived from the model, are virtually identical to the actual percentage of Democratic identifiers.

b. Figures derived from taking the mean predicted probability of Democratic identification for a group in a particular year (table 10.1) multiplied by that group's number of respondents, and dividing this product by the number of Democratic identifiers.

Continued . . . .

TABLE 10.3. — CONTINUED

Percentage of Democratic identifiers in group continuing to claim Democratic identification after removing Democratic tendency of defining group characteristic[c]

	1952	1956	1960	1964	1968	1972	1976	1980	1984	1988	1990	1992	1994	1996
Black	68	61	76	59	41	45	39	36	45	38	51	41	41	51
Catholic	62	61	52	69	66	61	57	67	68	75	72	64	63	75
Jewish	46	48	65	65	62	47	38	32	43	54	47	37	44	50
Female	102	111	91	98	92	89	94	81	87	79	94	86	89	83
Native southern white	42	41	43	54	62	64	57	74	82	72	88	83	84	98
Union household member	75	77	74	72	85	81	76	76	72	74	71	69	77	85
Regular churchgoer	100	104	106	103	101	93	93	110	111	96	97	109	89	120
Income: top third	17	110	116	136	117	122	134	119	121	123	125	136	188	127
White Protestant fundamentalist	—	—	—	—	—	82	88	55	75	80	97	87	119	91
Hispanic, non-Cuban	—	—	—	—	—	—	—	68	86	70	74	81	87	79
Born 1959–70	—	—	—	—	—	—	—	148	150	170	163	150	134	120
Born 1943–58	—	—	—	—	—	—	—	122	132	127	112	114	136	106

Relative size (in percentages) of Democratic coalition after removing group characteristic

	1952	1956	1960	1964	1968	1972	1976	1980	1984	1988	1990	1992	1994	1996
Black	97	96	98	94	89	91	89	87	90	85	89	85	86	90
Catholic	90	90	86	92	91	88	86	91	90	93	91	89	88	93
Jewish	97	98	99	99	99	98	98	96	98	99	98	98	98	98
Female	101	106	94	99	95	93	96	89	92	86	97	92	94	89

Native southern white	85	84	84	90	93	92	91	94	96	94	98	97	97	100
Union household member	92	93	91	92	96	94	93	93	92	94	93	93	95	97
Regular churchgoer	100	102	103	101	101	97	97	104	104	98	98	104	95	107
Income: top third	106	103	106	110	105	106	110	105	106	106	107	110	115	107
White Protestant fundamentalist	—	—	—	—	—	97	98	91	96	96	100	98	103	99
Hispanic, non-Cuban	—	—	—	—	—	—	—	99	99	98	98	98	98	98
Born 1959–70	—	—	—	—	—	—	—	102	106	111	114	112	109	105
Born 1943–58	—	—	—	—	—	—	—	108	111	109	104	105	109	102

SOURCE: 1952–96 National Election Studies.

c. Figures derived by recalculating the probabilities of Democratic identification without the effect of, say, white Protestant fundamentalist identification then taking the mean of these probabilities for all respondents who were white Protestant fundamentalists. The ratio of this revised mean probability to the mean probability that includes the effect of white Protestant fundamentalism gives the ratio of the hypothetical size to the actual one.

TABLE 10.4. SIZE AND COMPOSITION OF THE REPUBLICAN COALITION, 1952–96

	1952	1956	1960	1964	1968	1972	1976	1980	1984	1988	1990	1992	1994	1996
Republican identification in the United States[a]														
predicted probability	27	29	29	25	24	24	24	23	28	29	25	26	32	27
Percentage of Republican coalition with a given group characteristic[b]														
Black	5	6	4	3	1	3	2	2	1	3	3	2	1	1
Catholic	15	15	10	16	14	15	18	21	21	24	26	20	22	22
Jewish	0	1	1	1	1	1	1	0	1	1	1	0	1	0
Female	57	61	56	56	54	57	65	57	56	58	51	49	53	46
Native southern white	5	7	7	5	6	10	10	15	15	15	15	19	25	19
Union household member	22	20	15	14	20	17	14	15	16	14	14	10	14	10
Regular churchgoer	40	43	47	47	39	42	47	49	45	43	47	51	50	49
Income: top third	47	36	42	47	37	40	46	40	40	39	44	48	39	42
White Protestant fundamentalist	—	—	—	—	—	13	12	11	12	17	21	21	27	19
Hispanic, non-Cuban	—	—	—	—	—	—	—	2	2	1	3	4	5	3
Born 1959–70	—	—	—	—	—	—	—	3	14	20	31	27	28	24
Born 1943–58	—	—	—	—	—	—	—	33	38	34	30	35	35	33

SOURCE: 1952–96 National Election Studies.

a. These estimates, derived from the model, are virtually identical to the actual percentage of Republican identifiers.

b. Figures derived from taking the mean predicted probability of Republican identification for a group in a particular year (table 10.2) multiplied by that group's number of respondents, and dividing this product by the number of Republican identifiers.

The movement away from the Democratic Party by native southern whites, for example, began in the 1960s, and members of union households began to move in the 1970s. The Hispanic population, and hence its contribution to the party coalitions, has been on the rise for at least fifteen years. Yet several watershed changes have occurred very recently. First, native southern whites, perhaps for the first time ever, had an incremental push (very slightly) favorable to the Republicans, and in the past two elections they were estimated to be a greater fraction of Republican than of Democratic identifiers. Second, members of union households sank to just one-fifth of all Democratic supporters in 1996. Third, Hispanics, while not increasing their marginal support for the Democrats, are now a much more substantial fraction of the coalition, while African Americans have stabilized in size or are possibly declining as a fraction of all Democrats.

A significant threshold was also passed when, in 1986 and in all but one subsequent year, white Protestant fundamentalists became a larger fraction of Republican than of Democratic identifiers. Despite overt Republican appeals since the early 1980s, the incremental push from being a fundamentalist was toward the Democrats until it evened out, or reversed, in the 1990s. Now Republicans are basically even in their appeal, and more of their identifiers claim to be a part of this group.

What of the future? Three developments highlighted by our analysis are especially worthy of note. The most visible is the changing gender composition of the parties. The gender gap has now existed for a decade and has reached the point where 60 percent or more of Democrats are women while a majority of Republicans are men. Yet, despite its size and salience, we think that this division is unlikely to continue for long, and it will certainly not be the basis on which either party attempts to build its coalition. Neither party can afford to ignore half the population; each, therefore, will attempt to build its support among both men and women. Republicans currently seem to be doing little to develop their appeal to women, and the gap among party identifiers may continue to grow for a few more elections. Yet it will not be the basis of a partisan realignment.

The second major development concerns the partisan support shown by Hispanics. If the anti-immigrant stance of the Republican Party continues unabated, we are likely to see a clear shift in favor of Democratic support in the electorate. Thus far, Republicans seem to have calculated that they can gain overall support by their position; that may be, but among Hispanics themselves, a continuation of recent party actions will clearly push them in a Democratic direction.

The third major development is related to the second, and it largely affects the Democratic Party. We were inclined a few years ago to ask whether the Democrats would become the party of minorities, as blacks continued their high level of support and Hispanics began to be a more meaningful presence. In part, that has happened; these two groups now constitute about a third of the coalition, rising quickly from about 20 percent in the early 1980s. At least as important, however, is that the Democratic Party is rapidly changing into a party with two sizable minority groups. As Hispanics increase in number, it may be increasingly difficult to satisfy both groups. It is difficult even to guess how the party system will change if future developments cause a major rift within the Democratic Party. Yet, however it turns out, this recent change in the pattern of group support may be the most significant new development to occur in the wake of the demise of the New Deal coalition.

PART III

The Elections for Congress

11

Reelecting the Republican Congress: Two More Years

Samuel C. Patterson and
Joseph Quin Monson

The election of President Bill Clinton to a second term in office in 1996 looked more and more imminent as the campaign unfolded. More uncertain was the outcome of the congressional elections. Would the Democrats win enough seats to recapture their majority in the House of Representatives? Was it even possible that the Democrats could capture control of the Senate, however narrowly? Or would the Republican majorities in the House and Senate, won only two years before, be reelected?

This chapter tells the story of the 1996 campaign for seats in Congress, first recounting who ran and how much political money was raised and spent in congressional races.* We then dissect how Americans voted—who voted for Republican congressional candidates and who voted for Democrats—what the final election results looked like, and what kinds of people won seats in Congress. Next, we trace trends in Americans' approval or disapproval of how Congress performs and contrast people who approve and those who disapprove of Congress. Before the November 1996 election, far more Americans approved of congressional performance than was true at the nadir of congressional approval just before the election of 1994. Interestingly, we show a historic reversal as political party control of the congressional houses changed, with Republicans generally disdaining the Democratic Congress followed by Democrats disapproving of the Republican Congress. Finally, we demonstrate the powerful influence of partisanship on congressional performance evaluation, even when other influences are taken

---

* We are indebted to Angela Rucker at the Federal Election Commission, Washington, D.C., who provided campaign finance data to us.

into account. And we show that Americans' approval or disapproval of congressional performance significantly influenced how people voted in the 1996 congressional election.

The contrasts between the congressional election in 1996 and its predecessors in 1992 and 1994 could not be more striking. The campaigns of candidates for Congress in 1992 took place in a climate of extraordinary negativism, highlighted by highly visible congressional scandals. Most prominent was the revelation that more than half the members of the House of Representatives were implicated in improprieties involving the House bank, an antiquated entity that provided extraordinary overdraft services for members. Members were charged with writing "bad" checks. Commentators bashed Congress in the media, and congressional approval plummeted to historic depths (see Patterson and Barr 1995). The bank overdraft scandal profoundly influenced the congressional election outcome, constituting "the major reason for the unusually high turnover of House seats in 1992" (Jacobson and Dimock 1994, 621). The party balance in the House and Senate was barely ruffled when the votes were counted—the Republicans gained nine House seats, and the Democrats gained one Senate seat. But the 103d Congress embraced a record proportion of new members, notably because a large number of incumbents retired.

The 1994 congressional election was altogether different. With Congress bashing unabated, House Republican leader Newt Gingrich (R-Ga.) masterminded an effort to nationalize the opposition party's congressional campaign in order to capture majority control of the House. Public approval of the performance of the Democrat-controlled Congress nose-dived, but, more important, the Republicans offered a credible avenue of change, a selection of generally impressive candidates, and a coherent manifesto they called the Contract with America. The voters responded by recording a historic change in congressional election politics—more than half the votes went to Republican House candidates, and Republicans won majorities in both the House of Representatives and the Senate for the first time in more than four decades.

This astonishing outcome inspired extravagant characterizations: the election was a "landslide," an "earthquake," a *tsunami*. One leading scholar emoted that the congressional election results "set off a political earthquake that will send aftershocks rumbling through national politics for years to come" (Jacobson 1996, 1). The Republicans' 52 percent popular vote majority was translated into capture of about 53 percent of the seats in the House and the Senate. In the aftermath of the 1994 election, the remarkably altered 104th Congress took up the challenges of the Republican agenda (see Kolodny 1996).

A House of Representatives sharply polarized along party lines passed most of the Contract with America proposals: internal House reforms, the line-item veto, crime control, federal mandates on the states, defense procurement, child support, reforms in welfare, tax policy, Social Security, product liability, and a constitutional amendment to require a balanced budget. The notable failure was term limits, which could not muster the 290 votes needed to amend the Constitution. Moreover, the Contract bills that were successfully considered by the House suffered a less enthusiastic reception in the Senate. The budgetary struggle by congressional Republicans, culminating in presidential vetoes and two partial shutdowns of the federal government in 1995, painted the backdrop for the 1996 election.

Our major curiosity in this analysis attends a perverse feature of congressional politics in the countryside, namely, the low state of Americans' attitudes toward Congress—its members and their performance. Citizens' dissatisfaction with congressional performance provides part of the alchemy of congressional elections, begging for an explanation of its causes and consequences. Who are the Americans who approve and who are the ones who disapprove of the way Congress does its job?

What effects do voters' appraisals of Congress have on their voting choices among congressional candidates? The 1996 National Election Study (NES) allows us to assay these questions in a different light from what previously has been done—where the target Congress bears a Republican majority in both houses.

The 1996 Congressional Election Campaign

The 1996 campaign for congressional seats, occurring as a companion to a somewhat one-sided and lackluster presidential contest, operated under relatively low media visibility. According to a study of fifty-two local television stations, "only thirty-seven carried any election coverage on a particular evening, of which only 1 percent of the reports dealt with House races and 9 percent with Senate contests" (Hershey 1997, 218). With little chance to regain control of the Senate, Democrats sought to find ways to return their party's majority to the House, mainly by demonizing Speaker Gingrich and denouncing the legislative agenda of the House Republicans. Republicans, desperate to retain their majority-party status, fought independently in the trenches, and their campaign sought aggressively to protect Republican incumbents.

Indeed, the probability that incumbents will win reelection, especially to the House, is enormous—95 percent of incumbents running for reelection won in 1996. The toughest congressional campaigns develop in open-seat districts where there is no incumbent in the contest. In 1996 there were fifty-three open House seats and fourteen open Senate seats (thirteen retired, and one was defeated in the primary). Open House seats multiplied throughout 1996, as members announced their retirement or their intention to run for other offices. As in 1992, the lion's share of the retirees were Democrats—57 percent of both representatives and senators—many of them in the South, where Democratic fortunes were declining.

In 1996 an unusually large number of open seats attracted an especially high proportion of experienced candidates—"quality challengers"—and it is generally acknowledged that the Republicans were more successful than the Democrats in recruiting outstanding candidates. It appears that "poor candidate recruitment by Democrats hampered their ability to win some of the most competitive races," and "many observers attribute this to the poor political climate for Democrats during that key recruiting period in early and mid-1995, when the party was still reeling from devastating 1994 losses" (Cook 1997). In contrast, under the leadership of Representative Bill Paxon (R-N.Y.), chairman of the National Republican Congressional Committee, an aggressive candidate recruitment program was launched in 1994 to cultivate excellent future candidacies (Ceaser and Busch 1997, 129–30; Cohen 1997, 181–84).

Republicans also developed a substantial advantage in raising campaign money. Indeed, 1996 was a record-breaking year for congressional elections; House and Senate candidates raised 20 percent more than they had in 1992, and they spent 12 percent more. The campaign spending increase went primarily to House candidates, with Republican candidates far outdistancing their Democratic rivals in raising and spending money. Figure 11.1 depicts how much it cost a typical House candidate campaigning in 1996 and in the two previous congressional elections. Average incumbent spending went well above a half a million dollars, largely due to the sizable number of Republican incumbents running for reelection. More prominently, spending in open-seat races escalated from 1992 to 1996, approaching a $600,000 average, with Republican open-seat winners averaging $743,577 and Democratic open-seat winners spending $791,590.

The most expensive House races in 1996 were run by first-term members. The seventy-one freshman Republicans exceeded the average fund raising of their counterparts in open-seat races. Republican first-termers' fund raising averaged about $850,000, compared to only about $400,000 for their Democratic opponents (Corrado 1997, 161). Little wonder that overall campaign spending by House candidates reached record levels. So-called soft money poured into the coffers of national and state party organizations, augmenting the ferocious fund-raising efforts of congressional candidates. One House member lamented, "Today, for a modestly spirited race, you have to raise a million dollars. That's ten thousand dollars a week, two thousand dollars a day. I would think, 'If I have not made arrangements to make two thousand dollars today, I'm behind.' And I will have to raise four thousand dollars tomorrow" (Koszczuk 1997, 774).

Campaign spending by senatorial candidates looks somewhat different

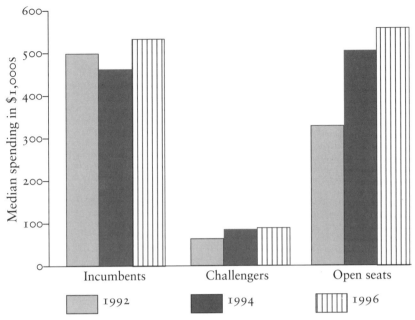

FIGURE 11.1. HOUSE CANDIDATES' CAMPAIGN SPENDING:
1992, 1994, 1996

SOURCE: Federal Election Commission, *Record*, vol. 23 (June 1997), 10.

(see Abramowitz and Segal 1992, 123–43). Only a third of the 100 Senate seats are up for election every two years. Because an unusual number of 1996 senatorial contests occurred in the less-populated states of the South and West, with relatively low campaign costs, spending levels were moderate (and less than in 1994, when there were vigorous Senate races in the larger states). Altogether, Senate candidates raised and spent about $220 million, with Republicans spending $114 million and Democrats spending $106 million. Incumbents spent 38 percent of the senatorial campaign money, challengers spent 25 percent, and open-seat contenders spent 37 percent. A very sizable share of spending, $47.2 million, was attributable to the thirteen incumbent Republican senators (Corrado 1997, 156).

The 1996 election was nearly as much a contest for political money as it was for popular votes. The postelection conflict between congressional Democrats and Republicans over the legality of contributions and "soft money" distributions extended the 1996 campaign for a full year after the election was over. Indeed, one scholar has argued that the decline in public trust of Congress lies partly in the detailed and timely disclosure and reporting of candidates' campaign spending, reflecting the suspicion Americans harbor about the nefarious role of money in electoral politics (Herrnson 1997, 238).

Two More Years: The Election Outcome

A sagacious scholar has said that one of the main peculiarities of "elections American style ... is that so few eligible citizens vote in them" (Burnham 1987, 97). Unfortunately, record levels of spending in the 1996 congressional campaigns did not translate into similarly high voter turnout on election day. Quite the contrary. Far fewer than half the Americans of voting age (45.7 percent) voted for House candidates, down from just over half (50.8 percent) in 1992 but a percentage point above congressional election turnout in 1988 (44.7 percent). Some analysts attribute the low voter turnout to widely generalized disinterest in the campaign and election, one in which the foreordained presidential contest attracted the lowest voter turnout in nearly three-quarters of a century (see Ceaser and Busch 1997, 154–56).

Observers of election outcomes pronounced that the exercise had produced little congressional change, that the results were "unsurprising," and that 1996 was a status quo election (see Cohen 1997; Hershey 1997; Jacobson 1997a). Indeed, Americans' voting pattern in 1996 was largely one of continuity. President Clinton was reelected handily, and almost all incumbents who sought to be returned to Congress by their constituents were, in fact, reelected.

Table 11.1, reporting results from the NES, indicates how Americans reported they voted in contests for seats in the House of Representatives, cross-tabulated by gender, race and ethnicity, age, income, education, region, partisan identification, and political ideology. For the sake of comparison, we have included the 1994 breakdowns along with those for 1996 in the table. Some "gender gap" continued to distinguish the congressional voting of women and men: a majority of women voted Democratic for Congress, while a substantial majority of men voted Republican. African Americans and Hispanics voted overwhelmingly for Democratic congressional candidates, while a majority of whites voted Republican. Republicans won the votes of high-income and college-educated voters. Democrats did better among lower-income and less-well-educated voters. These differences between Democratic and Republican support are all statistically significant ($p < .05$ or stronger), judging from chi-square statistics, shown in table 11.1.

Regional aspects of voting behavior portrayed in table 11.1 are striking. In 1996 a majority of voters reported voting Democratic in House races in the East; in other regions more than half the voters indicated they voted Republican for Congress. Except that Democratic congressional candidates apparently did somewhat better in the Midwest and South in 1996, these results substantially replicate those of 1994 (but see Bannon 1997, 36). These statistics underscore the dramatic loss of support for Democratic congressional candidates in the South, compared to previous decades.

As is always the case, Democratic versus Republican congressional elec-

TABLE 11.1. HOW PEOPLE VOTED IN THE 1996 AND 1994 CONGRESSIONAL ELECTIONS
(IN PERCENTAGES)

Voter characteristics	1996			1994		
	Democrat	Republican	Percentage of population	Democrat	Republican	Percentage of population
Gender, race, and ethnicity						
Men	43	58	48	43	58	48
Women	52	48	52	50	50	52
		$\chi^2 = 8.517, p < 0.004$			$\chi^2 = 4.814, p < .028$	
Whites	44	56	85	42	58	87
Blacks	86	14	12	84	16	11
Other	35	66	3	59	41	3
		$\chi^2 = 63.229, p < .0001$			$\chi^2 = 53.913, p < .0001$	
Hispanics	74	26	10	69	31	8
		$\chi^2 = 23.477, p < .0001$			$\chi^2 = 12.152, p < .0001$	
Age						
18–24	53	47	8	51	49	10
25–34	47	53	21	42	58	23
35–44	43	57	27	41	60	25
45–54	45	55	15	42	58	14
55–64	51	49	12	55	45	11
65 and older	50	50	17	55	46	17
		$\chi^2 = 4.36, p < .499$			$\chi^2 = 15.289, p < .009$	
Income						
Under $15,000	63	37	19	68	32	18
$15,000–24,999	67	33	14	63	38	16
$25,000–34,999	54	46	15	46	54	16
$35,000–49,999	43	57	18	45	55	20

$50,000–74,999	35	65	20	35	65	19
$75,000 and above	37	63	15	31	69	12
Education						
	$\chi^2 = 52.921, p < .0001$			$\chi^2 = 52.408, p < .0001$		
Less than high school	73	27	13	71	30	15
High school graduate	52	48	32	50	50	34
Some college	47	53	27	48	52	26
College graduate	37	63	19	36	64	18
Postgraduate	40	60	10	40	60	8
Region						
	$\chi^2 = 37.287, p < .0001$			$\chi^2 = 30.246, p < .0001$		
East	51	49	20	52	48	20
Midwest	46	54	24	44	56	24
South	46	54	35	44	56	35
West	46	54	22	47	53	21
Party identification						
	$\chi^2 = 1.496, p < .683$			$\chi^2 = 3.584, p < .31$		
Strong Democrat	87	13	19	90	10	15
Weak Democrat	72	28	20	73	27	19
Leaning Democrat	70	30	14	66	34	13
Independent	42	58	8	53	47	10
Leaning Republican	22	78	12	24	76	12
Weak Republican	18	82	16	21	79	15
Strong Republican	3	97	13	8	93	16
Political ideology						
	$\chi^2 = 434.052, p < .0001$			$\chi^2 = 373.859, p < .0001$		
Liberal	76	25	25	76	24	20
Moderate	60	40	31	56	44	33
Conservative	20	80	44	24	76	47
	$\chi^2 = 214.508, p < .0001$			$\chi^2 = 151.027, p < .0001$		

SOURCE: 1994 and 1996 National Election Studies.

tion voting traveled strongly along lines of partisan attachment in 1996. Strong Democrats voted overwhelmingly for Democratic congressional candidates; by the same token, strong Republicans voted for Republican candidates. Interestingly, far fewer strongly identified Republicans voted for the opposite party's candidates for Congress than did strongly identified Democrats. Ideologically, voters' choices were divided in the expected way between the major-party candidates. Overwhelmingly, voters who designated themselves liberal voted for Democratic House candidates; most self-styled conservatives voted Republican. Party and ideological differences here are very powerful, yielding highly significant chi-square statistics, as displayed in table 11.1.

When all the votes were counted, the Republicans had maintained their majority-party status in Congress. But they captured only the slimmest of margins in House races and won the narrowest House seat margin of any majority party in over forty years. The overall election outcomes are provided in table 11.2 (p. 192). House Republican contenders won a total of four-tenths of a percent more votes than Democratic candidates; Republicans' nearly 49 percent of the vote yielded them just over 52 percent of the House seats. While Democratic House candidates won nearly as many popular votes as Republicans (48.5 percent), this yielded them only about 47 percent of the seats. Compared to 1994 congressional contests, the Republicans' vote share was down 3.5 percentage points, while the Democrats' vote share went up 3.1 percentage points. It should be noted that the 49 percent vote share captured by the Republican congressional candidates exceeded the vote of their party's presidential candidate, Bob Dole, by fully 8 percent (see Weisberg and Patterson 1998, 271–82).

Republican candidates won a majority of House seats in the South, Midwest, and West. Democrats won a majority of seats only in the East (Weisberg and Patterson 1998, 277). Democratic seat gains in the East, Midwest, and West Coast states were offset by striking Republican successes in the South, Plains, and Mountain states. One keen observer of congressional elections calls the 1996 outcome "a geographic polarization of major proportions" (Cook 1997, 442). Southern states, once the "solid South" of the Democratic Party, have transmogrified into the solid Republican South. The Republican House members newly elected in 1994 fared reasonably well, although they were challenged vigorously by Democrats—only 13 of 73 freshman Republicans lost. And Republican House candidates did well in open-seat districts, winning the fifty-three open races 29–24.

Thirteen senators—a record number—retired in 1996, eight of them Democrats. The Republicans lost only one Senate seat, that of Larry Pressler of South Dakota, and picked up three of the eight formerly Democratic open seats. No party change occurred in thirty of the thirty-four Senate seats contested in 1996, giving the Republicans a net gain of two seats overall, and a

TABLE 11.2. THE 1996 CONGRESSIONAL ELECTION RESULTS

Votes and seats	House of Representatives		Senate	
	Number	Percentage	Number	Percentage
National popular vote				
Republican vote	43,890,897	48.9	24,785,394	49.5
Democratic vote	43,611,257	48.5	23,961,917	47.8
Other vote	2,334,123	2.6	1,346,163	2.7
Total	89,836,277	100.0	50,093,474	100.0
Republican plurality	279,640	.4	823,477	1.7
Congressional seats				
Republican seats	228	52.4	55	55.0
Democratic seats	206	47.4	45	45.0
Other seats	1	.2	0	0
Republican seat change from 1992	+52		+12	
Republican seat change from 1994	−2		+2	
Incumbents reelected				
Republicans	196	92.0	12	92.3
Democrats	165	98.2	7	100.0
Incumbents defeated				
Republicans	17	8.0	1	7.7
Democrats	3	1.8	0	0

SOURCES: Rhodes Cook, "Thinnest of Margins Shows Country's Greatest Divide," *Congressional Quarterly Weekly Report*, 55 (15 February 1997), 444; Gary C. Jacobson, "Extension of Remarks: The Congressional Elections of 1996," *APSA Legislative Studies Section Newsletter*, 20 (January 1997), 2–3.

NOTE: House of Representatives voting results are for 431 districts; in four districts, three in Louisiana and one in Florida, candidates ran unopposed and no vote was recorded.

55–45 majority in the Senate. But moderate Republicans and middle-of-the-road Democrats tended to be replaced by conservative Republicans. As with the House outcomes, the Senate results firmly strengthened the Republicans' hold on Senate seats in the South. Indeed, Mary Landrieu's election to replace J. Bennett Johnston made Louisiana the only state in the South with two Democratic senators. Republicans won Senate seats in Alabama (replacing Democrat Howell Heflin) and Arkansas (replacing Democrat David Pryor). In Arkansas, the new Republican senator, Tim Hutchinson, became the first of his party elected to the Senate since Reconstruction. Of the dozen seats gained by Senate Republicans since 1992, seven were southern.

The 105th Congress, with its reduced House Republican majority and only slightly larger Senate majority, faced a reelected Democratic president whose veto probably could not be overridden. The new Congress opened its deliberations in January 1997 in a rather smitten state, far different from the efficient overconfidence of the previous Congress's Republican majority. Seventy-three House members and fifteen senators were newcomers to their chambers, although eight of the fifteen new senators had served previously as members of the House. But the membership turnover is, realistically, much higher: 232 of the 435 representatives (53.3 percent) and 40 of the 100 senators (40 percent) in the 105th Congress had come to the institution since 1992. About two-thirds of the members of the 105th House had served in public office prior to their election to Congress, and nearly half the members of the 105th Senate served previously in the House of Representatives.

The 105th Congress was a more politically conservative body, more polarized ideologically, with a smaller political "center" than before. Its leaders—Speaker Newt Gingrich (R-Ga.) and his lieutenants in the House, and Majority Leader Trent Lott (R-Miss.) in the Senate—muted the impact of the polarized houses in the early days of the 105th Congress. But partisan and ideological conflict amplified as the 1998 election came into view.

Public Response to the New Republican Congress

Over the post–World War II years, the popularity of Congress has waxed and waned, but favorable public opinion about Congress has generally been rather low since the peak approval levels of the mid-1960s. Public esteem for Congress fluctuates over time mainly as a function of citizens' party orientations, the popularity of the president, the generally negative media coverage of the institution, variations in reporting about unethical conduct, and highly visible congressional actions (see Durr, Gilmour, and Wolbrecht 1997; Hibbing and Theiss-Morse 1995; Patterson and Caldeira 1990; Patterson, Ripley, and Quinlan 1992). The disparity between what citizens think Congress ought to be like and their perceptions of what Congress actually is like powerfully drives public evaluations of congressional performance (Kimball and Patterson 1997). More broadly, one scholar has argued that electoral system biases that award enhanced congressional majorities to the dominant party for many years—witness the forty-year hegemony of the congressional Democrats after World War II—indirectly contributed to the decline of public favor toward Congress (see Campbell 1996, 198).

Scandals, charges of corruption, and allegations of ethical impropriety have mushroomed in media preoccupation since the 1970s, feeding negativism about Congress and influencing voter choice in congressional elections (see Peters and Welch 1980; Welch and Hibbing 1997). Although citizens generally offer much more favorable appraisals of their own representative than they do of congressmen generally, incumbents can fall to unfavorable public evaluations, as did many in 1992 who had written "bad" checks at the infamous House bank (see Asher and Barr 1994; Ripley et al. 1992).

We portray the trajectory of congressional popularity from spring 1993 through early 1998 in figure 11.2. These "approval/disapproval" ratings reflect the response to "Do you approve or disapprove of the way Congress is handling its job?" It is apparent from figure 11.2 that disapproval far exceeds approval in the minds of Americans most of the time.

Public support was notably unfavorable in the weeks leading up to the 1994 election. After the Republican takeover of Congress, congressional approval rates climbed modestly, only to shrink to 20–30 percent levels through much of 1995–96 (Patterson and Kimball 1997). The Republican leadership, facing public disapproval of two government shutdowns and fearing potential electoral consequences, turned a political pirouette. It passed several highly touted bills in the months prior to the election in a strategic effort to bolster Republican chances in the upcoming campaign (see Dewar and Pianin 1996).

In the wake of perceived comity between the publicly more moderate President Clinton and the chastened congressional Republican leadership in autumn 1996, levels of approval of congressional job performance climbed to percentages in the mid-30s just in time for the election. The polls welcomed a renewed Republican Congress early in 1997 with somewhat kinder and gentler approval ratings. But the turnabout was short lived; as 1997 wore along, congressional approval levels often receded to the long-term average of about 30 percent, although Congress enjoyed historically higher marks during the summer and fall.

In the course of its surveys, the NES asks its respondents to evaluate the performance of both Congress as a whole and their own representative. In figure 11.3 (p. 196), we show the results as the difference between the percentage of respondents who said they "approve" and those who said they "disapprove." For instance, the 1996 NES showed that 45.1 percent ap-

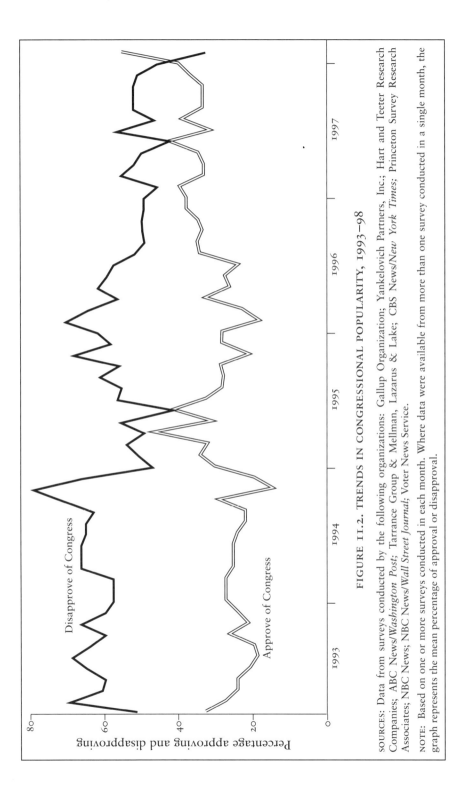

FIGURE 11.2. TRENDS IN CONGRESSIONAL POPULARITY, 1993–98

SOURCES: Data from surveys conducted by the following organizations: Gallup Organization; Yankelovich Partners, Inc.; Hart and Teeter Research Companies; ABC News/*Washington Post*; Tarrance Group & Mellman, Lazarus & Lake; CBS News/*New York Times*; Princeton Survey Research Associates; NBC News; NBC News/*Wall Street Journal*; Voter News Service.

NOTE: Based on one or more surveys conducted in each month. Where data were available from more than one survey conducted in a single month, the graph represents the mean percentage of approval or disapproval.

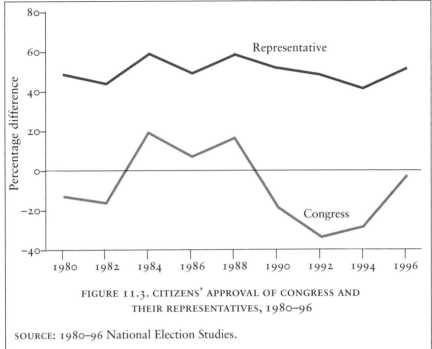

FIGURE 11.3. CITIZENS' APPROVAL OF CONGRESS AND
THEIR REPRESENTATIVES, 1980–96

SOURCE: 1980–96 National Election Studies.

NOTE: The entries in the figure are the differences between the percentage of respondents who "approved" minus the percentage who "disapproved" for each year. The questions were "In general, do you approve or disapprove of the way the U.S. Congress has been handling its job?" and "In general, do you approve or disapprove of the way Representative _____ has been handling his/her job?"

proved the performance of Congress and 46.8 disapproved, a difference of only −1.7 percent. The trace line for net approval of Congress dramatizes the spectacular plunge in approval in 1990, and again in 1992, with moderate recovery thereafter. On the eve of the 1992 election, the NES indicated that almost two-thirds of Americans disapproved of congressional performance. At the time of the 1994 midterm election, net approval had recovered only slightly; by 1996, the level of disapproval was nearly offset by the level of approval. As expected, approval/disapproval differences for the survey respondents' own representatives remained quite stable over these election years despite the public volatility in assessments of the performance of Congress as a whole.

A healthy share of the recent public discourse about Congress and Americans' attitudes toward it has focused on Speaker Newt Gingrich, the controversial, outspoken, and aggressive leader of House Republicans. Gingrich has been perceived as so central to Republican electoral and policy successes that public opinion polls have begun to assay his popularity. In the 1980s, while still a junior member of Congress, Gingrich gained notoriety by shrewdly exploiting C-SPAN coverage of House floor proceedings, coordinating televised speeches given under "special orders" after the regular House business had been conducted. Republicans giving these speeches attacked the Democratic majority and its leaders, and Gingrich acquired sufficient stature to get elected minority whip in 1989, then Speaker in 1995. In that year, *Time* magazine designated Gingrich "Man of the Year," lionizing him as an "exceptional leader . . . Gingrich has changed the center of gravity" (quoted in Hershey 1997, 213).

The negative public opinion about Congress also encompassed its most visible leader, Newt Gingrich. The Gallup poll began reading the public pulse of Gingrich before the 1994 election. In October of that year, fewer than half the Gallup poll respondents had heard of Gingrich or had any opinion about him; only 19 percent expressed a "favorable" opinion of him (see figure 11.4, p. 198). "Unfavorable" appraisals grew throughout 1995 and 1996 as more and more poll respondents became acquainted with Gingrich and his performance as Republican leader. The electoral reconfirmation of the Republican congressional majorities and the renewal of Gingrich's speakership did little to endear him to his fellow citizens. A July 1997 NBC News/*Wall Street Journal* poll gave him only an 18 percent "favorable" rating, compared to a 54 percent "unfavorable" rating.

The American public is pretty hard on its national, freely elected, highly responsive representative assembly, the U.S. Congress. Furthermore, public scorn can readily be visited on congressional leaders, such as Speaker Gingrich. Yet, members of Congress usually win applause from their own constituents, and often win reelection even in the face of human error and perfidy. It is, perhaps, only human nature to embrace and have affection for what is proximate and well worn, and to scorn and distrust what is unknown and distant. In such climates, one can wonder who approves of Congress's performance and who disapproves.

Who Approves of Congress?
Who Disapproves?

Following long-standing practice, respondents in the 1996 NES were asked their views of congressional performance by the question, "Do you approve or disapprove of the job the U.S. Congress is doing?"

The most interesting characteristics of those who answered this question are shown in table 11.3 (p. 200), where we compare results from 1994 and 1996 surveys. Table 11.3 dramatizes the strikingly higher levels of congressional approval in 1996 over 1994. Differences between groups of re-

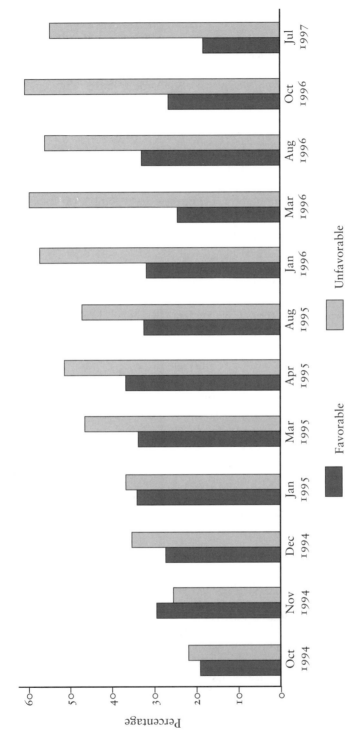

FIGURE 11.4. EVALUATIONS OF NEWT GINGRICH, 1994–97

SOURCE: *Gallup Poll Monthly*, August 1997, 41.

NOTE: The interview item read as follows: "Next, I will read the names of some people in the news. As I read each name, please say whether you have a favorable or unfavorable opinion of this person—or if you have never heard of him or her."

spondents—in terms of gender, race or ethnic origin, age, income, and so forth—are assessed using chi-square statistics. Considered one by one, some of the usual expectations about approvers and disapprovers are correct, and some are wrong. For instance, Americans who are relatively well-off—with higher incomes and better education—were less supportive of Congress in 1994 than people with relatively low socioeconomic status, but this pattern was weak, if not reversed, in 1996. In the aggregate, men and women evaluated Congress in about the same measure in 1996, although the sexes were statistically different in 1994 (where $\chi^2 = 5.233$, and $p < .022$). In 1996 African Americans disapproved of congressional performance more than they approved, but whites and Hispanics were about evenly divided that year (statistically significant racial or ethnic differences are confined to 1994). Regionally, there was a bit of a western tilt to public disapproval of Congress's performance, with proportionally more westerners and midwesterners disapproving and more easterners and southerners approving, but again regional differences were, as a whole, not statistically significant in 1996.

The strongest characteristics that divide approvers and disapprovers revolve around partisan commitments, political involvement, and orientations toward the government generally. Table 11.3 underscores the influence of political party affiliation and strength of partisan attachment on congressional performance evaluation. The contrast between 1996 and 1994 is remarkable. In 1996, party identifiers were reacting to a Republican-controlled Congress; the "strong Democrats" in the public (along with "leaning Democrats" and "independents") registered substantial disapproval of that Congress. In marked contrast, in 1994 Republican identifiers were far more likely than Democratic identifiers to disapprove of the performance of a Democrat-controlled Congress. In both election years, party differences are very significant statistically—with $p < .0001$.

This partisan differentiation is reflected in ideological differences: in 1996, most self-styled "liberals" disapproved of Congress, and most "conservatives" approved. In the 1994 survey, disapproval of Congress spread across ideological groups, but conservatives were far more disapproving than liberals. Again, voters who supported Democratic congressional candidates in the 1996 election disapproved of Congress's performance, while voters for Republican candidates tended to approve, the reverse of the 1994 pattern. Finally, 1996 respondents favorable to Democratic president Bill Clinton's performance also tended to disapprove of the Republican Congress, while Clinton disapprovers were more positive toward Congress. In contrast, in 1994 those who disapproved of President Clinton's performance were also very prone to disapprove of the then-Democratic Congress. Again, these differences bear very significant chi-square statistics.

Americans' appraisals of the work of Congress are related to their more general orientations toward the governmental process and the extent of their

TABLE 11.3. WHO APPROVES AND WHO DISAPPROVES OF CONGRESS?
(IN PERCENTAGES)

Respondent characteristics	1996		1994	
	Approve	Disapprove	Approve	Disapprove
Gender, race, and ethnicity				
Men	49	51	31	69
Women	50	51	36	64
	$\chi^2 = .106, p < .745$		$\chi^2 = 5.233, p < .022$	
Whites	50	50	31	69
Blacks	44	57	56	44
Other	45	55	29	71
	$\chi^2 = 3.065, p < .216$		$\chi^2 = 42.092, p < .0001$	
Hispanics	50	50	42	58
	$\chi^2 = .077, p < .781$		$\chi^2 = 5.132, p < .023$	
Age				
18–24	66	34	52	48
25–34	49	51	39	61
35–44	47	53	29	71
45–54	46	54	30	70
55–64	52	48	32	68
65 and older	46	54	25	75
	$\chi^2 = 17.324, p < .004$		$\chi^2 = 46.041, p < .0001$	
Income				
Under $15,000	47	54	42	58
$15,000–24,999	47	53	41	59
$25,000–34,999	48	52	32	68
$35,000–49,999	49	51	32	68

$50,000–74,999	53	47	27	73
$75,000 and above	49	51	28	72
		$\chi^2 = 3.282, p < .657$		$\chi^2 = 23.873, p < .0001$
Education				
Less than high school	44	56	40	60
High school graduate	51	49	40	60
Some college	49	51	32	68
College graduate	50	50	22	78
Post graduate	48	52	24	76
		$\chi^2 = 2.842, p < .585$		$\chi^2 = 38.577, p < .0001$
Region				
East	51	49	39	61
Midwest	47	53	31	69
South	52	48	35	65
West	46	54	28	72
		$\chi^2 = 4.307, p < .230$		$\chi^2 = 11.102, p < .011$
Party identification				
Strong Democrat	41	59	48	52
Weak Democrat	50	50	40	60
Leaning Democrat	34	66	41	59
Independent	37	63	29	72
Leaning Republican	50	50	28	73
Weak Republican	61	39	32	68
Strong Republican	68	33	15	86
		$\chi^2 = 78.74, p < .0001$		$\chi^2 = 83.663, p < .0001$

Continued . . .

TABLE 11.3. — CONTINUED

Respondent characteristics	1996		1994	
	Approve	Disapprove	Approve	Disapprove
Political ideology				
Liberal	38	62	39	61
Moderate	44	56	35	65
Conservative	59	41	24	76
	$\chi^2 = 40.689, p < .0001$		$\chi^2 = 25.979, p < .0001$	
How often trust government				
Just about always	55	46	77	23
Most of the time	63	37	52	48
Only some of the time	45	55	28	72
None of the time	13	87	20	80
	$\chi^2 = 53.128, p < .0001$		$\chi^2 = 98.017, p < .0001$	
Satisfaction with the way democracy works				
Satisfied	56	44	—[a]	—
Fairly satisfied	50	50	—	—
Not very satisfied	35	65	—	—
Not at all satisfied	39	61	—	—
	$\chi^2 = 27.367, p < .0001$			
Number of groups with whom you discuss politics				
0	52	48	—	—
1	45	55	—	—
2	47	53	—	—
3	52	58	—	—
4 or more	39	62	—	—
	$\chi^2 = 10.459, p < .033$			

Vote for Congress				
Democratic candidate	40	60	39	61
Republican candidate	60	40	20	80
	$\chi^2 = 39.545, p < .0001$		$\chi^2 = 42.685, p < .0001$	
Clinton job performance				
Approve	47	53	46	54
Disapprove	55	45	20	81
	$\chi^2 = 8.753, p < .003$		$\chi^2 = 128.592, p < .0001$	

SOURCE: 1994 and 1996 National Election Studies.

NOTE: Respondents were asked: "Do you approve or disapprove of the job the U.S. Congress is doing?"

a. Not available from the 1994 American National Election Study data.

political involvement. Citizens who generally trust the government, and who are satisfied with the way democracy works, tend to approve of Congress, while the untrustful and dissatisfied disapprove. As table 11.3 shows, trust in government and congressional approval are highly correlated in both election years (χ^2s = 98.017 and 53.128 respectively, with $p < .0001$). Similarly, satisfaction with democracy responses bears a parallel pattern for 1996, equally robust statistically. Political involvement—here measured from the 1996 data as the extent of discussing politics in groups—is inversely related to congressional support ($\chi^2 = 10.459$, $p < .033$). Those who discuss politics in a larger number of groups are less approving of Congress than those who do not indulge in group-based discussion of politics. These results present a crude taxonomy of people, one category made up of citizens who are quite trusting and satisfied, who are rather disassociated from politics, and who think Congress is doing pretty well; another category is composed of hard-nosed critics who distrust government, express dissatisfaction with the system, and may engage in active political discussion about the Congress they find so wanting.

These interpretations and speculations are all well and good, but many of the factors considered in table 11.3 are interrelated and overlapping —such as party affiliation and ideology, or education and income. How much leverage in explaining variation in congressional performance evaluation can we acquire by considering a number of predictors simultaneously? In table 11.4, we present a logistic regression model of congressional approval. Our model includes a dozen explanatory variables, assaying the independent effect of each on views of congressional job performance. The variables in this manifold provide an acceptable statistical model, predicting over 60 percent of the evaluative behavior. As we suspected, socioeconomic status—income and education—has little independent effect on support for Congress. Gender differences have only a marginal effect and are not as strong as the bivariate comparison suggested.

Political party identification powerfully divides supporters of Congress from its detractors. Even with the weighty party factor in the fray, differences among Americans in their ideological orientations, their attitudes toward government generally, and their involvement in political discussion are independently correlated with their appraisals of congressional performance. Among Americans, party identification and ideological orientation are not redundant—a considerable proportion of Democratic identifiers declare themselves "conservative," and a nontrivial percentage of Republican identifiers think of themselves as "liberal" (in the 1996 NES data, party and ideological identifications are not the same, but they are substantially correlated: $-r = .52$, $p < .01$).

Consistent with the findings of other studies, our results indicate that Americans' favorable attitudes toward their local member is associated with

TABLE 11.4

DETERMINANTS OF CONGRESSIONAL PERFORMANCE
APPROVAL, 1996

Variable	Coefficient (Standard error)	P value	Probability change
Constant	-1.534 (.432)	.000	—
Party identification	.154 (.099)	.000	.23
Political ideology	.157 (.057)	.006	.23
Education level	.035 (.026)	.175	—
Family income	−.002 (.011)	.834	—
Gender	−.230 (.122)	.059	.06
Race	−.033 (.179)	.852	—
Trust in government	.793 (.128)	.000	.38
Satisfaction with democracy	.386 (.115)	.001	.19
Presidential evaluation	.110 (.107)	.303	—
Evaluation of own member of Congress	.382 (.097)	.000	.19
Number of political discussion groups to which respondent belongs	−.103 (.045)	.021	.29
Media exposure	−.345 (.180)	.055	.09

N	1291
χ^2	130.749 (12 df / $p < 0.000$)
Pseudo-R^2	.073
-2 log likelihood	1658.113
Percentage correctly predicted	62.7
Percentage baseline prediction	48.6

SOURCE: 1996 National Election Study.

NOTE: The dependent variable in this analysis is the respondents' approval of Congress, scored 1 if the respondent approved of the performance of Congress and 0 if the respondent disapproved of the performance of Congress.

their approval of Congress (see Hibbing and Theiss-Morse 1995, 117–18; Patterson, Ripley, and Quinlan 1992). This result confirms the possibility that Americans' congressional evaluations are influenced, at least partly, by how well they regard their own representative.

Finally, we estimated media effects. We know that media coverage of Congress tends to be negative and that, over time, media negativity and levels of disapproval of Congress tend to go hand in hand (Durr, Gilmour, and Wolbrecht 1997, 187–91; Patterson and Caldeira 1990). For the 1996 data, our own estimations indicate that as exposure to campaign programs increases, congressional disapproval increases, though statistically the relationship is only marginally significant. Regrettably, our data do not include estimates of the valence of media content, but we can assert that Americans who watch a lot of television are more prone to disapprove of Congress than people who are less exposed to media. Our results concerning media effects, however limited, run contrary to the claims of recent investigations where direct media exposure effects on evaluations of Congress are thrown into some doubt (see Hibbing and Theiss-Morse 1998).

One means of interpreting logistic regression coefficients is to calculate the individual impact of each variable in the model on the predicted probability of approving or disapproving of Congress. To do this, the predicted probability of approval is recalculated while changing the value of each independent variable, one by one, from its minimum to its maximum value, holding all the other variables in the model constant at their means (see Long 1997, 66–69). In table 11.4 we have given the probability change potential of each statistically significant predictor variable. Accordingly, trust in government has the greatest impact on congressional change (with probability change = .38), closely followed by the number of political discussion groups, political ideology, party identification, satisfaction with democracy, approval of own member of Congress, media exposure, and gender.

The main results presented in table 11.4 share important similarities with the findings of other investigations, particularly in the prominent impact on congressional appraisal of party identification, trust in and satisfaction with government, and political involvement. But our analysis shows little persistent, systematic effect of socioeconomic variables such as income or education (consistent with Kimball and Patterson 1997 and Patterson, Ripley, and Quinlan 1992, but different from Hibbing and Theiss-Morse 1995, 118).

What is more interesting is that ideological differences matter in the analysis shown in table 11.4, even with the partisan differences controlled; all other things equal, in 1996 respondents who considered themselves "conservatives" were significantly more favorable toward the Republican Congress than were self-styled "liberals." In earlier work, based on data gathered before the change in the congressional-party majority, respondents' ideological orientations were not independently related to their evaluations of Congress (Hibbing and Theiss-Morse 1995, 118; Kimball and Patterson 1997, 717; Patterson, Ripley, and Quinlan 1992, 324). The party and ideological polarization of American politics may have made the ideological basis of congressional evaluation more salient to many citizens. Moreover, citizens' evaluations may have been given sharper relief by the visibility of the Republican Congress, spurred particularly by the highly publicized institutional changes and leadership activity in the House of Representatives. Furthermore, the fact that today ideological differences seem to equal the strength and direction of party identification as predictors of congressional performance evaluation may testify to elevated levels of ideological awareness and salience in the American public. Ideology, attitudes, and involvement are not merely artifacts of partisan attachments and loyalties; instead, these factors reinforce Americans' orientations toward Congress.

Our analysis permits a twofold argument. First, Americans approve or disapprove of Congress because of their partisan and ideological commitments. The more Republican and conservative they are, the more firmly they approve of the Republican-controlled Congress; the more Democratic and liberal, the more they disapprove. As partisan polarization grows and strengthens, evaluations of congressional performance are likely to remain relatively low (see King 1997). In this vein, presumably, citizens are evaluating congressional performance on the basis of public policy preferences. Second, whether Americans approve or disapprove of Congress hinges on their more generalized sense of external trust and satisfaction, beyond their partisan or ideological attachments. The trustful and the satisfied, and those who participate little in discussing politics, are the most likely to approve of Congress; those who disapprove tend also to distrust government, express dissatisfaction, and, perhaps on the basis of their disenchantments, discuss politics in group settings.

Voting in the Congressional Election

Given the nexus between Americans' partisan affinities and their appraisal of an institution such as Congress, it would come as no surprise if congressional performance evaluation bore some relationship to voting in congressional elections. For the 1996 congressional election, the expectation would be that voters who approve of the Republican-controlled Congress would likely vote for Republican congressional candidates. By the same token, voters who disapproved of Congress might well be expected to "throw the scoundrels out" by voting for Democratic candidates. The bivariate crosstabulation of congressional approval/disapproval, on the one hand, and of Democratic and Republican voting for House candidates in 1996, on the other hand, bears out this expectation. A sizable majority (62.2 percent) of survey respondents who expressed approval of Congress reported voting for Republican candidates for the House of Representatives in the 1996 election. Similarly, a solid majority (57.8 percent) of those expressing disapproval of Congress voted for Democratic candidates.

We undertook to estimate the impact of a variety of predictors on the 1996 congressional vote, using the NES data. Here, the modeling effort embraces a baker's dozen of independent variables that, taken together, correctly predicted 84 percent of the voting choices. The vote model in table 11.5 takes a somewhat different shape from the congressional evaluation model in table 11.4, partly because evaluation of Congress is itself embraced in the vote model and partly because research on congressional voting calls for a somewhat different recipe. For instance, the congressional vote model includes "interest in the election" and the candidate incumbency variables appropriate to it but not particularly suitable to the congressional evaluation model. The latter model, in turn, includes independent variables of special theoretical interest to evaluation of Congress—"trust" and "satisfaction," member evaluation, group discussion, and media exposure—that are less directly relevant to voting.

The "performance evaluation" effect in congressional voting survives handsomely in a multivariate model of 1996 congressional voting behavior, as table 11.5 shows. Variables that tap partisan orientations directly—party identification, liberalism-conservatism, the presence of a Republican incumbent, approval or disapproval of the Democratic president—are all significantly related to voting for the Republican House candidate in 1996. In contrast, possible predictors of voting behavior, such as blame for the budget deficit, interest in the election, or personal or socioeconomic factors such as race, gender, or family income do not bear independently and significantly on voting (though education comes close to statistical significance). At the same time, it is interesting to note that approval or disapproval of Congress, which carries its own trace of partisan bias, nevertheless is related to congressional voting, even when patently partisan considerations are included in the model and are, in effect, controlled.

Americans who felt the economy was better tended to vote Democratic for Congress, though the relationship is statistically only marginally significant. Those dissatisfied with the economy tended to vote against congressional candidates of the president's party, in the 1996 election for Republican candidates for Congress. Moreover, voters who gave President Clinton a favorable performance evaluation were, all other things equal, likely to vote for Democratic congressional candidates.

To evaluate the relative impact of congressional evaluations on congressional vote choice it is again useful to calculate the predicted probability change effect of each statistically significant independent variable in the model, while holding the other variables constant at their means. When

TABLE II.5

DETERMINANTS OF THE 1996 VOTE FOR CONGRESS

Variable	Coefficient (Standard error)	P value	Probability change
Constant	−5.249 (.953)	.000	—
Evaluation of Congress	.424 (.149)	.004	.20
Presidential evaluation	−.774 (.201)	.000	.35
Republican incumbent	2.313 (.372)	.000	.51
Democratic incumbent	−.423 (.372)	.255	—
Party identification	.545 (.071)	.000	.66
Ideology	.336 (.101)	.001	.46
Blame for budget deficit	.157 (.162)	.335	—
Interest in the election	−.069 (.152)	.649	—
Race	.010 (.346)	.976	—
Gender	−.011 (.211)	.957	—
Family income	.013 (.020)	.509	—
Education level	.088 (.047)	.062	.36
Retrospective national economy	−.473 (.264)	.073	.22

N	907
χ^2	648.123 (13 df / $p < .000$)
Pseudo-R^2	.516
−2 log likelihood	608.318
Percentage correctly predicted	83.7
Percentage baseline prediction	58.2

SOURCE: 1996 National Election Study.

NOTE: The dependent variable for this analysis is the vote that respondents' cast for congressional candidates, scored 1 if the respondent voted for the Republican candidate and 0 if the respondent voted Democratic.

this is done, the relative effect of congressional approval on voting, in terms of probability change, is smaller than for the other significant variables (probability change = .20). Unsurprisingly, variables that are on the list of usual suspects as predictors of congressional voting—party identification, ideology, presidential popularity, and so forth—have relatively large effects. Party identification exhibits the largest probability change, followed by whether or not a Republican incumbent was running, political ideology, presidential approval, education, evaluation of the economy, and finally, congressional approval. Interestingly, two variables that are powerful predictors of congressional approval, party identification and liberalism-conservatism, also significantly predict congressional voting. In this shooting match, it is indeed remarkable that congressional approval survives as a predictor of voting in an environment in which so many heavy-duty predictors of voting choice are at play.

In short, voting in congressional elections is partly grounded in voters' appraisal of the performance of Congress and its members. Although voters' congressional evaluations are themselves colored by partisan attachments, they are significantly correlated with the congressional vote even when partisan affinities are taken into account. In 1996, voters who thought the Republican Congress was doing a good job tended to vote Republican above and beyond the call of the party affiliation, and, by the same token, voters who evaluated the Republican Congress unfavorably tended to vote for Democratic congressional candidates.

Conclusion

The 1996 congressional election transpired in a climate more polarized along political party lines than has been normal for American politics. The parties struggled stridently to raise money, recruit candidates, and use the media to attack the turpitude of opposition candidates and expose cracks in their posture on crucial political issues. The election outcome, somewhat deflating for the partisans on both sides, renewed Republican majorities in both House and Senate, diminished in the former and enhanced in the latter.

It has been effectively demonstrated that Americans reflect their views about the processes of legislation, and abuses of them, in their evaluations of congressional performance (Hibbing and Theiss-Morse 1995, 115–17). Americans' approval or disapproval of Congress are summary evaluations of congressional processes and how they work, congressional party majorities and partisanship, the performance of the leaders, relations between Congress and the president, and the public policies Congress adopts. However impressionistic their evaluations of Congress may be, in the 1996 election Americans were inclined to carry their assessments of congressional performance with them into the voting booth.

TABLE 11.6
VARIABLES IN THE MULTIVARIATE ANALYSES

The database for tables 11.4 and 11.5 derives from the 1996 National Election Study. Variables drawn from this database have been scored as follows:

Congressional approval-disapproval	Strongly approve = 1; approve, not strongly = .5; don't know or no answer = 0; disapprove, not strongly = −.5; strongly disapprove = −1.
Congressional vote	Voted for Republican congressional candidate = 1; voted for Democratic congressional candidate = 0. In the voting analysis, nonvoters are excluded.
Evaluation of respondent's own representative	Strongly approve = 1; approve, not strongly = .5; don't know or no answer = 0; disapprove, not strongly = −.5; strongly disapprove = −1.
Republican incumbent	Republican incumbent running = 1; Republican candidate not incumbent = 0.
Democratic incumbent	Democratic incumbent running = 1; Democratic candidate not incumbent = 0.
Party identification	Strong Democrat = 1; weak Democrat = 2; leaning Democratic = 3; independent = 4; leaning Republican = 5; weak Republican = 6; strong Republican = 7.
Political ideology	Conservative = 1; moderate or don't know or refused = 0; liberal = −1.
Blame for budget deficit	Clinton or Democrats in Congress = 1; both/neither Democrats and Republicans = 0; Reagan/Bush or Republicans in Congress = −1.
Presidential popularity	Approval or disapproval of President Bill Clinton: strongly approve = 1; approve, not strongly = .5; don't know or no answer = 0; disapprove, not strongly = −.5; strongly disapprove = −1.
Interest in the election	Very much interested = 1; somewhat interested = 2; not much interested = 3.
Race	A dummy variable: white = 1; nonwhite = 0.
Gender	A dummy variable: female = 1; male = 0.
Family income (dollars per year)	1 = 0–2,999 9 = 13K–13,999 17 = 35K–39,999 2 = 3K–4,999 10 = 14K–14,999 18 = 40K–49,999 3 = 5K–6,999 11 = 15K–16,999 19 = 50K–59,999 4 = 7K–8,999 12 = 17K–19,999 20 = 60K–74,999 5 = 9K–9,999 13 = 20K–21,999 21 = 75K–89,999 6 = 10K–10,999 14 = 22K–24,999 22 = 90K–104,999 7 = 11K–11,999 15 = 25K–29,999 23 = 105K and 8 = 12K–12,999 16 = 30K–34,999 above
Education	Less than high school = 1; high school graduate = 2; some college = 3; college graduate = 4.
Better/worse off economically than last year	Much better = 1; somewhat better = .5; same or don't know or no answer = 0; somewhat worse = −.5; much worse = −1.
Trust in government	Just about always = 3; most of the time = 2; only some of

	the time = 1; none of the time = 0.
Satisfaction with democracy	Satisfied = 3; fairly satisfied = 2; not very satisfied = 1; not at all satisfied = 0.
Political discussion group membership	Scored as the raw number of groups to which respondent belongs.
Media exposure to campaign programs	A good many = 1; several = .67 ; just one or two = .33; none = 0.

12

The Impact of Incumbents' Levels of Competence and Integrity in the 1994 and 1996 U.S. House Elections

JEFFERY J. MONDAK, CARL McCURLEY,
AND STEVEN R.L. MILLMAN

THE REELECTION of Republican majorities in the House and Senate in 1996 has prompted considerable speculation regarding voters' choices. Most conjecture concerns the possibility that these were "nationalized" elections —that voters used their ballots as part of a broad referendum on the direction of American politics. Such a perspective has generated many specific questions: Was 1994 a repudiation of the Clinton administration and Democratic congressional leadership? Do these electoral results signal a partisan realignment? In 1996, did voters reelect the Republican majority in a conscious attempt to deny President Clinton a Democratic Congress? Was it a backlash against House Speaker Newt Gingrich that led to a weakening of the Republican majority?

This chapter offers a different view. Focusing on the House elections, we suggest that voters in 1994 and 1996 were not motivated primarily by concern with national politics. Instead, they made up their minds much as they had in earlier years—on the basis of district-specific considerations. Our analysis demonstrates that most voters in 1994 did not consciously participate in a referendum on the Clinton administration and that, similarly, attitudes toward Newt Gingrich did not affect support for Republican House incumbents in 1996. Instead, voting in these elections did not differ from the norm: voters supported the most competent and principled incumbents; well-funded challengers outperformed challengers with less money; and challenger spending hinged largely on such district-specific factors as the incumbent's prior vote margin and his or her levels of competence and integrity. National political forces may have mattered, but mostly as an indirect influence on the decision-making process of the individual voter. In short, House voters did not participate in a national referendum when they voted in the 1994 and 1996 congressional elections.

We examine several district-level phenomena, but we are concerned primarily with what we define as *incumbent quality*. Members of the House differ from one another in their levels of competence and integrity. By "competence," we mean traits important for effective service, such as intelligence, motivation, and skill at working with others. "Integrity" refers to whether representatives are principled, and whether they can be trusted to act in the best interests of their constituents. These attributes should matter to voters. First, attention to competence and integrity can bring efficiency to the task of deciding which House candidate to support. Voters in congressional elections often do not know a great deal about the policy positions advanced by candidates. But all of us evaluate the competence and integrity of others on a regular basis, and thus it may be easier for the voter to choose the competent or principled candidate than to vote on the basis of ideological or policy considerations.[1] Second, voting on the basis of competence and integrity offers a reasonable decision-making process. If voters rightly conclude that their member of Congress is a skilled legislator who can be trusted to act conscientiously on difficult questions of policy, then the process of representation will have been well served.

It may make sense that voters should care about the competence and integrity of their House members, but do they? Or is the vote driven by partisanship, perceptions of the economy, and, especially in 1994 and 1996, the desire to bring a fundamental change to the American political landscape? We would be foolish to deny that such forces influence the individual-level House vote. But competence and integrity also matter. In past research using both data from the National Election Studies (NES) (McCurley and Mondak 1995) and a laboratory experiment (Kulisheck and Mondak 1996), we have demonstrated that voters do respond to information regarding the quality of congressional incumbents. Incumbents' levels of integrity directly influence the vote choice. In contrast, competence exerts indirect influence: the least-competent incumbents tend to draw the best, and best-funded, challengers, increasing the likelihood that voters will opt to replace the incumbent. The competence and integrity of House incumbents may have influenced voting in past elections, but did these traits matter in 1994 and 1996? We believe that they did.

Gary Jacobson and Samuel Kernell (1983) describe in detail how national conditions can affect congressional campaigns without exerting direct influence on how individual voters choose a candidate. They reason that strategic political actors adjust their behaviors to the political climate of the time. Consider, for example, an election year that promises to be favorable to Republicans—such as 1994, when the Clinton administration was struggling in Congress, the president was unpopular with the American public, and criticism of the Democratic-controlled Congress was on the rise. How will strategic political actors respond? First, Republicans who have contemplated running for Congress will jump in because the time seems right. As a result, the Republican Party should have more and better candidates on the ballot. Second, many Democrats who have thought about running for Congress likely will wait until times seem more promising.[2] Third, Republican leaders, seeing an opportunity for victory, may attempt to organize the party's candidates and mount a cohesive assault on Democrats in Congress. Fourth, when it becomes clear that Republicans may do well, prospective financial contributors will give much more to Republican candidates than they would have otherwise.

Collectively, these strategic decisions mean that voters in a district defended by a Democratic incumbent will see an experienced and qualified challenger who likely will run an effective campaign on the strength of party support and substantial financial contributions. In contrast, congressional districts defended by Republican incumbents may draw only weak Democratic opposition. If voters simply vote for those viewed as the best candidates, the party on the positive side of national political trends will gain seats in the House. National forces will have influenced who ran, how much money they had, and how effectively they campaigned. Hence, in the most extreme case, voters may have completely ignored national politics when voting in local House races and yet national political developments will have made a difference.

If voters in House races act to signal their collective satisfaction or dissatisfaction with a political party, the process degenerates into one of *electoral roulette*. Members of Congress hold no control over their fates if the vote represents only a referendum on national politics. In 1994, for instance, if the Republican victory marked a repudiation of the Clinton administration, then the thirty-five House Democrats who lost simply were in the wrong place at the wrong time. But if national forces matter by heightening attention to the strengths and weaknesses of congressional incumbents, as may have occurred in 1994, then the process is better described as *electoral Darwinism*. Strategic opponents seek out the weakest incumbents and do their best to convince voters that those incumbents should be replaced.

Our central hypothesis is that the competence and integrity of House incumbents influenced the individual-level vote choice in 1994 and 1996. In neither election did most voters consciously participate in a national referendum. Instead, challengers received votes largely because they waged campaigns that effectively questioned the qualifications of incumbents. In short, the process was one of electoral Darwinism, not electoral roulette.

Preliminary Indicators of the Importance
of Incumbent Quality

Before examining the possible direct link between incumbent quality and the vote choice in 1994 and 1996, we first consider whether more circumstantial evidence may be of relevance. A reasonable starting point is the proposition that national political forces, not the individuating characteristics of congressional incumbents, resonated with voters. This proposition is of particular importance for 1994, the year Republican congressional candidates rallied behind Newt Gingrich and the Contract with America. Republicans gained fifty-two seats in 1994 and captured control of the House. Given the magnitude of the Republican victory, it seems likely that many voters based their choices at least partly on concern with a national political agenda.

Many political scientists have diagnosed 1994 as an instance in which national political factors trumped local considerations. For instance, Stephen Wayne writes of the 1994 elections

> Tip O'Neill's much-quoted aphorism (that "all politics is local") is accurate for most midterm elections. Local personalities and issues usually dominate the campaign and explain the outcome from state to state. The elections of 1994 were different. They were the closest we have come to a national referendum in a midterm election since 1946. They were a vote of no confidence in Democratic leadership in general and the Clinton administration in particular. But they were more than that. They were also a protest against politics as usual, against the way that Congress worked and its members behaved, and against the policies and leadership in Washington and many of the states.[3]

From this perspective, voters had a lot on their minds in 1994, little or none of which concerned the specific strengths and weaknesses of House members. Legislators' levels of competence and integrity may have mattered in prior years, but 1994 appears to have been a different story. According to this view, some Democratic House incumbents (thirty-five, to be exact) were the innocent victims of electoral roulette. Voters were angry at Congress and at the Clinton administration, and someone in Washington had to pay the price. But do national forces operate in such a powerful and indiscriminate manner? Despite the intuitive appeal of this idea, some analysts have suggested that a closer look is warranted. The red flag was public opinion regarding the Contract with America. Although billed by Republican leaders as the centerpiece of a policy mandate, national opinion polls conducted immediately before the 1994 election repeatedly showed that a substantial majority of Americans had not even heard of the Contract. Moreover, of those who had heard of the Contract, many opposed it.[4] How could national factors be decisive when the most salient of those factors escaped the notice of most voters?

A review of data from the 1994 and 1996 NES heightens our skepticism that House voters in either year participated in some form of national referendum. In both years, NES respondents were asked how often their representatives supported President Clinton's legislative proposals. For the 1994 election to have been a referendum on the Clinton administration, voters seemingly would have required at least some sense of whether their representatives stood with Clinton or against him—something many voters seemingly may have been able to deduce from partisanship alone. Yet over two-thirds of respondents would not even offer a guess on this item! Likewise, over half the respondents refused to guess at how their representatives voted on the crime bill in 1994 or on welfare reform in 1996.

Our point is not that voters should be criticized for their apparent lack of political awareness. Indeed, it would be wrong to blame only voters for any knowledge they lacked. Elsewhere (Mondak 1995c, 161–68), one of us has criticized local news media for their coverage of events relevant to congressional elections. Local media, particularly when reliant on national wire services, underplay or ignore the local implications of national news. Local newspapers devote most of their front-page coverage to national and international news, often without highlighting any link between national politics and local political leaders. The crime bill and the welfare bill received prominent attention from newspapers, but information about how local House members voted on those pieces of legislation typically was relegated to the political equivalent of a box score: a list of who voted which way, printed in small font, stuck in the back pages, and devoid of accompanying explanation or analysis. For present purposes, though, the bottom line concerns what took place in 1994 and 1996; it is difficult to reconcile the claim that a congressional election was a national referendum with the reality that most voters simply do not see much of a link between the local House member and prominent questions of policy.

If the 1994 election was not primarily a referendum on President Clinton, or on the Contract with America, then what explains the vote? One answer hinges on the idea that national forces can matter in an election even if voters do not respond directly to a national agenda. Gary Jacobson (1997b) has noted that the Republicans recruited a particularly high-quality group of candidates in 1994 and that those candidates tended to be well funded. Republicans won, not because voters sent a signal of dissatisfaction with President Clinton and his fellow Democrats, but because Republican congressional candidates were experienced, organized, and well funded. From this perspective, perhaps the game did not change in 1994; instead, the Republicans just played it better than they had in previous years (for a similar argument, see Lacy 1998). This view is consistent with our description of electoral Darwinism: better challengers with more money should effectively locate and defeat the weakest congressional incumbents. That is, Democratic

House members should not have suffered equally in 1994. Instead, the most vulnerable incumbents should have faced the most difficult bids for reelection. We put this explanation to the test later, when we examine determinants of the individual-level House vote. If 1994's losing Democrats were the victims of electoral roulette, then factors such as respondents' attitudes toward President Clinton will be found to exert strong influence on the vote. But if electoral Darwinism was at work, then voters should be found to have turned against the least-principled and least-able incumbents.

We have one more bit of circumstantial evidence, this time from 1996. Incumbent quality can influence the composition of the U.S. House even if voters do not play a direct role in the process. This is because low-quality incumbents do not leave office exclusively through electoral defeat. Some incumbents, particularly those embroiled in scandal, decline to seek reelection. Voluntary retirement makes for a much more graceful exit than does a loss at the polls. Many such retirements occurred in 1992 in the wake of the controversy surrounding the House bank (see, for example, Patterson and Barr 1995, 288), and a general pattern of scandal-driven retirement has been found in other years as well (Mondak 1995b). How do we know that a House member has retired for strategic reasons? Although there is no conclusive evidence, one obvious sign is an early departure. Incumbents who retire after only one or two terms in the House typically have not yet reached their golden years, and thus early retirements are worth a closer look. Sometimes, it is quite obvious why an incumbent has departed.

In 1996 thirty-three House incumbents retired.[5] The average tenure of these retirees was 8.88 terms, or just under eighteen years in office. But two of these representatives retired after only a single term: Enid Greene Waldholtz (R-Utah) and Wes Cooley (R-Ore). Of the seventy-three Republicans first elected in 1994, all but three ran for reelection in 1996; Waldholtz and Cooley retired, while Sam Brownback of Kansas was elected to the Senate. Waldholtz and Cooley "retired" when their respective scandals washed away any meaningful opportunity for them to win reelection.

In Oregon, it is against the law to make false claims in campaign literature. In March 1997, soon after leaving office, Wes Cooley was convicted of breaking that law.[6] Cooley's campaign literature advanced false claims about his military record and wrongly indicated that Cooley was a member of Phi Beta Kappa. Cooley elsewhere told tall tales about having once been a champion motorcycle racer. Also, controversy existed regarding Cooley's marriage. Although Cooley claimed that he and his wife were married in 1994, they had always told friends that they were married in Mexico in the mid-1980s. Why does this matter? Because Mrs. Cooley was the widow of a veteran and received widow's benefits of up to $900 per month until she remarried.[7]

When Enid Greene Waldholtz was elected to the House in 1994, she was viewed as a rising star in the Republican Party. She was named to the prestigious Rules Committee, the first Republican freshman so honored in seventy years. But Waldholtz's career disintegrated a year later when she conceded that she had gained office in 1994 on the strength of nearly $2 million in illegal campaign funds. The congresswoman claimed in a five-hour televised soliloquy that she had no idea that the $1.8 million pumped into her 1994 campaign in its final two months was anything but legal. Media blasted her in editorials such as "Trust Me, I Don't Have a Clue."[8]

Incumbent quality does affect the composition of the U.S. House, and the voluntary departures of Wes Cooley and Enid Waldholtz in 1996 exemplify one means by which the influence of quality is felt. In these instances, the partisan composition of the House remained the same, since both Cooley and Waldholtz were replaced by fellow Republicans. Nonetheless, incumbent quality—or the lack thereof—prompted turnover. We believe that voters also respond to incumbent quality and that they did so in 1994 and 1996. If we are right, then neither election represented a true national referendum. To test this proposition, we first must devise a means to measure the competence and integrity of congressional incumbents.

Measuring Incumbent Quality

Testing the hypothesis that the vote choice in the 1994 and 1996 House elections was determined partly by the competence and integrity of incumbent legislators requires two types of data. Our primary dependent variable will be the individual-level congressional vote choice (i.e., whether a person voted for or against the incumbent House member). Appropriate data are available from the 1994 and 1996 NES. Matters became more complicated when we turn to the question of how to measure levels of competence and integrity. The NES surveys identify voters' perceptions and behaviors, not the actual attributes of elected officials. Hence we must look to sources outside the NES for data on incumbent quality; then, once appropriate indicators are obtained, we must merge those data with the 1994 and 1996 NES surveys.

We measure competence and integrity by deriving numerical estimates of these traits from published assessments of each House member. Two biennial volumes, the *Almanac of American Politics* and *Politics in America*, provide invaluable data on all members of Congress. In prior research, we compiled data from the 1972–94 editions of the *Almanac of American Politics* by conducting a systematic content analysis of its written descriptions of House members (Mondak 1995a). In a follow-up study (Millman 1997), similar data were drawn from *Politics in America*. This second study provides the indicators of competence and integrity used in this chapter.[9]

In our initial research on candidate quality (Mondak 1995a), one group of coders listed all words and phrases used in the *Almanac of American Politics* to describe the competence and integrity, broadly defined, of members of Congress. The content analysis centered on general rather than policy-specific descriptions. That is, all references to specific bills, policies, and political issues were excluded. For instance, "tireless" in the phrase "a tireless opponent of abortion rights" would have been excluded, whereas it would have been included had the phrase read "a tireless legislator."[10] A second group of coders then used a numerical scale to rate each word and phrase (see table 12.1). Hence, qualitative data (written descriptions, such as "knowledgeable" and "associates with bigots") were transformed into quantitative indicators (numbers on a 0 to 1 scale, including .83 for "knowledgeable" and .07 for "associates with bigots"). This second group of coders also determined whether each word and phrase spoke primarily to competence or to integrity. Finally, numerical values for the competence and integrity of a particular House member were obtained simply by calculating the average score for the various words and phrases used to describe that representative. When these data were merged with the 1976–92 NES surveys, we found that voters responded directly to incumbent integrity, whereas incumbent competence influenced challenger spending, yielding indirect influence on the individual-level vote choice (McCurley and Mondak 1995).

Our initial coding procedure was replicated in virtually identical form to obtain competence and integrity data from *Politics in America* (Millman 1997), and we merge this set of scores with the 1994 and 1996 NES surveys.[11] Although we have done much to attempt to ensure the reliability and validity of our coding procedure (for details, see Mondak 1995a and Millman 1997), our measures of competence and integrity clearly remain imprecise relative to other, more familiar variables such as vote choice, partisanship, and campaign spending. But this does not mean that our indicators are *too* imprecise to function as predictors of the congressional vote. We offer two simple tests of face validity. First, we can consider whether the scores given to particular words and phrases seem intuitively plausible. That is, do the attributes identified by our coding procedure as desirable (or undesirable) warrant the scores they have received, or are those scores without true meaning? We report a brief sample of words and phrases in table 12.1, with those terms divided into three quality categories (0–.49 = low, .50–.70 = medium, .71–1.00 = high). The placement of these words and phrases demonstrate the validity of the first step in our coding procedure. One might quibble about specific entries, but we believe that all voters would prefer a legislator who is thoughtful, effective, and reliable to one who is good-humored, a moderating force, and a faithful ally of the president, and certainly to one who is adversarial, boorish, and delinquent on child-support payments.

Table 12.2 (p. 221) displays a sample of House members categorized

TABLE 12.1

SAMPLE WORDS AND PHRASES BY LEVEL OF QUALITY

Low quality (0 to 0.49)	Medium quality (0.50 to 0.70)	High quality (0.71 to 1.00)
Adversarial	Affable	Effective
Boorish	Courtly	Near-legendary status
Failed to pay child support	Faithfully backed the president	Reliable
Not a major presence	Good humored	Thoughtful
Rarely visible	A moderating force	Trusted

SOURCE: From Millman 1997.

using our coding procedure. As with the words and phrases, the placement of representatives into quality categories seems reasonable. For instance, the five members in the lowest-quality category all have been embroiled in either legal or political scandal, whereas the five high-quality members are prominent and respected political figures. Again, room exists for disagreement. The bottom line, though, is that the quality scores derived from *Politics in America* provide functional estimates of House members' levels of competence and integrity.[12] Thus, by merging these data with data from the NES, we can use the competence and integrity scores to determine whether these traits influenced the vote choice in 1994 and 1996.

Incumbent Quality and the Congressional Vote

Financing plays a vital role in determining a challenger's prospects for electoral success (see, for example, Jacobson 1980), meaning that incumbents' levels of competence affect voters indirectly by influencing the quality and visibility of challengers. We must consider whether this pattern of effects existed in 1994 and 1996. Thus, prior to study of the possible link between in-

TABLE 12.2

SAMPLE HOUSE MEMBERS BY LEVEL OF QUALITY

Low quality (0 to 0.49)	Medium quality (0.50 to 0.70)	High quality (0.71 to 1.00)
Alcee Hastings	Sonny Bono	William Archer
Jay Kim	Duncan Hunter	Richard Gephardt
Joseph McDade	Joseph Kennedy	Lee Hamilton
Bill Paxon	Bernard Sanders	Jim Leach
Mel Reynolds	Gerald Solomon	Susan Molinari

SOURCE: From Millman 1997.

cumbent quality and vote choice, we first examine whether the quality of House members partly determined how much money challengers spent in their campaigns.

A District-Level Analysis of Incumbent Quality and Challenger Spending

Prospective candidates for political office act strategically. Before entering any race, the wise politician determines if it will be possible to obtain the resources needed to run a viable campaign and if there exists a meaningful chance to win. In U.S. House elections, strategic behavior occurs when the best challengers run in open seats and when high-quality challengers target vulnerable incumbents. But what factors identify imperiled incumbents? National political conditions clearly stand as one critical indicator, a point discussed in detail by Jacobson and Kernell (1983). For instance, in years when public sentiment strongly favors one party, that party can be expected to field an especially strong group of candidates. This is because ambitious (and opportunistic) politicians will attempt to capitalize on the inviting national climate. As we have seen, Jacobson (1997b) argues that precisely this sort of strategic behavior took place in 1994 and contributed to the Republican takeover of Congress.

District-specific signals of electoral vulnerability also encourage prospective challengers. Poor performance by an incumbent in an earlier election offers perhaps the clearest evidence that the incumbent can be defeated. Thus, strategic challengers should be expected to target districts in which incumbents previously won by especially narrow margins (Bond, Covington, and Fleisher 1985). Similarly, we expect that the best challengers will seek out low-quality incumbents. House members who are of low competence or integrity should be more easily defeated than their high-quality counterparts, meaning that a quality deficit should attract opportunistic opponents.

We use challenger spending as our indicator of challenger quality. Challenger quality can be measured in various ways, with such indicators as prior political experience or status in the community. But access to money marks the bottom line. Funding is essential if a challenger is to have any chance of defeating an incumbent (see, for example, Jacobson 1980, 1997b). Moreover, weak, inexperienced challengers typically struggle to raise funds because potential donors do not wish to waste their resources on likely losers. At question is whether challenger spending increases in response to national political forces, district-level factors, and, most important for present purposes, the competence and integrity of congressional incumbents. Previously (McCurley and Mondak 1995), we found challenger spending to be inversely related to incumbent competence (i.e., the best incumbents drew poorly funded challengers), but we identified no link between integrity and challenger spending.

In constructing our challenger-spending variable, we start with Federal Election Commission data on challenger disbursements. We include data only from major-party challengers, and we exclude challengers who reported no expenditures. The disbursement data then are adapted to account for two technical factors. First, because two elections are to be examined, spending data should be inflation neutral. Second, challenger spending suffers from diminishing returns (see, for example, Jacobson 1985), meaning, for instance, that increasing spending from zero to $300,000 likely will yield many more votes for a challenger than will increasing spending from $300,000 to $600,000. We account for these factors by dividing each challenger's disbursements by the average level of challenger spending for the year and then taking the natural log of the resulting values. This procedure generates values that range, theoretically, from positive to negative infinity. In actuality, the range is −5.29 to 2.24 in 1994, and −5.57 to 2.54 in 1996. As a simple example, a value of zero on the spending variable means that the challenger's spending matched the year's average; in contrast, a score of −1.10 means that the challenger spent only one-third of the year's average, while a score of 1.10 corresponds with spending three times greater than the average.

Regression models include three independent variables in addition to competence and integrity. The first is the incumbent's previous margin of victory (defined as the percentage of the total vote in the district received by the incumbent). Again, our expectation is that House members elected in close races last time will draw well-funded challengers this time. We also include a dummy variable to distinguish seats held by Democrats from those held by Republicans. This variable enables us to test whether national events worked to the collective advantage of candidates from one of the parties. The third independent variable is seniority (defined as the number of terms the incumbent has been in office). We expect that prospective challengers will be unlikely to take on veteran incumbents unless other factors, such as a poor showing last time, make a senior member appear vulnerable.

Table 12.3 (p. 224) depicts regression estimates.[13] As expected, the incumbent's previous margin strongly influences challenger spending, although it is somewhat surprising that the effect in 1996 doubles that of 1994 in magnitude. Results for the *Democratic incumbent* dummy variable provide a partial explanation: in 1994, national forces favored Republicans, and thus challenger funding was elevated against all Democratic incumbents. That is, the impact of national politics in 1994 may have somewhat dampened the impact of district-level electoral vulnerability. This partisan difference in spending did not recur in 1996, and thus challenger spending hinged more heavily on district-level factors. The seniority variable did not produce the expected effect. At least in 1994 and 1996, seniority failed to deter well-financed challengers.

TABLE 12.3

DETERMINANTS OF CHALLENGER SPENDING,

1994 AND 1996

	1994		1996	
Independent variable	Coefficient (Standard error)	P value	Coefficient (Standard error)	P value
Constant	2.678 (.997)	.008	4.408 (1.265)	.001
Political variables				
Previous election margin	−.028 (.008)	.001	−.056 (.011)	.001
Democratic incumbent	.475 (.230)	.041	−.095 (.282)	.736
Incumbent's seniority	−.038 (.025)	.135	.015 (.033)	.651
Incumbent quality variables				
Incumbent integrity	−1.443 (.638)	.025	.167 (.749)	.824
Incumbent competence	−1.122 (1.257)	.374	−3.094 (1.332)	.022
N	142		114	
R^2	.14		.22	

SOURCE: For the dependent variable, Federal Election Commission.

Table 12.3 also demonstrates that levels of challenger spending vary in response to incumbent quality, but the specific nature of these effects differs in 1994 and 1996. In 1994, the competence and integrity variables produce negative coefficients of similar magnitude, although only the latter reaches statistical significance. In contrast, we see a large competence effect in 1996 and the utter absence of an integrity effect. Results for 1996 closely resemble those from our pooled analysis for the years 1970–92 (McCurley and Mondak 1995). The outlier is 1994. We can offer no conclusive explanation why integrity influenced challenger spending only in 1994. One possible reason is that the effect reflects the residual impact of the House banking scandal. Given the various allegations of impropriety faced by the Clinton administration, another explanation is that Republican challengers targeted ethically questionable incumbents in an attempt to link them to Clinton on the issue of integrity. These explanations, however, are only speculative.

This analysis provides the first step in determining if incumbent quality influenced the vote choice in 1994 and 1996. Table 12.3 demonstrates that incumbents who were of the lowest quality were targeted by well-funded challengers. Hence, if challenger funding influences the individual-level vote choice, that effect would establish at least an indirect role for competence and integrity. The impact of incumbent quality and prior vote margin on challenger spending also means that any effect of national forces in 1994 and 1996 was not entirely indiscriminate. Republican challengers did out-spend Democratic challengers in 1994, but the strongest and most consistent predictors of challenger spending are incumbent-specific.

THE CONGRESSIONAL VOTE

We have come to the bottom line: why did voters opt for or against their House incumbents in 1994 and 1996, and did incumbents' levels of compe-tence and integrity play any role? Here we shift from an aggregate-level analysis of incumbents in their districts to an individual-level examination of voter assessments of incumbents, a move that provides us with a substantial increase in the number of cases. Data on the congressional vote are drawn from the 1994 and 1996 NES. The vote variable is coded 1 if the respondent voted for the incumbent, and 0 if the respondent voted for the district's ma-jor-party challenger.[14] We exclude open-seat districts and districts in which the incumbents did not face major-party opposition.

Our logistic regression models include several groups of independent variables. First, we use a dummy variable to distinguish seats held by Re-publican incumbents from those held by Democrats, plus a series of four dummy variables to account for the relationship between the party of the in-cumbent and respondents' self-identified party affiliations (e.g., incumbent and respondent both are Democrats, incumbent is a Democrat and respon-dent is a Republican). Our dummy variables account for five of the six pos-sible combinations of incumbent party identification (whether the current House member is a Democrat or a Republican) and voter party identifica-tion (whether the survey respondent is a Democrat, a Republican, or an in-dependent). This means that the reference category for the effect of the dummy variables is independent voters in districts with Republican incum-bents and that the effects for the five dummy variables should be interpreted relative to this reference category.

Second, the challenger-spending measure that served as our dependent variable in the preceding section is included as an independent variable here. As challenger spending increases, the likelihood that a respondent will vote for the incumbent should decrease. Thus, a negative coefficient is expected. Given the relationship between incumbent quality and challenger spending identified earlier, any direct effect of spending on the vote choice would im-ply the presence of an indirect link between quality and the vote.

The third group of variables captures the possible relationship between respondents' attitudes toward prominent national politicians and the con-gressional vote choice. These variables enable us to test the extent to which voting in 1994 and 1996 was a form of national political referendum. In 1994 we include a measure of presidential approval (1 = respondent approves of President Clinton's performance, 0 = otherwise). The effect of this variable should differ depending on whether a district's incumbent is a Democrat or a Republican. The impact of presidential approval in districts held by Republican incumbents will be given by the coefficient for the variable *Clinton approval*. The sign should be negative on this measure because respondents who approve of President Clinton are expected to be less likely to vote for a Republican congressional incumbent than respondents who disapprove of Clinton. The corresponding effect in districts held by Democratic incumbents is given by the sum of the coefficients for the variable *Clinton approval* and the interaction term *Clinton approval* × *Democratic incumbent*. This sum should be positive, which would mean that respondents who approve of Clinton are more likely to vote to retain Democratic House incumbents.

In addition to the Clinton variables, the 1994 analysis also includes a feeling thermometer concerning then-Senate majority leader Bob Dole, and the interaction between that feeling thermometer and the dummy variable identifying Democratic congressional incumbents. These perceptions of a second nationally prominent politician are included so that we may assess whether the congressional vote choice was in part a response to GOP leadership. In 1996 we replace the Clinton and Dole approval measures with dummy variables that identify whether the respondent voted for Clinton or Dole for president.[15] In 1996 many Democratic challengers seemingly campaigned more against House Speaker Newt Gingrich than against their actual Republican opponents (see, for example, Hershey 1997). To test whether this strategy resonated with voters, we include a feeling thermometer concerning Newt Gingrich as part of our 1996 analysis (this variable is not available in 1994).

Our final variables are the indicators of incumbent competence and integrity. We face a problem in merging these data with the NES surveys because competence and integrity scores are not available for all House incumbents. If *Politics in America* did not publish a sufficiently detailed assessment of an incumbent, then no score could be obtained.[16] We could estimate models of the vote that include only those instances where both competence and integrity data are available, but in doing so we would greatly limit the number of cases in our models. One consequence would be a possible distortion of the sample weight. Additionally, we would be discarding useful information: the effects of our other independent variables on the vote for those cases for which competence or integrity scores are unavailable. To avoid these problems, we use all available NES data and simply include our competence and integrity measures when they are available. This approach slightly complicates model construction because we need not only the competence and integrity measures but also a second pair of variables indicating whether competence and integrity scores were available for the case in question. Thus, the variable *integrity measure available* is coded 1 if we have integrity data for the respondent's House incumbent, and 0 if we do not. The variable *incumbent integrity* is the integrity score obtained from our coding procedure, provided that such a score is available, and 0 if no score was obtained.[17] An identical pair of variables is used to measure incumbent competence.[18] This procedure allows a relatively straightforward interpretation of the effects of competence and integrity without requiring the sacrifice of large portions of the NES samples.

Logistic regression results are depicted in table 12.4 (p. 228). We see evidence in both 1994 and 1996 that national political forces did influence the congressional vote. Nevertheless, some of the reported effects conflict dramatically with past explanations of these elections. Most striking is that in 1994, approval of President Clinton affected the vote in House seats defended by Republican incumbents, but not in seats defended by Democrats! The −1.18 coefficient for Clinton approval is the effect in districts with Republican incumbents. Under average conditions (i.e., average challenger spending, and the respondent has the mean score on the Dole feeling thermometer), the likelihood that a nonpartisan respondent will vote to retain a Republican incumbent varies from 0.30 (respondent approves of Clinton) to 0.58 (respondent disapproves of Clinton). In contrast, the coefficient for Clinton approval in districts defended by Democrats is equal to −1.18 + 1.42, or 0.24. This negligible coefficient produces a swing of only 6 points in the likelihood that a respondent voted to retain a Democratic incumbent (.38 if disapprove of Clinton, .44 if approve). Also, note that the coefficient for *Democratic incumbent*, the dummy variable that distinguishes seats held by Democrats from those held by Republicans, is statistically insignificant, and positive. It was not the case that voters exhibited any blanket tendency to reject Democratic incumbents in 1994. Likewise, disapproval of President Clinton brought no direct backlash against Democratic House members.

The coefficients for the Gingrich feeling thermometer variables also warrant emphasis. If a national referendum took place in 1996, one obvious focal point was Republican leadership in Congress, particularly as personified by Newt Gingrich. In 1996, many Democratic challengers attempted to cast Republican House incumbents as guilty by association with the unpopular Speaker, but current results suggest that this strategy failed to sway voters. The logit coefficient for the Gingrich variable is insignificant and substantively weak in seats defended by Republican incumbents. In other words, antipathy toward Gingrich did not cause backlash against Republican House members in 1996, just as ill will toward Clinton failed to hurt Democrats in 1994. Feelings about Gingrich brought some effect in seats defended by Democrats—a high score on the Gingrich feeling thermometer

TABLE 12.4
DETERMINANTS OF INCUMBENT HOUSE VOTE,
1994 AND 1996

Independent variable	1994		1996	
	Coefficient (Standard error)	P value	Coefficient (Standard error)	P value
Constant	−.697 (.835)	.404	1.269 (.700)	.067
Incumbent and voter partisanship				
Democratic incumbent, all voters	.721 (1.013)	.476	−.111 (.941)	.906
Democratic incumbent, Democratic voter	2.370 (.545)	.001	.912 (.669)	.173
Democratic incumbent, Republican voter	−.847 (.525)	.107	−1.248 (.621)	.044
Republican incumbent, Republican voter	2.257 (.811)	.005	1.177 (.741)	.112
Republican incumbent, Democratic voter	.254 (.754)	.736	−1.550 (.626)	.132
Campaign variables				
Challenger spending	−.463 (.085)	.001	−.138 (.067)	.041
Clinton approval (1994), Clinton vote (1996)	−1.177 (.525)	.025	−.424 (.426)	.320
Clinton approval/vote × Democratic incumbent	1.423 (.645)	.027	2.047 (.746)	.006
Dole feeling thermometer (1994), Dole vote (1996)	.024 (.010)	.013	2.229 (.692)	.001
Dole feeling thermometer/vote × Democratic incumbent	−.033 (.012)	.007	−2.335 (.919)	.011
Gingrich feeling thermometer (1996 only)			.005 (.007)	.450
Gingrich feeling thermometer × Democratic incumbent			−.026 (.011)	.014

Continued . . .

corresponds with a decreased likelihood that the respondent voted to retain a Democratic House incumbent—but this effect obviously was no threat to Republican House members.

The results described thus far reveal that neither the 1994 nor 1996 congressional election was an across-the-board referendum. But recall that our analysis centers on House seats defended by incumbents. In open seats—where there is no evidence of an incumbent's competence and integrity—national considerations may have played a more prominent role.

TABLE 12.4 — CONTINUED

	1994		1996	
Independent variable	Coefficient (Standard error)	P value	Coefficient (Standard error)	P value
Incumbent quality variables				
Integrity measure available	−2.097 (1.306)	.108	−1.720 (.890)	.053
Competence measure available	−4.566 (1.671)	.006	−1.494 (1.196)	.212
Incumbent integrity	3.949 (1.946)	.042	3.438 (1.300)	.008
Incumbent competence	6.130 (2.395)	.011	1.407 (1.779)	.429
N	574		781	
χ^2	301.187 (14 df / p < .001)		417.027 (16 df / p < .001)	
Pseudo-R^2	.41		.41	
−2 log likelihood	430.81		511.80	
Percentage correctly predicted	83.61		84.05	
Percentage baseline prediction	65.85		71.57	

SOURCES: 1994 and 1996 National Election Studies.

Previously, we saw that incumbents' levels of quality partly determine how well funded their challengers will be. Likewise, incumbents who won by narrow margins in prior elections also tend to draw well-funded challengers. In table 12.4, the coefficients for the challenger-spending variable reveal that these effects ultimately influence the vote choice: the more money a challenger spends, the less likely a respondent is to vote for the district's incumbent. This effect simply makes good sense. What is striking in table 12.4 is the enormous difference in the magnitude of the spending coefficients in 1994 and 1996. The coefficient is –0.14 in 1996, which is comparable in size to the overall effect of –0.16 we found elsewhere for 1976–92 (McCurley and Mondak 1995, table 6). Table 12.4's spending coefficient for 1994 exceeds this level by a factor of three. That is, challenger spending in 1994 yielded much greater electoral returns than normal.

The Republican Party led an orchestrated and well-publicized campaign to capture the House in 1994. Our results suggest that the success of this campaign was not indiscriminate. In the presence of a prominent national campaign, we might expect challenger spending to decline in importance due to the effects of free media coverage and party spending. But this did not occur. Challenger success was linked directly, and quite strongly, to spending. And, as we saw in the previous section, levels of challenger spending varied inversely with incumbent quality and electoral vulnerability. Collectively, these results demonstrate that 1994's defeated House incumbents were the victims of electoral Darwinism, not electoral roulette—challenger spending influenced the vote, and the weakest House members drew the best-funded challengers.

Coefficients for the competence and integrity variables reveal a second difference between 1994 and 1996. In 1996 incumbent integrity directly influences the House vote, but competence does not. This is the precise pattern we found previously for 1976–92 (McCurley and Mondak 1995). Integrity also matters in 1994, and, in fact, the integrity coefficients are quite similar in magnitude in 1994 and 1996. The anomaly concerns competence. In 1994, unlike in any other year we have studied, incumbent competence produces a substantively large and statistically significant direct effect on the individual-level vote choice.[19] When the going got tough, the weak crumbled like a fallen TV preacher. In a laboratory experiment (Kulisheck and Mondak 1996), we found that voters do respond to information about competence when that information is presented in clear form. Thus, we suspect that the strong competence effect in 1994 reflects the unusual success of challengers in highlighting incumbents' deficiencies.

To help make clear the substantive impact of competence and integrity, we graph their effects in figures 12.1, 12.2, and 12.3.[20] Figures 12.1A and 12.1B show the effect of competence in 1994; figures 12.2A and 12.2B depict the impact of integrity that year; and figures 12.3A and 12.3B show the integrity effect in 1996. Each graph includes three lines, distinguishing respondents on the basis of self-identified partisanship. Voters who identify with the same party as their House member seem somewhat immune to the influence of incumbent quality. This effect is most pronounced in 1996. Self-identified Democrats were highly likely to vote to retain Democratic incumbents, just as Republicans were inclined to reelect Republicans. Consequently, even incumbents with appallingly low integrity scores received strong support from their fellow partisans in 1996.

Few congressional incumbents can remain in office without at least some support from independents or affiliates of the opposing party. Figures 12.1, 12.2, and 12.3 reveal that competence and integrity can be instrumental in securing such support. More often than not, such voters will support the challenger when the district's representative is of dubious quality, but these same constituents will vote to retain a high-quality incumbent. This is the basic logic underlying the concept of the personal vote (see, for example, Cain, Ferejohn, and Fiorina 1987). Current results show that this logic was not suspended in 1994 or 1996. Yes, national political forces brought some influence on voting in these elections. But the effects of national forces did not preclude a role for incumbent quality. To the contrary, we have found especially strong effects for competence and integrity in 1994, a year in

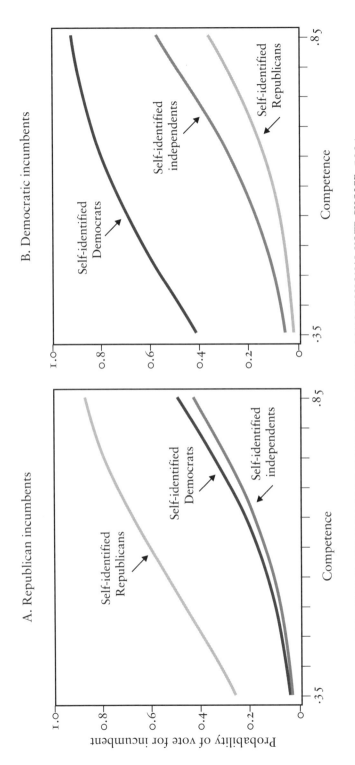

B. Democratic incumbents

Self-identified Democrats

Self-identified independents

Self-identified Republicans

Competence

A. Republican incumbents

Self-identified Republicans

Self-identified Democrats

Self-identified independents

Competence

Probability of vote for incumbent

FIGURE 12.1. THE IMPACT OF COMPETENCE ON THE CONGRESSIONAL VOTE CHOICE, 1994

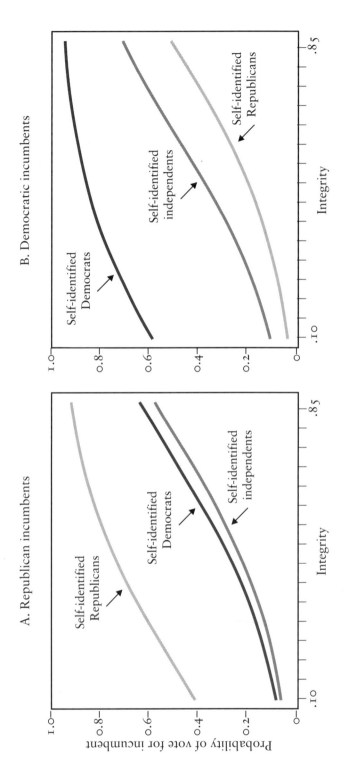

FIGURE 12.2. THE IMPACT OF INTEGRITY ON THE CONGRESSIONAL VOTE CHOICE, 1994

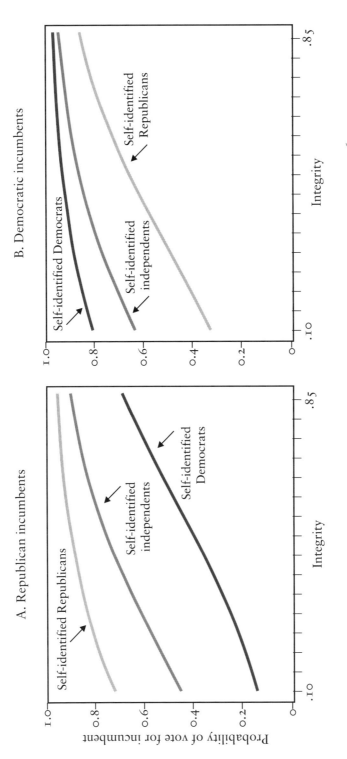

A. Republican incumbents

B. Democratic incumbents

Probability of vote for incumbent

Integrity

Self-identified Republicans

Self-identified independents

Self-identified Democrats

Self-identified Democrats

Self-identified independents

Self-identified Republicans

FIGURE 12.3. THE IMPACT OF INTEGRITY ON THE CONGRESSIONAL VOTE CHOICE, 1996

which national political forces were unusually prominent. National political forces and incumbent quality are mutually reinforcing; the winds of change make it easier to sweep away incumbents who are mediocre or weak.

Conclusion

Danger lurks whenever analysts attempt to deduce voters' individual-level motivations from aggregate election results. The outcomes of the 1994 and 1996 U.S. House elections differed dramatically from all those from the previous forty years in that the Republicans captured control of Congress in 1994, and this Republican majority was reelected in 1996. Given such a fundamental shift in American politics, it is tempting to conclude that the back-to-back Republican victories in 1994 and 1996 reflect a deliberate, conscious effort by voters to dethrone the Democrats. But such a conclusion is wrong. Voters did not participate in a national referendum when they voted in the 1994 and 1996 U.S. House elections.

This chapter argues that voters in 1994 and 1996 made up their minds in House elections much as they had in earlier years, in large part by assessing the relative strengths and weaknesses of competing candidates. Incumbents' levels of competence and integrity form an important part of such a decision calculus. Developments in national politics may influence the vote, but the effects of national forces typically are indirect. National factors can help determine which candidates run and how effectively they campaign. Hence, voters need not participate in a national referendum for national forces to make a difference. In 1994, Americans as a whole knew very little about the Contract with America, and most would not even guess which way their local House member had voted on the crime bill, or even whether their representative generally tended to support or oppose the president. Most people simply did not perceive any link between national politics and their House members. Consequently, in our analysis of the vote choice we saw no blanket rejection of Democratic House incumbents in 1994 and no sign that antipathy toward President Clinton prompted voter backlash against Democratic incumbents.

Republicans won in 1994 because they played the game well. In table 12.4, we saw that challenger spending exerted extremely strong influence on the House vote in 1994. Republican challengers outspent their Democratic counterparts, and thus the challenger-spending effect worked to the net advantage of Republicans. But levels of challenger spending also hinged on two district-specific forces: the incumbent's prior vote margin (incumbents who won by narrow margins in 1992 drew well-funded challengers in 1994) and the incumbent's level of integrity (the most principled incumbents were challenged by poorly funded opponents). Strong, well-funded challengers ran against weak incumbents. Moreover, incumbents' levels of competence and integrity brought direct influence on individual-level voting. Collectively, these findings suggest that voters did not indiscriminately choose Republicans over Democrats in 1994. Instead, they voted much as they had in prior years: for the better candidate. The Republican Party made gains in 1994 by fielding good candidates who succeeded in pointing out the limitations of the most vulnerable congressional incumbents.

The story of Republican reelection in 1996 is similar to that of the party's initial victory in 1994. The House vote in 1996 did vary in response to the presidential election (Clinton voters were likely to prefer Democratic House incumbents, and Dole voters were likely to prefer Republican incumbents). But the 1996 election was not a referendum on Newt Gingrich's first two years as House Speaker: the vote in districts held by Republican incumbents did not vary as a function of respondents' attitudes toward Gingrich. As in 1994, challenger spending influenced the House vote in 1996, with levels of spending determined largely by incumbents' levels of competence and their previous vote margins. Voters also were likely to retain highly principled congressional incumbents. Competence and integrity did not fully determine the vote choice in 1994 and 1996—some high-quality incumbents were defeated in these years, and some low-quality incumbents were reelected—but these traits clearly had some impact.

Despite our emphasis on district-level explanations for voting, we do not disregard the effects of national political forces, although these forces typically operate well before voters go to the polls. When party fortunes decline, potential high-quality challengers become more likely to postpone election bids, and vulnerable incumbents become more likely to retire. National forces certainly do influence House elections, yet these forces appear to bring only indirect influence on the process by which the voter decides which candidate to support.

We have distinguished between two views of the electoral process: electoral Darwinism and electoral roulette. The latter perspective is troubling because it suggests that voters care little or nothing about the attributes of the actual candidates for office. Results presented in this chapter offer much greater support for the former perspective. Voters seek to elect competent and principled representatives. For their part, challengers work to defeat incumbents by targeting those who appear most vulnerable and by emphasizing the House members' weaknesses. Thus, House elections are determined on a district-by-district basis. It sometimes happens, as in 1994, that these 435 separate contests collectively produce systemic change. When such change occurs, it is because one party's candidates fared particularly well in the district-level battles for office, not because voters have decided en masse to send some sort of signal to Washington

Appendix:
Chronology of the 1996
Presidential Campaign

BARRY C. BURDEN

1995

3 January	Former defense secretary Dick Cheney (R-Wyo.) announces that he will not pursue the Republican nomination for president.
30 January	Jack Kemp (R-N.Y.), former member of the House of Representatives and HUD secretary, announces that he will not seek the presidency.
9 February	After hinting that he would begin his presidential campaign in April, former vice-president Dan Quayle shocks the political community by stating that he will not run in 1996. He claims that fund-raising difficulties are the reason for his withdrawal.
24 February	Senator Phil Gramm (R-Tex.) becomes the first major figure to announce his presidential candidacy.
27 February	Former governor and secretary of education Lamar Alexander (R-Tenn.) declares his candidacy for the Republican nomination.
20 March	After challenging President Bush in 1992, conservative columnist Pat Buchanan becomes a presidential candidate again. Symbolically, his announcement takes place in New Hampshire. Alan Keyes, an African American talk show host from California, also announces his candidacy today.
30 March	Senator Arlen Specter (R-Pa.) officially becomes a presidential candidate. He is noted for being the moderate among the Republican candidates and for his role in the Clarence Thomas Supreme Court nomination hearings in 1991.
10 April	Senate Majority Leader Bob Dole (R-Kans.) announces his candi-

dacy. His campaign experience and national visibility make him an early front-runner.

13 April   Ultraconservative Congressman Robert Dornan (R-Calif.) announces his intention to run for president.

19 April   Senator Richard Lugar (R-Ind.) becomes a candidate for president, running on his experience in foreign affairs.

11 June   At a town meeting in New Hampshire, President Clinton and House Speaker Newt Gingrich agree to create a bipartisan commission to deal with campaign finance and lobbying reform. Despite their handshake, the commission does not materialize.

22 September Malcolm ("Steve") Forbes Jr., CEO of *Forbes* magazine, announces the beginning of his presidential campaign. He focuses almost exclusively on economic issues, especially the "flat" national income tax.

25 September Ross Perot announces that he will back a third political party, later to be named the Reform Party.

29 September Governor Pete Wilson (R-Calif.) drops out of the Republican nomination race despite never having formally entered it. Wilson was criticized by California Republicans for seeking higher office soon after being reelected governor.

8 November   Retired general Colin Powell announces that he will not run for president after publicly pondering the decision for weeks. He also will not accept the vice-presidential nomination but promises to work within the Republican Party. Dole is helped by this withdrawal and the newly announced support of Governor Steve Merrill of New Hampshire.

14 November Much of the federal government shuts down for six days after the president and Congress fail to approve a measure to fund its daily operations. About 800,000 employees are put on furlough. Congressional Republicans and particularly Speaker Gingrich seem to suffer publicly for the impasse.

22 November Senator Arlen Specter suspends his nomination campaign. He claims lack of financing has forced his withdrawal, though many believe that his pro-choice message was too moderate for Republican activists.

27 November Speaker of the House Newt Gingrich (R-Ga.) ends speculation that he will run for president in 1996.

16 December After a congressional funding resolution expires, the federal government again shuts down, this time for twenty-one days. Fewer than 300,000 employees are laid off this time, though more are working without pay.

1996

15 January   Steve Forbes unexpectedly becomes the second-runner in the Republican nomination race. His plans for a 17-percent flat in-

come tax rate, and millions of dollars in campaign advertising, draw enough attention to make him the main alternative to leader Dole.

23 January   President Clinton delivers the State of the Union address. The speech is well received as Clinton declares that "the era of big government is over." It looks as though Clinton is moving to the center to steal the Republican agenda.

26 January   Hillary Clinton becomes the only first lady to testify before a grand jury after she is subpoened regarding the Whitewater financial affair.

6 February   Though the leading Republican candidates chose not to participate, Louisiana holds the first nominating event in the country. Buchanan beats Gramm handily and claims that he is the representative of the Republican right.

12 February   Favorite Bob Dole narrowly wins the first round of the Iowa caucuses. Dole finishes with 26 percent and Buchanan 23 percent. Forbes finishes fourth, despite having spent $4 million in the state.

14 February   After a dismal fifth-place showing in Iowa, Phil Gramm quiety exits the Republican nomination race to focus on retaining his Senate seat in Texas. Meanwhile, polls show Dole and Buchanan tied in New Hampshire.

18 February   Phil Gramm adds to Senator Dole's long list of endorsements just two days before the crucial New Hampshire primary.

20 February   After months of leading all other candidates in the polls, Bob Dole finishes a close second to Pat Buchanan in the New Hampshire primary. Buchanan gets 27 percent of the vote to Dole's 26 percent. Alexander is not far behind with 23 percent, and Forbes trails with 12 percent. A poor showing in New Hampshire ended Dole's campaign in 1988.

21 February   Upset by the New Hampshire results, Colin Powell declares that he will not support Pat Buchanan even if he becomes the Republican nominee. This statement is indicative of the efforts of mainstream Republicans to stop Buchanan's candidacy.

24 February   Steve Forbes finishes first in the Delaware primary, but he was the only major candidate to visit the state.

27 February   After spending millions of dollars in the state, Steve Forbes (33 percent) wins the winner-take-all Arizona primary. Dole is second in Arizona (30 percent) and Buchanan is third (27 percent). Dole sweeps primaries in the Dakotas.

2 March   Dole reestablishes himself as leader of the pack with a decisive win in the South Carolina primary (45 percent). Buchanan is second, Forbes third, and southerner Lamar Alexander a disappointing fourth.

5 March   Senator Dole sweeps all eight Junior Tuesday primaries and

makes a great leap toward the Republican nomination. He seems unstoppable, as his vote totals range from 40 percent in Vermont to 64 percent in Rhode Island. Buchanan finishes second in most of the primaries, with about a fourth of the Republican vote.

6 March | After failing to win a single primary and doing poorly in the South, Alexander ends his campaign. Lugar also quits. Both express support for Bob Dole as they exit the race. Dole draws the endorsements of former president Bush and his son, Governor George W. Bush (R-Tex.). Jack Kemp publicly backs Forbes just one day before the New York primary. Kemp's move does not sit well with Republican leaders.

7 March | Bob Dole easily wins the New York primary with 92 of 93 possible delegates. He begins to focus on President Clinton rather than other Republicans as his main opponent.

12 March | Dole takes all seven Super Tuesday primaries, which include populous states such as Florida and Texas. Meanwhile, President Clinton quietly locks up the Democratic nomination, passing the required 2,146 delegates.

14 March | Steve Forbes ends his presidential campaign. Saying that he has no regrets about spending $25 million on an unsuccessful campaign, he praises and endorses Dole.

19 March | Dole wins the "Big Ten" primaries in Ohio, Michigan, Illinois, and Wisconsin. Perot states that he will run for president once again if Reform Party supporters ask him to do so.

26 March | Dole easily takes the California primary and declares that he is the Republican nominee.

15 May | Lagging by 20 percentage points in the polls, Dole tries to jump-start his general election campaign by resigning from the Senate to pursue the presidency full-time. Dole will leave his majority leader post in June after thirty-five years in Congress.

28 May | A federal jury renders guilty verdicts for Clinton associates Jim and Susan McDougal and Governor Jim Guy Tucker (D-Ark.). Jurors indict all three in the complicated Whitewater scandal despite seeing taped presidential testimony on their behalf.

13 June | One day after Dole's departure from the Senate, Trent Lott (R-Miss.) is elected majority leader. Both the House and Senate are now led by conservative southern Republicans.

17 June | The Senate Special Whitewater Committee chaired by Alphonse D'Amato (R- N.Y.) releases its 769-page report implicating Hillary Clinton and White House staff in the scandal. Democrats deliver a counterreport over 500 pages long.

9 July | Former Colorado Governor Richard Lamm announces that he will seek the Reform Party nomination, running on a platform of cleaning up government and reducing the national debt. His

	candidacy attracts little attention.
5 August	Dole introduces a new $551 billion tax-cut plan to an audience in Chicago. In addition to a capital gains tax cut and a child credit for some families, it promises a 15-percent cut in the individual tax rate and a balanced budget. The "15%" plan becomes a central part of Dole's campaign.
7 August	Abortion rights advocates within the Republican Party end their efforts to soften language in the Republican platform. Despite Dole's endorsement of a "tolerance plank," abortion opponents succeed in keeping the antiabortion language.
10 August	Outside his boyhood home in Russell, Kansas, Bob Dole announces that Jack Kemp will be his running mate. Though Dole and Kemp have disagreed in the past, the ticket seems to click. Republicans are once again excited about the campaign.
11 August	Buchanan calls a truce with the Republican Party, claiming that the party platform reflects his views. He does not explicitly endorse Dole as the nominee.
12 August	The Republican National Convention begins in San Diego. The featured speakers include Colin Powell, George Bush, Gerald Ford, Dan Quayle, and Nancy Reagan on behalf of her husband. Elizabeth Dole gives a glowing account of her husband's military service and life in Kansas. Several speakers contrast Dole's character with Clinton's. The Republicans use their television time to convince viewers that they are a "big" party, accepting of people with differing views. A flawless convention coupled with the addition of Kemp to the ticket allow the Republicans to cut into Clinton's lead for a short time. Meanwhile, Perot's Reform Party begins meeting in California.
18 August	Perot accepts his party's nomination as the Reform Party's convention concludes in Valley Forge, Pennsylvania. Over a million people were sent nominating ballots; of the 50,000 returning their ballots, Perot beat Lamm by a ratio of 2 to 1.
22 August	President Clinton signs a historic welfare reform bill into law, making the biggest changes to the welfare system since its introduction sixty years earlier. It requires welfare recipients to work after two years and limits their benefits to five years total. Much of the responsibility for welfare is turned over to the states. Clinton vetoed two earlier versions of the bill.
26 August	The Democratic National Convention gets under way in Chicago. Al Gore, Christopher Reeve, Jim and Sarah Brady, and Hillary Clinton get prime-time speaking spots. The convention, devoted more to President Clinton than to his party, focuses on the administration's accomplishments and its role in carrying America into the twenty-first century. The final day is marred by a tabloid report that presidential adviser Dick Mor-

ris was involved with a prostitute. Morris resigns, but Clinton's performance seems unaffected. The convention bounce allows the Democrats to retake their double-digit lead over Dole and Kemp.

10 September   Perot uses one of his "infomercials" to announce that he has selected Pat Choate as his running mate. Choate is an economist, commentator, and Perot campaign adviser. Polls show Perot with about 5 percent voter support.

18 September   Bob Dole falls from an outdoor stage in Chico, California, when a retaining wall gives way. The incident reinforces feelings about Dole's age, though he jokes about it later.

6 October   The first of two presidential debates is held in Hartford, Connecticut. In this traditional format with a single moderator, Clinton defends his record while Dole challenges it. Topics include Dole's 15-percent tax-cut idea, the economy and budget generally, as well as peace in Bosnia and the Middle East. The debate is quite civil and Dole is intentionally humorous, even choosing not to criticize Clinton's character when given the chance. He appears more congenial than before, but does little to improve his standings in the polls. Perot was excluded by the commission in charge of the debates and subsequently filed charges, which failed in court.

9 October   The vice-presidential candidates hold their only debate in St. Petersburg, Florida. As in the presidential debate, the candidates are respectful of one another personally but clearly differ on the issues. Kemp argues that the Clinton administration imposes too many taxes and government regulations. Gore claims that Kemp and Dole disagree on many issues and that Kemp has changed his positions since joining the ticket. Like Clinton, he is particularly critical of the Dole tax-cut plan, which he claims will increase the deficit. Though the debate is uneventful, the consensus is that Gore is the winner.

12 October   After considerable bickering within the Dole-Kemp camp, Dole decides to concentrate on California's 54 electoral votes at a weekend strategy meeting in Washington. The campaign will pour millions of dollars into the state in an attempt to narrow Clinton's lead there.

16 October   Clinton and Dole debate for a second time in San Diego, California. This time it is a "town hall" format where citizens, not journalists, ask the questions. Dole brings up the shaky character of the Clinton administration several times but the president does not respond. Partly as a result, Clinton is seen as the winner.

18 October   John Huang is relieved of his fund-raising duties at the Democratic National Committee (DNC) after being the target of a

campaign finance scandal. Huang raised nearly $1 million in illegal campaign contributions from Indonesian businessman Mochtar Riordy. Riordy runs the Lippo Corportation where Huang used to work. Dole makes "foreign contributions" to the Democrats a campaign issue.

23 October   In an effort to broach Clinton's lead in the polls, Dole campaign aide Scott Reed asks Perot to leave the race and endorse the Republican ticket. Perot refuses and vows to stay in "until the bitter end."

5 November   Voters reelect the Clinton/Gore ticket. The Democrats receive 49 percent of the popular vote and a total of 379 electoral votes. Dole and Kemp get 41 percent of the popular vote (159 electoral votes). The Perot/Choate ticket gets less than 9 percent support and no electoral votes. Though Clinton wins handily, his coattails do not bring many Democrats to Washington with him. Republicans maintain their congressional majority, losing nine seats in the House and gaining two in the Senate. Voter turnout in the presidential election falls below 50 percent for the first time since 1924.

Notes

CHAPTER 1 — REELECTION: THE 1996 U.S. ELECTION

1. The success rate for nonelected presidents in this century was also actually quite high: Johnson kept the presidency (1964), as did Truman (1948), Coolidge (1924), and Roosevelt (1904); only Ford (1976) could not hold on to the presidency. The record of heirs apparent was more problematic. Only Reagan (1988) succeeded in passing his presidency on to his vice-president, whereas Johnson (1968) and Eisenhower (1960) were not able to do so, but Coolidge (1928) and Roosevelt (1908) were able to pass the presidency on to their designated heirs in their cabinets. See the discussion of "successor effects" in Mattei and Weisberg 1994.

2. The lack of emphasis on reelection in our voting models may have been due to the first full-blown SRC National Election Study being conducted in 1952, the only presidential election of the century other than 1920 not to have an incumbent or heir apparent running for the presidency.

3. A recent variant of this approach has been offered by modern political psychology, which seeks to understand voting as a case in which people have to make decisions using their limited information (Rahn, Aldrich, Borgida, and Sullivan 1990).

4. This analysis was performed in conjunction with Stephen Mockabee and was initially included in Weisberg and Mockabee 1997. The 1996 data are from the National Election Study survey collected with the support of the National Science Foundation. Results shown in this chapter use the appropriate sampling weights (i.e., v960003 in the dataset).

5. The data in table 1.4 also show that Elizabeth Dole was more of a plus for her husband's campaign than Hillary Clinton was for her husband's. At the same time, it is worth noting that public reactions to Mrs. Clinton were not negative; regardless of all the attacks on her role in the Whitewater real estate deal, commodities trading, and health-care reform, her mean rating was slightly positive and actually on par with that of Bob Dole. Yet the standard deviation of her ratings was higher than that for any other political personality, illustrating how controversial a figure she had become.

CHAPTER 2 — VOTER TURNOUT IN THE 1996 ELECTION

1. This is the figure offered by turnout expert Curtis Gans, director of the Committee for the Study of the American Electorate, and Scammon and McGillivray

(1997); other estimates, including that of the Federal Election Commission (49.1 percent), differ slightly. The disparities reflect the fact that calculating voter turnout is a complicated and somewhat controversial undertaking. For more on the difficulties of accurately estimating turnout, see Bruce 1997a and 1997b and Gans 1997.

2. Of course, a decline in roll-off could be indicative of heightened interest in the congressional races rather than, as we argue here, a measure of declining interest in the presidential race. There is evidence to suggest that the former interpretation is incorrect, however: turnout in House contests declined from 50.8 percent in 1992 to 45.9 percent in 1996 (Scammon and McGillivray 1997). It thus appears that the 1996 roll-off decline is indeed a reflection of lessened interest in the presidential contest and not a relative increase in excitement about House contests.

3. The same roll-off pattern is evident when we compare presidential turnout to Senate turnout in 1992 and 1996. In the fifteen states that held Senate elections in 1992 and 1996, Senate roll-off amounted to roughly 840,000 votes in 1992 (4 percent of presidential turnout) as compared to 307,000 votes in 1996 (only 1 percent of presidential turnout).

4. One Neilsen ratings point represents 1 percent of all American households with television.

5. A statistical significance test is an assessment of the probability of a relationship between two variables occurring by random chance. To say, as we do here, that an explanatory variable is "significant" is to say that its observed relationship with the dependent variable is substantial enough that it is unlikely to have occurred by chance alone. That being the case, we conclude instead that the observed relationship reflects a real relationship between the variables. Statistical *in*significance, in contrast, describes an association that is weak and may well have occurred randomly, and thus we conclude that the explanatory variable appears to have no effect on the dependent variable. The "p value" reported here and in several of our tables is related to the statistical significance test described in the previous note. The p value, a number between 0 and 1, is an estimate of the probability of obtaining a given correlation if no relationship actually existed between the variables. In other words, the p value estimates the likelihood that the observed correlation could have occurred by chance. The smaller the p value, the stronger the evidence that there is, in fact, a relationship between the variables.

6. Some analysts recommend weighting the observations by the statewide voting-age population in order to account for population differences and correct for nonconstant error variance in this use of OLS regression (Knack 1995). When we weighted the data in this manner, the results were very similar to those presented in table 2.2.

7. In this and the ensuing tables, the reader may notice that turnout levels among even those in the low-turnout categories seem quite high, given a national turnout rate of only 49 percent. Turnout estimates in surveys are usually higher than actual turnout rates, in part because survey samples tend to underrepresent some groups of unlikely voters (e.g., those who are hospitalized or homeless, or who travel or move frequently). In addition, participation in a survey about politics tends to increase one's political awareness and thus the likelihood of voting. Finally, some survey respondents claim to have voted when they did not (for a discussion of which groups are most likely to overreport their turnout, see Silver, Anderson, and Abramson 1986).

8. External political efficacy is the extent to which people feel they can influence the political process. We use two NES survey questions—"I don't think public

officials care much about what people like me think" and "People like me don't have any say about what the government does"—to create an index of political efficacy.

9. The specific statistical technique used here is logistic regression, or "logit" for short. The advantage of the logit model is that the dependent variable (whether or not one voted in 1996) is a nonlinear function of the explanatory variables. This allows us to restrict the expected values of the dependent variable (the probability that one voted in 1996) to a range of values between 0 and 1. The disadvantage of the logit model is that the marginal effect of each explanatory variable is not constant, as in OLS regression. The effect of a single unit change in an explanatory variable depends on the values of the other variables in the model, so logit coefficients do not have a straightforward interpretation. As a result, we use the logit coefficients to calculate a change in probability score when varying each explanatory variable from its minimum to maximum value while holding the other explanatory variables constant at their mean values. This change in probability score (presented in the final column of table 2.8) is interpreted as the change in the respondent's probability of voting given a shift from the lowest to highest value of the explanatory variable.

10. The dependent and independent variables are measured in exactly the same way in the 1992 and 1996 models. The occupation measure employed in our previous 1996 multivariate turnout analysis was dropped because we lacked an identical measure for 1992. We also dropped the variable assessing contact by a religious group; this question was not asked in 1992, and we found no suitable alternative.

11. The feeling thermometer is an assessment question asking respondents to rate an object (a political figure, political party, etc.) on a "temperature" scale ranging from 0 (indicating greatest disfavor) to 100 (extremely favorable) degrees.

12. Another glimpse into the contribution of Perot's decline to the 1996 turnout downturn is provided by 1996 NES respondents' recollection of whom they supported in the 1992 presidential race. Eighty-six percent of those who recall having voted for Perot in 1992 also turned out to vote four years later, as compared to the 91.4 percent turnout among those who voted for Bush or Clinton in 1992.

13. But some argue that low voter turnout is a sign of contentment with the way things are going and that the uninterested segment of the American public provides a buffer between the extreme partisans at either end of the political spectrum (Berelson et al. 1954). In addition, some argue that people abstain from voting when the ideological differences between the competing parties are negligible (Downs 1957). The similarity of competing parties may be another reason why turnout is lower in the United States than in other democracies.

CHAPTER 3 — ATTITUDINAL CORRELATES
OF THE 1996 PRESIDENTIAL VOTE

1. Tau_c is a coefficient of association that is appropriate for ordinal variables with unequal numbers of categories, with 1 as its maximal value and 0 for statistical independence.

2. To obtain a "seat-of-the-pants" estimate of the net effect of these issues, how much a candidate was favored on the issue (the difference column in the table) was multiplied by how strongly that scale was related to the major-party vote (the correlation column in the table), and these products were averaged over the 9 scales (omitting the general ideology scale). The average of these products was .00, showing that they essentially washed each other out. This estimate should not be taken too literally, since the use in the NES preelection survey of a different set of scales

covering some other issue divisions might have obtained a different result. Yet it is striking that these scales were not unidirectional in their effects.

3. There is an interesting pattern in table 3.5, with Perot losing votes and Dole gaining support from 1992 to 1996 among those giving conservative answers (rows 1, 3, and 5), while Perot lost votes and Clinton gained support among those giving liberal answers (rows 2, 4, and 6). Without looking at the panel data, we cannot safely say that Perot's conservative supporters largely moved to Dole while his liberal supporters moved to Clinton, but these results are suggestive of that dynamic.

4. The potential impact of these issues was at least partially neutralized by the concern that Hispanic voters, who are largely Catholic, had with the Republican positions on immigration and especially the cutoff of welfare benefits to some immigrants. See also chapter 10.

5. To the extent possible with NES questions, we follow the Kellstedt et al. (1996) classification of ten distinct religious traditions in America. After respondents are grouped according to their specific religious affiliations, people who have low levels of commitment or who do not express an affiliation are classified as secular along with atheists and agnostics. Our religious commitment measure is constructed using the following items: attendance at religious services, prayer outside of religious services, religious affiliation, and importance of religion in one's life. Each item counts as one "point" on the religious commitment scale. Those who score at the highest level on each of the four items receive an additional point, resulting in a scale which can range from 0 to 5. Those who score below 2 are classified as seculars.

6. The conventional wisdom is that the public is more likely to hold the incumbent responsible for a poor economy than to reward the incumbent for a strong economy. Indeed, as shown in table 3.7, the relationships between economic evaluations and the vote were somewhat stronger in 1992 than in 1996, but there were sizable relationships in both years.

7. Meanwhile, the average rating of Reform Party candidate Ross Perot among independents was only 47. Perot needed the support of independents if he was to repeat his strong showing of 1992, but they did not view him as favorably as they viewed the major-party nominees.

8. The coding of these variables was standard, except that people who could not answer the ideology question were coded as 4 to cut down the amount of missing data. Clinton won a bare majority of the two-party vote of those who could answer the ideology question, so the equation would not have properly represented the population without this adjustment.

9. We have run an equation with similar variables for other religions, but those terms are not statistically significant.

10. We have made several basic assumptions in this model. First, we restrict ourselves to the major-party vote; Perot received too little of the vote to be worth adding complexity to our modeling effort. Second, we use only closed-ended questions in the NES survey. Open-ended questions also provide valuable information, but the closed-ended questions are less affected by verbosity differences between respondents and provide an opportunity to investigate the importance of variables (such as empathy), which the campaign does not raise to a level of consciousness for the voters. (See Nisbett and Wilson 1977 for a more general negative view of the ability of people to verbalize the reasons behind their actions.)

11. A logistic equation based on party identification by itself can predict 87 percent of these cases correctly. Adding the 3 other non-candidate variables increases this only to 88 percent, while the use of all 8 variables moves the prediction level up

to 94 percent. Thus the candidate variables are critical to improving the prediction beyond the level that partisanship alone can predict.

12. The *competence* variable is the only one of the original 8 variables that does not remain significant in this larger equation. It is the least robust variable in the 8-predictor equation, barely reaching the .05 level of significance.

Chapter 4 — The Partisan Choice

1. This list omits Lyndon Johnson, who succeeded from the vice-presidency.

2. We do not consider Perot voters in this chapter. For reasons why we restrict our analysis to the two major-party candidates, see Smith and Kessel 1995, 112–13.

3. Unless otherwise specified, all subsequent references to recent elections, other elections, the best performance by a candidate in a particular category, and the like should be understood as referring to elections since 1952.

4. A general discussion about the advantages and disadvantages of open-ended and closed-ended questions appears in chapter 5.

5. This model has a little history. The model used in this chapter was designed to compare the influence of different factors on presidential vote choice across time. It was first applied to the elections of 1952 through 1976 and published in *Presidential Campaign Politics* (Kessel 1980). Subsequent elections were added in succeeding editions of the book. For data on all elections from 1952 through 1988, see Kessel 1992.

6. Party comments were between 13 and 17 percent of all responses during the 1950s and 1960s. They have not been over 10 percent since that time.

7. Closed-ended questions based on these policy areas were used in a 1972 survey of presidential voting that was part of a larger study directed by C. Richard Hofstetter. No voting analyses from this study were ever published, but the policy area questions worked quite well.

8. We should point out that all comments about groups are assigned to the appropriate issue category. This practice assumes that respondents use references to groups as a way to discuss policy. Thus, for example, when there is a reference to African Americans, the response is grouped with those under the heading of civil rights. When farmers are mentioned, since the probable topic is agricultural policy, these responses are grouped under that issue heading; and so forth. Including groups in this way increases the prominence of issues.

9. NES surveys typically include both preelection and postelection interviews. The candidate and the party likes/dislikes questions are asked in the preelection wave of interviewing. Vote choice, of course, is measured in the postelection wave. In 1996 the candidate likes/dislikes questions were asked of all respondents, but the party likes/dislikes questions were asked only of a randomly selected half of the sample. Therefore the 506 respondents in this study are those who answered both the candidate and party questions in the preelection survey and reported their presidential vote in the postelection interview.

10. No attempt is made to distinguish between direct and indirect effects (an indirect effect using the variables in this model might be that the voters' party affect would lead them to have a favorable perception of a candidate's personality, which in turn might lead them to favor that candidate's economic policy, which would finally lead them to vote choice). Rather than make any assumption about a particular sequence of attitudes that would lead to each other and ultimately to vote choice,

each attitude category is given equal standing in terms of causal proximity; the vote is estimated from all of them.

11. The probit model expresses the probability that the dichotomous dependent variable is equal to one of its values as a nonlinear function of its right-hand-side variables. Ordinary regression models are inappropriate in this circumstance because they do not. See Aldrich and Nelson 1984 for a more complete treatment of probit with binary variables and McKelvey and Zavoina 1975 for an extension to multi-category variables.

12. Specifically, we calculate the estimated differences in the predicted probabilities of a Democratic vote that result from shifting each independent variable *one standard deviation* about its mean (with the other regressors held constant at their mean values). Interested readers should consult Smith and Kessel 1995 for more detail about the nature and relevance of these indicators.

13. All comments are classified by NES as pro-Democratic, anti-Democratic, pro-Republican, or anti-Republican. In the process of generating our valences, we begin by classifying all comments falling within a given category as pro-Democratic or pro-Republican (antipartisan comments are treated as propartisan in the other direction). We then divide the pro-Democratic comments by the total number of comments in that attitude category to determine the *proportion* of the comments that favor the Democratic Party. Finally, we adjust the neutral point on the measures so that they take on the value of zero when neither party has an edge. This makes the signs of the measures indicate the partisan directions of the advantages.

14. The measures that show whether a probit coefficient is statistically significant are its standard error and its probability value (abbreviated as p value in tables 4.1 and 4.2). Since we are using a 95 percent confidence level as our criterion for statistical significance, the probability value must be .05 or lower. A probability value of exactly .05 means there are only 5 chances out of 100 that the given probit coefficient could have occurred by chance. A probability value lower than .05 means there are fewer that 5 chances out of 100.

15. Notice that an attitude category may not be significant even though one party or the other has a strong advantage in partisan valence. The valence figures in table 4.2 tell us that voters regarded President Clinton as the more intelligent candidate and that Senator Dole was seen as having more experience. Nevertheless, President Clinton was not advantaged by his intelligence and Senator Dole was not helped by his experience because neither attitude was statistically related to vote choice.

16. The American economy was very strong in both 1964 and 1996, and it was not a source of concern. There was a mild recession in 1960, but other attitudes were more important that year for a variety of reasons.

17. Our criterion is the 95 percent confidence level, meaning that in 95 cases out of 100, the observed relationship could not have occurred by chance. With international involvement, we have only 92.5 percent confidence. Aldrich, Sullivan, and Borgida argue that international affairs will have the least impact on vote choice when it is not salient and/or there is little difference between candidate positions (1989, 136). In 1996, foreign policy was not salient.

18. Another issue category, *natural resources*, was also statistically insignificant. *Agriculture*, mentioned by only a single respondent, simply dropped out of the analysis. These two minor attitudes are often inconsequential in vote choice.

19. This NES coding is unfortunate because it robs us of the chance to separate management skill per se from having a conservative fiscal posture.

20. The remaining candidate categories, *record and incumbency, intelligence, personality,* and *experience,* were not significant in determining vote choice in 1996.

21. Tests of coefficient and standard deviation differences are conducted using direct comparisons of these statistics from 1992 and 1996 data. The test associated with the valence differences is simply a mean difference test.

22. Since there have been few statistical comparisons of changes between elections, it is worth emphasizing that there are three *different* kinds of change. A change in a probit coefficient indicates that an attitude is more tightly, or more loosely, associated with vote choice. A change in partisan valence means that a given party is more advantaged, or more handicapped, by a change in the partisan direction (or extremity) of an attitude. A change in standard deviation means that persons are more tightly grouped, or more widely dispersed, on an attitudinal continuum. Various combinations of these changes are possible. For instance, when 1996 is compared to 1992, trust had significant changes in its probit coefficient, partisan valence, and standard deviation. Economic management had significant changes in partisan valence and standard deviation. Social benefits had a significant change only in its standard deviation.

CHAPTER 5 — COMPARING MODELS OF THE VOTE

1. Some social psychologists instead view candidate evaluation as "memory based," in which respondents are able to retain all those individual pieces of information and then list them as the pro's and con's when asked for a summary evaluation of a candidate. This can be viewed as closer to what open-ended questions assume about the capabilities of respondents. The evidence provided by Lodge, McGraw, and Stroh (1989) directly challenges the memory-based model of candidate evaluation.

2. These response categories are the independent variables in chapter 4.

3. These are presented in the section of chapter 4 entitled "The Building Blocks of Vote Choice."

4. The value of this consideration can be seen in the section of chapter 4 entitled "Change from 1992 to 1996." Here the 1996 results are compared directly with results obtained using the same model in 1992.

5. We will use the phrase "in the full sample" to alert readers when we are referring to statistical relationships that are significant with the 1034 voters, but not with the 506.

CHAPTER 6 — THE IMPACT OF THE ECONOMY
ON THE 1996 ELECTION

1. Lee, Lifeson, and Peart (1980) also suggest including abstention as a choice, arguing "if you choose not to decide, you still have made a choice."

2. Multinomial logit assumes that the covariances in the error terms across choices are all equal to zero. The error variance covariance matrix is the identity matrix, with all the error variances for all choices equal to 1. Multinomial probit allows one to estimate the covariances in error terms across pairs of alternatives. We estimated the model using both MNL and Limdep's MNP procedure. We set to 0 the error covariance between a choice of Clinton and Dole, enabling us to estimate five covariances: Clinton-Abstain, Dole-Abstain, Perot-Abstain, Clinton-Perot, and Dole-Perot. To avoid problems of fragile identification (Keane 1992), we also constrained to zero the effect of education on Dole and Perot, and the effect of partisanship on

Perot. Using the Broyden-Fletcher-Golfardb-Shanno algorithm, we found no significant differences between the MNP and MNL results. We have chosen to report results and base our simulations on the MNL results, which are much easier to interpret in a four-choice model than the MNP results.

3. In estimates not shown, we also included other controls, including political issues (e.g. abortion, defense spending, health care, and government guarantee of a good standard of living), union membership, religious tradition and commitment, and a 3-category income variable to assess nonlinearity in income's effect on vote choice. Inclusion of these variables has no impact on the effect of the economy in the 1996 election. To minimize the number of observations we exclude from the analysis due to incomplete data, we dropped the issue questions and religious preference measures. See chapters 3 and 4 for a complete discussion of other factors influencing vote choice in the 1996 election.

4. We do not use the traditional 7-point partisanship scale, since evaluations of Perot may be a nonlinear function of the 7-point scale. That is, strong Democrats and strong Republicans may dislike Perot equally, while moderates of both parties may be more inclined to vote for him.

5. The average voter is characterized by the following parameters on the other independent variables: 2.77 on personal financial situation, .53 Democrat, .39 Republican, 3.58 on ideology, 15.11 on income, .54 on female, 13.37 on education level, .15 on age 18–29, .36 on age 30–44, .23 on age 45–59, and .11 on African American. For the dummy variables, such as partisanship, age, race, and gender, these values indicate the probability that a voter is a Democrat, or female, or African American.

6. In results not shown, we estimated our model using a 3-category dummy for income to capture nonlinear effects. It had a substantively similar same effect.

7. Since slightly over 50 percent of eligible voters failed to vote in the 1996 election, the NES sample obviously misrepresents the extent of abstention. As Brehm (1993) demonstrates, even rigorous scientific surveys such as the NES fail to reach the "phantom respondents," an overwhelming proportion of whom are perennial nonvoters. There is also a well-documented tendency for many nonvoters to claim they voted, usually for the winner, in every postelection survey (Wright 1993).

8. To estimate vote shares when a choice is excluded, divide each voter's predicted probability of choosing each alternative by by 1 minus the predicted probability of the excluded choice. In the case of excluding abstention, divide each percentage by (1–.39). The predicted vote share for each alternative is the mean across all respondents.

Chapter 7 — Hillary Clinton
and the President's Reelection

1. Our argument is not that previous first ladies were inconsequential actors in White House politics (see Caroli 1987), nor that many first ladies of the past did not possess their own public personas—Eleanor Roosevelt is a clear enough example of a presidential spouse who was publicly her own woman. We do argue, however, that the novelty of the 1990s is that the spouses of presidential candidates became campaign issues and were consciously exploited as such by their husbands and by opponents.

2. A Lexis/Nexis search on the wives' names revealed that the mean number of *New York Times* stories about them was 177.7 in 1980, 1984, and 1988. In 1992 it

jumped to 583, and in 1996 it regressed somewhat to 295, still much higher than before Hillary Clinton was a presidential candidate's spouse.

3. Hillary Clinton's drop in popularity is also reflected in the spontaneous comments given in response to the open-ended candidate "like/dislike" questions in the 1996 NES. In 1992, respondents made 28 positive and 32 negative comments about her. In 1996, these figures were 21 and 70 respectively. We are grateful to John Kessel for bringing these data to our attention.

4. All these correlations are significantly different from 0 and 1.

5. To incorporate Perot voters, we also estimated multinomial logit models of the three-candidate vote. The substantive conclusions remained the same, so for simplicity we discuss only the simpler binary logit results in the text.

6. As table 7.2 showed, there is substantial multicollinearity between the thermometer ratings. This problem leads to larger standard errors and thus lower probabilities of finding statistically significant independent variables. Despite this hurdle, the coefficients on the wives' thermometer scores are highly significant, boosting our confidence in their effects on the vote. It might also be mentioned here that Hillary Clinton's effect is especially robust, with reaction to her remaining statistically significant throughout a wide variety of specifications of the logit model in table 7.3. The coefficient for Elizabeth Dole, by contrast, tends to move in and out of statistical significance, which is consistent with her relatively weak impact in table 7.3.

7. As one would expect, the candidate trait questions are moderately correlated with thermometer ratings of the candidates.

8. Predictions are based on the logit formula $1/(1 + e^{-Z})$ where Z is the sum of all of the coefficients multiplied by the modal values of the variables associated with them.

9. Working in favor of the second of these explanations is the fact that when individuals assigned the highest thermometer score of 100 to both wives, almost 86 percent of them voted for Clinton (see table 7.4).

10. This is likely the reason for the stronger 1996 correlation in table 7.2. This is not the case for Barbara Bush and Elizabeth Dole. Groups' ratings differed by small amounts, and the differences were equivalent for both women. For instance, Democrats' and Republicans' mean ratings differed by only 15 points compared to differences of roughly 50 points for the Clintons in 1996.

11. The omnibus CBS News/*New York Times* survey interviewed 1,001 American adults one month after the general election. The data are available from the Roper Center at the University of Connecticut, archive number USCBS96-96012A.

12. There are certainly partisan and ideological effects on how an individual perceives Hillary Clinton's White House influence, but they are muted when compared to these effects on other attitudes. Also, demographic group memberships seldom affect responses to this question.

13. It is likely that her success was made easier by the 1996 campaign's lack of dominant issues and by the Democratic and Republican candidates' convergence on the ideological center ground. Under these circumstances, she became more prominent than she might otherwise have been and reassured committed Democrats concerned about her husband's courting of moderate voters.

CHAPTER 8 — THE MEDIA
AND THE 1996 PRESIDENTIAL CAMPAIGN

1. Respondents were asked to talk about the "ad they remembered best," and

up to five responses were collected. These responses were then placed in categories; the original codes are in the Political Advertisement Master Code in the appendix to the 1996 NES. We recoded these into the categories of an attack ad, a negative ad, a positive ad, a dishonest ad or misleading ad, and whether the ad had a positive or negative effect on the respondent. In the NES codes, "attack" ads are negative ads in which the respondent recalled the actual content of a specific ad. If the respondent did not mention the content of the ad beyond the sponsor, but did mention "mud-slinging" or "backbiting" or some similar term, the ad was coded as a negative commercial. There was also one code for Clinton comparison ads, but it received very few mentions. All the recoding was based on the NES codes and not the actual answers of the respondents. For parts of this chapter, the unit of analysis is the response to the ad and not the individual respondent; here we incorporate the multiple responses offered by citizens. For other parts of our work, the unit is the individual respondent; here we typically examine the first response offered about an ad.

CHAPTER 10 — PARTY COALITIONS IN TRANSITION

1. Party identification, or partisanship, has been measured regularly since 1952 by both commercial pollsters and academic researchers. There is a long history of research on the meaning and measure of partisanship, both in the United Sates and abroad. See, for example, Niemi and Weisberg 1993a and 1993b. For the distribution of partisanship over time, see Stanley and Niemi 1998.

2. Logistic regression is an appropriate method to use when the dependent variable is dichotomous. As we explain later, we have two dependent variables: whether a respondent is Democratic or not, and whether a respondent is Republican or not. In this circumstance, logit analysis is more appropriate than so-called ordinary least squares regression.

3. We might ideally have a single equation, one that assesses the contribution of every relevant group over the entire period under study. In fact, we need several models. This is primarily because the groups considered relevant change over time. Hispanics, for example, were simply not a large enough group to be considered politically significant before the 1980s. Religious fundamentalists were a large enough group, but they were not considered a coherent political force until the mid-1970s. As a result, survey questions needed to identify the appropriate groups have not been asked over the entire period. There was no reason to think about measuring religious fundamentalism in the 1950s and 1960s. In addition, how to measure this concept has been debated widely (see, for example, Rothenberg and Newport 1984). And, obviously, certain groups defined by birth dates—such as those born after 1958 —could not be relevant until recently.

4. The results reported here differ slightly from those in our earlier articles. In earlier analyses we included working class among the groups. That variable was not included in the 1996 NES data set; we opted to exclude it from all earlier years rather than begin yet another new model. Examination of the models for all prior years with and without the class variable reveals very small differences for the coefficients of all other variables.

5. The survey question used by the NES to measure partisanship is, "Generally speaking, do you usually think of yourself as a Republican, a Democrat, an independent, or what?" Democrats and Republicans are asked if they are "strong" or "weak," and independents are asked if they lean toward the Democratic or the Republican Party. For our analysis, we use respondents' answers to the first ques-

tion—on the direction of their partisanship—ignoring the follow-up response about intensity. (Regarding the handling of the "leaners," see Niemi and Weisberg 1993b, 278–79.)

6. That Republicans were able to maintain their majority in Congress despite the temporary nature of the shift in partisanship can be explained on the basis of the advantage of incumbency in congressional voting and to other, more temporary factors. See chapter 11 in this volume.

7. See chapter 9 in this volume for a full discussion of the gender gap.

8. One should not overinterpret fluctuations for relatively small groups, such as the Jewish population. Figures may change sharply simply because they are based on a small number of cases.

9. This kind of effect, in which people are influenced in their partisanship or voting behavior by what kinds of people are around them, was identified as long ago as 1954 in Berelson, Lazarsfeld, and McPhee's (1954) study of the largely Republican community of Elmira, New York. Taking a term from horse racing, they referred to this as the "breakage effect."

10. Vote on HR-2202, 25 September 1996 (*Congressional Quarterly Almanac* 1997, H-142).

11. Vote on S-1956, 23 July 1996 (*Congressional Quarterly Almanac* 1997, S-39). In addition, Republican Governor Pete Wilson continued to take a strong anti-immigrant stance in California.

12. Another striking change in the party coalitions, the greater proportion of the young, is politically significant but demographically inevitable as the older generations are replaced by the younger.

13. Historically, a greater proportion of men than women have been independent (Miller, Miller, and Schneider (1980, 88), so females constituted a majority of both parties.

14. This is a function, in part, of declining membership in unions.

15. Comparable results for Republicans would be convenient, but those results have a distorting mirror-image aspect. Given the general Democratic tendencies of the group ties, removing the group ties means that the groups' share of Republican identifiers, perhaps tiny to begin with, often swells to greater than 100 percent of its former size.

CHAPTER 12 — THE IMPACT OF INCUMBENTS' LEVELS OF COMPETENCE AND INTEGRITY IN THE 1994 AND 1996 U.S. HOUSE ELECTIONS

1. For a similar perspective on presidential elections, see Popkin 1994.

2. If the best prospective candidates from one party run in a particular year while the opposing party's political hopefuls stay home, one implication is that elections in open seats will be pivotal. This certainly was true in 1994; over half the freshman Republicans elected to the House in 1994 won in open-seat districts.

3. From the foreword (p. v) to Clyde Wilcox's book *The Latest American Revolution?* Also see Marjorie Randon Hershey's (1997, 206–8) discussion of the 1994 elections, which appears under the heading "The 1994 Campaign: Not All Politics Is Local."

4. See Wilcox 1995 (p. 21) and Jacobson 1997b (p. 162).

5. This number does not include those who ran for other offices or who resigned prior to the end of the 104th Congress.

6. "Former Congressman Is Convicted of Lying," *New York Times*, 19 March 1997.

7. "Representative Cooley's Mountain of Miscues: Blunt Oregonian Withholds Wedding Date as Controversy Cascades," *Washington Post*, 2 May 1996.

8. "Trust Me, I Don't Have a Clue," *New York Times*, 17 December 1995.

9. Our first study (Mondak 1995a) reported data only on House members who entered Congress between 1969 and 1981. Coding stopped with 1981 because one objective of that study was to assess the possible impact of a twelve-year legislative term limit on incumbent quality, so each House member had to have served in Congress for at least twelve years (see also Mondak 1995b). Because very few of these members remain in office today, our *Almanac* data are inappropriate for present purposes, since competence and integrity scores simply are not available for the vast majority of incumbents who ran for reelection in 1994 and 1996. In contrast, our second database focuses on the 104th Congress (Millman 1997), making it much more useful for the analysis conducted in this chapter.

10. We ignored policy and issue references for two reasons. First, doing so reduced the risk that the ideological preferences of the *Almanac's* authors would skew the incumbent quality scores. Second, given that opportunities for policy leadership increase with seniority, inclusion of references to policies and issues likely would have artificially inflated quality scores for the House's more senior members.

11. Two key improvements distinguish our second coding of incumbent quality from our initial effort. First, more coders were used to conduct the content analysis, enabling better tests of intercoder reliability. Second, words and phrases were rated on an 11-point (rather than 4-point) scale, allowing coders to pinpoint more precisely the distinctions between various attributes.

12. Again, current incumbent quality data are derived from the various volumes of *Politics in America*, and we previously constructed a similar data set that used as its starting point the available editions of the *Almanac of American Politics*. We highly recommend that readers who are unfamiliar with these works review both almanacs. The logic of our coding system will be much more clear once the reader has considered a few almanac entries, such as those for the representatives listed in table 12.2. Along the way, we suspect that most readers will come to share our view that these books are rife with fascinating narratives about American politics, history, and culture.

13. Because this is an examination of incumbents in their districts, one might expect the number of cases to equal the number of seats in the House. Yet, in table 12.3, the number of cases in both models is well below 435. Three factors account for this gap: (1) not all incumbents ran for reelection; (2) competence and integrity scores are not available for all incumbents; (3) for 1996, final FEC spending data were not yet available for all elections when our analysis was conducted. The second of these reasons stems from an inherent limitation of our coding procedure—if *Politics in America* did not comment on the competence or integrity of an incumbent, no score could be obtained. One solution to this problem is to code additional publications and merge the data from various sources. Unfortunately, this solution was impractical due to its cost.

14. Data are weighted using the NES full-sample weight variables.

15. The Clinton vote variable is coded 1 if the respondent voted for Clinton in 1996, and 0 if the respondent voted for some other candidate. Similarly, the Dole vote variable is coded 1 if the respondent voted for Dole, and 0 if otherwise. Respondents who voted for a presidential candidate other than Clinton or Dole are not

excluded from the model, they simply receive scores of 0 on both of the presidential vote variables.

16. This problem is especially severe for first-term House members because the authors of *Politics in America* do not yet have much information with which to evaluate most first-term legislators. Because our coding focused on the 104th Congress, the lack of data is more problematic for 1994 than for 1996. We have competence data on 52 percent of cases in 1996 and 44 percent in 1994, and integrity data on 34 percent in 1996 and 23 percent in 1994.

17. Again, the original competence and integrity scales are continuous measures with values potentially ranging from 0 to 1. For those incumbents included in the merged data file, the mean score for integrity is .61 in 1996 (range = .12 to .85, standard deviation = .19); for competence, the mean is .65 (range = .29 to .87, standard deviation = .11). Nearly identical descriptive statistics are obtained for 1994.

18. Given how our variables are defined, there are two reasons why an incumbent could receive a score of zero on integrity (or competence): either we have no integrity score for the incumbent, or we have a score, and that score happens to be zero. These are obviously very different scenarios. In one case, the zero means that the House member is woefully unprincipled, whereas in the second instance the zero means that we lack information about the incumbent's integrity. Clearly, the two scenarios should be treated as identical. The dummy variable *integrity measure available* is used to differentiate these scenarios. A negative coefficient is expected for this dummy variable, meaning that voters should be much less likely to support an incumbent whose actual integrity score is zero than to support the typical incumbents for whom we have no integrity score. That is, if an incumbent actually *earned* an integrity score of zero, constituents should be highly likely to vote against that incumbent.

19. At first glance, it appears that the effect of competence in 1994 is quite a bit larger than the effect of integrity. This is misleading because competence has both a smaller standard deviation and a more narrow range than integrity. In actuality, as shown below, the substantive effects of the two variables in 1994 are similar.

20. In computing the estimates for figures 12.1, 12.2, and 12.3, we hold other variables at their mean or mode values. In 1994, we set Clinton approval at 1, the Dole feeling thermometer at its mean (51.07), and challenger spending at the national average. In 1996, we assume that the respondent voted for Clinton, the respondent has an average opinion of Newt Gingrich (thermometer = 39.58), and challenger spending again was average.

References

Abramowitz, Alan I., and Jeffrey A. Segal. 1992. *Senate Elections.* Ann Arbor: University of Michigan Press.

Abramson, Jill, and Leslie Wayne. 1997. "Democrats Used the State Parties to Bypass Limits." *New York Times,* 2 October, A1, A8.

Abramson, Paul R., and John H. Aldrich. 1982. "The Decline of Electoral Participation in America." *American Political Science Review* 76:502–21.

Abramson, Paul R., John H. Aldrich, and David W. Rohde. 1994. *Change and Continuity in the 1992 Elections.* Washington, D.C.: CQ Press.

Aldrich, John H. 1997. "Positive Theory and *Voice and Equality.*" *American Political Science Review* 91:421–23.

Aldrich, John H., and Forrest D. Nelson. 1984. *Linear Probability, Logit, and Probit Models.* Sage University Papers on Quantitative Applications in the Social Sciences 07-045. Beverly Hills, Calif.: Sage.

Aldrich, John H., and Richard G. Niemi. 1996. "The Sixth American Party System: Electoral Change, 1952–1992." In *Broken Contract,* ed. Stephen C. Craig, 87–109. Boulder, Colo.: Westview Press.

Aldrich, John H., John L. Sullivan, and Eugene Borgida. 1989. "Foreign Affairs and Issue Voting: Do Presidential Candidates 'Waltz Before a Blind Audience?'" *American Political Science Review* 83:121–41.

Alvarez, R. Michael, and Jonathan Nagler. 1995. "Economics, Issues and the Perot Candidacy: Voter Choice in the 1992 Election." *American Journal of Political Science* 39:714–44.

Andersen, Kristi. 1997. "Gender and Public Opinion." In *Understanding Public Opinion,* ed. Barbara Norrander and Clyde Wilcox. Washington, D.C.: CQ Press.

Ansolabehere, Stephen, and Shanto Iyengar. 1995. *Going Negative: How Political Advertisements Shrink and Polarize the Electorate.* New York: Free Press.

Ansolabehere, Stephen, Shanto Iyengar, Adam Simon, and Nicholas Valentino. 1994. "Does Attack Advertising Demobilize the Electorate?" *American Political Science Review* 88:829–38.

Arnold, R. Douglas. 1982. "Overtilled and Undertilled Fields in American Politics." *Political Science Quarterly* 97:91–103.

Asher, Herb, and Mike Barr. 1994. "Popular Support for Congress and Its Members." In *Congress, the Press, and the Public,* ed. Thomas E. Mann and Norman J. Ornstein. Washington, D.C.: American Enterprise Institute and Brookings Institution.

References

Ayres, B. Drummond, Jr. 1995. "Law to Ease Voter Registration Has Added 5 Million to the Rolls." *New York Times,* 3 September.

Bannon, Brad. 1997. "A Populist Perspective on the 1996 Elections." *Public Perspective* 8 (December/January): 33–36.

Beck, Paul Allen. 1979. "The Electoral Cycle in American Politics." *British Journal of Political Science* 9:129–56.

———. 1997. *Party Politics in America.* 8th ed. New York: Longman.

Berelson, Bernard R., Paul F. Lazarsfeld, and William N. McPhee. 1954. *Voting: A Study of Opinion Formation in Presidential Campaigns.* Chicago: University of Chicago Press.

Bond, Jon R., Cary Covington, and Richard Fleisher. 1985. "Explaining Challenger Quality in Congressional Elections." *Journal of Politics* 47:510–29.

Bonk, Kathy. 1988. "The Selling of the 'Gender Gap': The Role of Organized Feminism." In *The Politics of the Gender Gap: The Social Construction of Political Influence,* ed. Carol M. Mueller. Newbury Park, Calif.: Sage.

Borquez, Julio, Edie N. Goldenberg, and Kim Fridkin Kahn. 1988. "Press Portrayals of the Gender Gap." In *The Politics of the Gender Gap: The Social Construction of Political Influence,* ed. Carol M. Mueller. Newbury Park, Calif.: Sage.

Brehm, John. 1993. *The Phantom Respondents: Opinion Surveys and Political Representation.* Ann Arbor: University of Michigan Press.

Brock, David. 1996. *The Seduction of Hillary Rodham.* New York: Free Press.

Broder, David. 1997. "Shameless Campaigning." *Washington Post National Weekly Edition,* 29 September, 4.

Brody, Richard A. 1978. "The Puzzle of Participation." In *The New American Political System,* ed. Anthony King. Washington, D.C.: American Enterprise Institute.

Bruce, Peter. 1997a. "How the Experts Got Voter Turnout Wrong Last Year." *Public Perspective* 8:39–43.

———. 1997b. "Reply to Gans." *Public Perspective* 8:44.

Bumiller, Elisabeth. 1996. "Running Against Hillary." *New York Times,* 13 October.

Burnham, Walter Dean. 1965. "The Changing Shape of the American Political Universe." *American Political Science Review* 59:7–28.

———. 1970. *Critical Elections and the Mainsprings of American Politics.* New York: Norton.

———. 1987. "The Turnout Problem." In *Elections American Style,* ed. A. James Reichley. Washington, D.C.: Brookings Institution.

Burrell, Barbara. 1997. *Public Opinion, the First Ladyship, and Hillary Rodham Clinton.* New York: Garland.

Bystrom, Dianne, Lori Melton McKinnon, and Carole Chaney. 1998. "First Ladies and the Fourth Estate: Media Coverage of Hillary Clinton and Elizabeth Dole in the 1996 Presidential Campaign." Paper presented at the annual meeting of the Midwest Political Science Association, Chicago, 23–25 April.

Cain, Bruce, John Ferejohn, and Morris Fiorina. 1987. *The Personal Vote: Constituency Service and Electoral Independence.* Cambridge, Mass.: Harvard University Press.

Campbell, Angus. 1960. "Surge and Decline." *Public Opinion Quarterly* 24:397–418.

Campbell, Angus, Philip E. Converse, Warren Miller, and Donald E. Stokes. 1960. *The American Voter.* New York: Wiley.

Campbell, James E. 1987. "The Revised Theory of Surge and Decline." *American Journal of Political Science* 31:965–79.

————. 1992. "Forecasting the Presidential Vote in the States." *American Journal of Political Science* 36:386–407.

————. 1996. *Cheap Seats: The Democratic Party's Advantage in U.S. House Elections.* Columbus: Ohio State University Press.

Caroli, Betty Boyd. 1987. *First Ladies.* New York: Oxford University Press.

Cassel, Carol A., and Robert Luskin. 1988. "Simple Explanations of Turnout Decline." *American Political Science Review* 82:1321–30.

Ceaser, James W., and Andrew E. Busch. 1997. *Losing to Win: The 1996 Elections and American Politics.* Lanham, Md.: Rowman and Littlefield.

Clausen, Aage R. 1973. *How Congressmen Decide: A Policy Focus.* New York: St. Martin's Press.

Cohen, Jacob, and Patricia Cohen. 1982. *Applied Multiple Regression/Correlation Analysis for the Behavioral Sciences.* 2d ed. Hillsdale, N.J.: Lawrence Erlbaum.

Cohen, Richard E. 1997. "Campaigning for Congress: The Echo of '94." In *Toward the Millennium: The Elections of 1996,* ed. Larry J. Sabato. Boston: Allyn and Bacon.

Congressional Quarterly Almanac. Vol. 52. 1997. Washington, D.C.: CQ Press.

Conover, Pamela J., and Virginia Sapiro. 1993. "Gender, Gender Consciousness, and War." *American Journal of Political Science* 37:1079–99.

Converse, Philip E. 1972. "Change in the American Electorate." In *The Human Meaning of Social Change,* ed. Angus Campbell and Philip E. Converse. New York: Russell Sage Foundation.

Cook, Charles E. 1997. "New Report Provides Insight to Dem Failure to Regain Control in '96." *Roll Call* 43 (7 August):5.

Cook, Elizabeth Adell, Ted G. Jelen, and Clyde Wilcox. 1992. *Between Two Absolutes: Public Opinion and the Politics of Abortion.* Boulder, Colo.: Westview Press.

Cook, Elizabeth Adell, Sue Thomas, and Clyde Wilcox, eds. 1994. *The Year of the Woman: Myths and Realities.* Boulder, Colo.: Westview Press.

Corrado, Anthony. 1997. "Financing the 1996 Elections." In *The Election of 1996: Reports and Interpretations,* ed. Gerald M. Pomper. Chatham, N.J.: Chatham House.

Devlin, L. Patrick. 1995. "Political Commercials in American Presidential Elections." In *Political Advertising in Western Democracies,* ed. Lynda Lee Kaid and Christina Holtz-Bacha, 186–205. Thousand Oaks, Calif.: Sage.

Dewar, Helen, and Eric Pianin. 1996. "Concession Supersedes Revolution: GOP Attempts to Appease Voters." *Washington Post,* 29 September, A1.

DiIulio, John J., Jr. 1997. "Conclusion: Valence Voters, Valence Victors." In *The Elections of 1996,* ed. Michael Nelson. Washington, D.C.: CQ Press.

Downs, Anthony. 1957. *An Economic Theory of Democracy.* New York: Harper and Row.

Duncan, Philip D. 1997. *Politics in America: 1998, the 105th Congress.* Washington, D.C.: CQ Press.

Durr, Robert H., John B. Gilmour, and Christina Wolbrecht. 1997. "Explaining Congressional Approval." *American Journal of Political Science* 41:175–207.

Erie, Steven P., and Martin Rein. 1988. "Women and the Welfare State." In *The Politics of the Gender Gap: The Social Construction of Political Influence,* ed. Carol M. Mueller. Newbury Park, Calif.: Sage.

Erikson, Robert S. 1990. "Economic Conditions and the Congressional Vote: A Review of the Macrolevel Evidence." *American Journal of Political Science* 34:373–99.

References

Erskine, Hazel. 1971. "The Polls: Women's Role." *Public Opinion Quarterly* 35: 275–90.

Fazio, Russell H. 1986. "How Do Attitudes Guide Behavior?" In *The Handbook of Motivation and Behavior,* ed. R.M. Sorrentino and E.T. Higgins. New York: Guilford.

Finkel, Steven E., and John G. Geer. 1998. "A Spot Check: Casting Doubt on the Demobilizing Effect of Attack Advertising." *American Journal of Political Science* 42:573–95.

Fiorina, Morris P. 1978. "Economic Retrospective Voting in American National Elections: A Microanalysis." *American Journal of Political Science* 22:426–43.

———. 1981. *Retrospective Voting in American National Elections.* New Haven: Yale University Press.

Fiske, Susan T., and Shelley E. Taylor. 1991. *Social Cognition.* 2d ed. New York: McGraw-Hill.

Fite, David, Marc Genest, and Clyde Wilcox. 1990. "Gender Differences in Foreign Policy Attitudes: A Longitudinal Analysis." *American Politics Quarterly* 18: 492–512.

Gans, Curtis. 1997. "It's Bruce Who Got the Turnout Story Wrong." *Public Perspective* 8:44–48.

Goldstein, Kenneth M. 1997. "Political Advertising and Political Persuasion in the 1996 Presidential Campaign." Paper presented at the annual meeting of the American Political Science Association, Washington, D.C., 28–31 August.

Grant, J. Tobin, Stephen T. Mockabee, and Quin Monson. 1997. "Specifying Religion Variables in Multivariate Models." Paper presented at the annual meeting of the Southern Political Science Association, Norfolk, Va., 5–8 November.

Green, John C., and James L. Guth. 1988. "The Christian Right in the Republican Party: The Case of Pat Robertson's Supporters." *Journal of Politics* 50:150–65.

Hastie, Reid, and Bernadette Park. 1986. "The Relationship between Memory and Judgment Depends on Whether the Task is Memory-based or On-Line." *Psychological Review* 93:258–68.

Herrnson, Paul S. 1997. *Congressional Elections: Campaigning at Home and in Washington.* 2d ed. Washington, D.C.: CQ Press.

Hershey, Marjorie Randon. 1997. "The Congressional Elections." In *The Election of 1996: Reports and Interpretations,* ed. Gerald M. Pomper. Chatham, N.J.: Chatham House.

Hibbing, John R., and Elizabeth Theiss-Morse. 1995. *Congress as Public Enemy.* New York: Cambridge University Press.

———. 1998. "The Media's Role in Public Negativity Toward Congress: Distinguishing Emotional Reactions and Cognitive Evaluations." *American Journal of Political Science* 42:475–98.

Jacobson, Gary C. 1980. *Money in Congressional Elections.* New Haven: Yale University Press.

———. 1985. "Money and Votes Reconsidered: Congressional Elections, 1972–1982." *Public Choice* 47:7–62.

———. 1996. "The 1994 House Elections in Perspective." In *Midterm: Elections of 1994 in Context,* ed. Philip A. Klinkner. Boulder, Colo.: Westview Press.

———. 1997a. "The 105th Congress: Unprecedented and Unsurprising." In *The Elections of 1996,* ed. Michael Nelson. Washington, D.C.: CQ Press.

————. 1997b. *The Politics of Congressional Elections*. 4th ed. New York: Longman.

Jacobson, Gary C., and Michael A. Dimock. 1994. "Checking Out: The Effects of Bank Overdrafts on the 1992 House Elections." *American Journal of Political Science* 38:601–24.

Jacobson, Gary C., and Samuel Kernell. 1983. *Strategy and Choice in Congressional Elections*. 2d ed. New Haven: Yale University Press.

Jewell, Malcolm E., and David M. Olson. 1988. *Political Parties and Elections in American States*. 3d ed. Chicago: Dorsey.

Kaufmann, Karen M., and John R. Petrocik. 1997. "The Revenge of the Soccer Moms? Gender as a Party Cleavage in American Politics." Paper presented at the annual meeting of the American Political Science Association, Washington, D.C., 28–31 August.

Keane, Michael P. 1992. "A Note on Identification in the Multinomial Probit Model." *Journal of Business and Economic Statistics* 10:193–200.

Keith, Bruce E., David B. Magleby, Candice J. Nelson, Elizabeth Orr, Mark C. Westlye, and Raymond E. Wolfinger. 1992. *The Myth of the Independent Voter*. Berkeley: University of California Press.

Kellstedt, Lyman A., John C. Green, James L. Guth, and Corwin E. Smidt. 1996. "Grasping the Essentials: The Social Embodiment of Religion and Political Behavior." In *Religion and the Culture Wars*, ed. John C. Green, James L. Guth, Corwin E. Smidt, and Lyman A. Kellstedt, 174–92. Lanham, Md.: Rowman and Littlefield.

Kenski, Henry C. 1988. "The Gender Factor in a Changing Electorate." In *The Politics of the Gender Gap: The Social Construction of Political Influence,* ed. Carol M. Mueller. Newbury Park, Calif.: Sage.

Kessel, John H. 1974. "The Parameters of Presidential Politics." *Social Science Quarterly* 55:8–24.

————. 1980. *Presidential Campaign Politics*. Homewood, Ill.: Dorsey.

————. 1992. *Presidential Campaign Politics*. 4th ed. Pacific Grove, Calif.: Brooks/ Cole.

Key, V.O., Jr. 1955. "A Theory of Critical Elections." *Journal of Politics* 17:3–18.

————. 1966. *The Responsible Electorate*. Cambridge, Mass.: Harvard University Press.

Kimball, David C., and Samuel C. Patterson. 1997. "Living up to Expectations: Public Attitudes toward Congress." *Journal of Politics* 59:701–28.

Kinder, Donald R. 1986. "Presidential Character Revisited." In *Political Cognition,* ed. Richard R. Lau and Donald O. Sears, 233–55. Hillsdale, N.J.: Lawrence Erlbaum.

Kinder, Donald R., and D. Roderick Kiewiet. 1981. "Sociotropic Politics." *British Journal of Political Science* 11:129–61.

Kinder, Donald R., and Walter R. Mebane Jr. 1983. "Politics and Economics in Everyday Life." In *The Political Process and Economic Change,* ed. Kristen Monroe. New York: Algathon.

King, David C. 1997. "The Polarization of American Parties and Mistrust of Government." In *Why People Don't Trust Government,* ed. Joseph S. Nye Jr., Philip D. Zelikow, and David C. King. Cambridge, Mass.: Harvard University Press.

Knack, Stephen. 1995. "Does 'Motor Voter' Work? Evidence from State-Level Data." *Journal of Politics* 57:796–811.

Knox, Richard A. 1996. "Medical Specialists Debate Electorate's Need to Know." *Boston Globe,* 15 October, A13

Kolodny, Robin. 1996. "The Contract with America in the 104th Congress." In *The*

References

State of the Parties, ed. John C. Green and Daniel M. Shea. 2d ed. Lanham, Md.: Rowman and Littlefield.

Koszczuk, Jackie. 1997. "Nonstop Pursuit of Campaign Funds Increasingly Drives the System." *Congressional Quarterly Weekly Report* 55 (5 April):770–74.

Kramer, Gerald H. 1965. *Decision Theoretic Analysis of Canvassing and Other Precinct Level Activities in Political Campaigning*. Ph.D. dissertation, Massachusetts Institute of Technology, Cambridge.

———. 1983. "The Ecological Fallacy Revisited: Aggregate- versus Individual-Level Findings on Economics and Elections and Sociotropic Voting." *American Political Science Review* 77:92–111.

Kulisheck, Michael R., and Jeffery J. Mondak. 1996. "Candidate Quality and the Congressional Vote: A Causal Connection?" *Electoral Studies* 15:237–53.

Lacy, Dean. 1998. "Back from Intermission: The 1994 Elections and the Return To Divided Government." In *Great Theatre: The American Congress in the 1990s*, ed. Samuel Patterson and Herbert Weisberg. New York: Cambridge University Press.

Lacy, Dean, and Barry C. Burden. 1999. "The Vote-Stealing and Turnout Effects of Ross Perot in the 1992 U.S. Presidential Election." *American Journal of Political Science* 43:233–55.

Layman, Geoffrey C. 1997. "Religion and Political Behavior in the United States." *Public Opinion Quarterly* 61:288–316.

Lee, Geddy, Alex Lifeson, and Neil Peart. 1980. "Freewill." From the album *Permanent Waves*. Mercury Records.

Leege, David C., and Lyman A. Kellstedt. 1993. *Rediscovering the Religious Factor in American Politics*. Armonk, N.Y.: M.E. Sharpe.

Lewis, Charles. 1996. *The Buying of the President*. New York: Avon Books.

Lewis-Beck, Michael S. 1988. *Economics and Elections: The Major Western Democracies*. Ann Arbor: University of Michigan Press.

Lodge, Milton, Kathleen M. McGraw, and Patrick Stroh. 1989. "An Impression-driven Model of Candidate Evaluation." *American Political Science Review* 83:399–419.

Long, J. Scott. 1997. *Regression Models for Categorical and Limited Dependent Variables*. Thousand Oaks, Calif.: Sage.

McCloskey, Herbert, and John Zaller. 1984. *The American Ethos*. Cambridge, Mass.: Harvard University Press.

McCurley, Carl, and Jeffery J. Mondak. 1995. "Inspected by #11840631113: The Influence of Incumbents' Competence and Integrity in U.S. House Elections." *American Journal of Political Science* 39:864–85.

McKelvey, Richard D., and William Zavoina. 1975. "A Statistical Model for the Analysis of Ordinal Level Dependent Variables." *Journal of Mathematical Sociology* 4:103–20.

MacKuen, Michael B., Robert S. Erikson, and James A. Stimson. 1989. "Macropartisanship." *American Political Science Review* 83:1125–42.

Mansbridge, Jane E. 1985. "Myth and Reality: The ERA and the Gender Gap in the 1980 Election." *Public Opinion Quarterly* 49:164–78.

Markus, Gregory B. 1988. "The Importance of Personal and National Economic Conditions on the Presidential Vote: A Pooled Cross-Sectional Analysis." *American Journal of Political Science* 32:137–54.

Mattei, Franco, and Herbert F. Weisberg. 1994. "Presidential Succession Effects in Voting." *British Journal of Political Science* 24:269–90.

Miller, Warren E. 1991. "Party Identification, Realignment, and Party Voting: Back to the Basics." *American Political Science Review* 85:557–68.

Miller, Warren E., Arthur H. Miller, and Edward J. Schneider. 1980. *American National Election Studies Data Sourcebook*. Cambridge, Mass.: Harvard University Press.

Miller, Warren E., and J. Merrill Shanks. 1996. *The New American Voter*. Cambridge, Mass.: Harvard University Press.

Millman, Steven Robert Lesh. 1997. "Effects of Term Limits on the Quality of Members of the U.S. House: Testing the Mondak Model." Master's thesis. Western Washington University.

Moen, Matthew C. 1992. *The Transformation of the Christian Right*. Tuscaloosa: University of Alabama Press.

Mondak, Jeffery J. 1995a. "Competence, Integrity, and the Electoral Success of Congressional Incumbents." *Journal of Politics* 57:1043–69.

———. 1995b. "Elections as Filters: Term Limits and the Composition of the U.S. House." *Political Research Quarterly* 48:701–27.

———. 1995c. *Nothing to Read: Newspapers and Elections in a Social Experiment*. Ann Arbor: University of Michigan Press.

Mueller, Carol M. 1988. "The Empowerment of Women: Polling and the Women's Voting Bloc." In *The Politics of the Gender Gap: The Social Construction of Political Influence*, ed. Carol M. Muller. Newbury Park, Calif.: Sage.

Mughan, Anthony, and Barry C. Burden. 1995. "The Candidates' Wives." In *Democracy's Feast: Elections in America*, ed. Herbert F. Weisberg. Chatham, N.J.: Chatham House.

Nelson, Rex. 1993. *The Hillary Factor*. New York: Gallen.

Nelson, Thomas E., and Zoe M. Oxley. 1999. "Issue Framing Effects on Belief Importance and Opinion." *Journal of Politics*, forthcoming.

Nichols, Stephen M., and Paul Allen Beck. 1995. "Reversing the Decline: Voter Turnout in the 1992 Election." In *Democracy's Feast: Elections in America*, ed. Herbert F. Weisberg. Chatham, N.J.: Chatham House.

Niemi, Richard G., and Herbert F. Weisberg. 1993a. *Classics in Voting Behavior*. Washington, D.C.: CQ Press.

———. 1993b. *Controversies in Voting Behavior*. Washington, D.C.: CQ Press.

Nisbett, Richard E., and Timothy D. Wilson. 1977. "Telling More Than We Can Know: Verbal Reports On Mental Processes." *Psychological Review* 84:231–59.

Norrander, Barbara. 1997a. "The Independence Gap and the Gender Gap." *Public Opinion Quarterly* 61:464–76.

———. 1997b. "The Independence Gap and the Gender Gap, Part II." Paper presented at the annual meeting of the American Political Science Association, Washington, D.C., 28–31 August.

O'Connor, Karen, Bernadette Nye, and Laura Van Assendelft. 1996. "Wives in the White House: The Political Influence of First Ladies." *Presidential Studies Quarterly* 26:835–53.

Patterson, Samuel C., and Michael K. Barr. 1995. "Congress Bashing and the 1992 Congressional Election." In *Democracy's Feast: Elections in America*, ed. Herbert F. Weisberg. Chatham, N.J.: Chatham House.

Patterson, Samuel C., and Gregory A. Caldeira. 1990. "Standing Up for Congress: Variations in Public Esteem since the 1960s." *Legislative Studies Quarterly* 15:25–47.

Patterson, Samuel C., and David C. Kimball. 1997. "Unsympathetic Audience: Citizens' Evaluations of Congress." In *Great Theatre: The American Congress in the*

References

1990s, ed. Herbert F. Weisberg and Samuel C. Patterson. New York: Cambridge University Press.

Patterson, Samuel C., Randall B. Ripley, and Stephen V. Quinlan. 1992. "Citizens' Orientations Toward Legislatures: Congress and the State Legislature." *Western Political Quarterly* 45:315–38.

Peters, John G., and Susan Welch. 1980. "The Effects of Charges of Corruption on Voting Behavior in Congressional Elections." *American Political Science Review* 74:697–708.

Petrocik, John R. 1974. "An Analysis of Intransitivities in the Index of Party Identification." *Political Methodology* 1:31–47.

Popkin, Samuel L. 1994. *The Reasoning Voter: Communication and Persuasion in Presidential Campaigns.* 2d ed. Chicago: University of Chicago Press.

Powell, G. Bingham, Jr. 1986. "American Voter Turnout in Comparative Perspective." *American Political Science Review* 80:17–44.

Prior, Markus. 1997. "All Advertising Is Local: Content, Sequence, and Targeting in the 1996 Presidential Campaign Ads." Master's thesis, Ohio State University.

Radcliff, Benjamin. 1992. "The Welfare State, Turnout, and the Economy: A Comparative Analysis." *American Political Science Review* 86:444–54.

Ragsdale, Lyn. 1980. "The Fiction of Congressional Elections as Presidential Events." *American Politics Quarterly* 8:375–98.

Rahn, Wendy M., John H. Aldrich, Eugene Borgida, and John L. Sullivan. 1990. "A Social-Cognitive Model of Candidate Appraisal." In *Information and Democratic Processes,* ed. John Ferejohn and James Kuklinski. Urbana: University of Illinois Press.

Rahn, Wendy M., Jon A. Krosnick, and Marijke Breuning. 1994. "Rationalization and Derivation Processes in Survey Studies of Political Candidate Evaluation." *American Journal of Political Science* 38:582–600.

Rhine, Staci L. 1995. "Registration Reform and Turnout Change in the American States." *American Politics Quarterly* 23:409–26.

Ripley, Randall B., Samuel C. Patterson, Lynn M. Maurer, and Stephen V. Quinlan. 1992. "Constituents' Evaluations of U.S. House Members." *American Politics Quarterly* 20:442–56.

Rosenstone, Steven J. 1982. "Economic Adversity and Voter Turnout." *American Journal of Political Science* 26:25–46.

Rosenstone, Steven J., Roy L. Behr, and Edward H. Lazarus. 1996. *Third Parties in America.* 2d ed. Princeton: Princeton University Press.

Rothenberg, Stuart, and Frank Newport. 1984. *The Evangelical Voter.* Washington, D.C.: Free Congress Research and Education Foundation.

Rusk, Jerrold G. 1970. "The Effect of the Australian Ballot Reform on Split Ticket Voting." *American Political Science Review* 64:1220–38.

Sabato, Larry J. 1997. *Toward the Millennium: The Elections of 1996.* Boston: Allyn and Bacon.

Scammon, Richard M., and Alice V. McGillivray. 1993. *America Votes 20.* Washington, D.C.: CQ Press.

———. 1997. *America Votes 22.* Washington, D.C.: CQ Press.

Schlozman, Kay Lehman, and Sidney Verba. 1979. *Injury to Insult.* Cambridge, Mass.: Harvard University Press.

Shapiro, Robert Y., and Harpreet Mahajan. 1986. "Gender Differences in Policy Preferences: A Summary of Trends from the 1960s to the 1980s." *Public Opinion Quarterly* 50:42–61.

Silver, Brian, Barbara Anderson, and Paul Abramson. 1986. "Who Overreports Voting?" *American Political Science Review* 80:613–24.

Simon, Rita J., and Jean M. Landis. 1989. "The Polls—A Report: Women's and Men's Attitudes about a Woman's Place and Role." *Public Opinion Quarterly* 53: 265–76.

Smith, Charles E., Jr., and John H. Kessel. 1995. "The Partisan Choice: George Bush or Bill Clinton." In *Democracy's Feast: Elections in America,* ed. Herbert F. Weisberg. Chatham, N.J.: Chatham House.

Smith, Tom W. 1984. "The Polls: Gender and Attitudes toward Violence." *Public Opinion Quarterly* 48:384–96.

Stanley, Harold W., and Richard G. Niemi. 1991. "Partisanship and Group Support, 1952–1988." *American Politics Quarterly* 19:189–210.

———. 1992. "Partisanship and Group Support Over Time." In *Controversies in Voting Behavior,* ed. Richard G. Niemi and Herbert F. Weisberg. 3d ed. Washington, D.C.: CQ Press.

———. 1995. "The Demise of the New Deal Coalition: Partisanship and Group Support, 1952–1992." In *Democracy's Feast: Elections in America,* ed. Herbert F. Weisberg. Chatham, N.J.: Chatham House.

———. 1998. *Vital Statistics on American Politics, 1997–1998.* Washington, D.C.: CQ Press.

Stimson, James A. 1991. *Public Opinion in America: Moods, Cycles, and Swings.* Boulder, Colo.: Westview Press.

Stokes, Donald E., Angus Campbell, and Warren E. Miller. 1958. "Components of Electoral Decision." *American Political Science Review* 52:367–87.

Stokes, Donald E., and John J. DiIulio Jr. 1993. "The Setting: Valence Politics in Modern Elections." In *The Elections of 1992,* ed. Michael Nelson. Washington, D.C.: CQ Press.

Sundquist, James L. 1973. *Dynamics of the Party System.* Rev. ed. Washington D.C.: Brookings Institution.

Teixeira, Ruy A. 1987. *Why Americans Don't Vote: Turnout Decline in the United States, 1960–1984.* Westport, Conn: Greenwood Press.

Tufte, Edward R. 1975. "Determinants of the Outcomes of Midterm Congressional Elections." *American Political Science Review* 69:812–26.

Verba, Sidney, and Norman H. Nie. 1972. *Participation in America.* New York: Harper and Row.

Wald, Kenneth D. 1997. *Religion and Politics in the United States.* 3d ed. Washington, D.C.: CQ Press.

Weisberg, Herbert F. 1987. "The Demographics of a New Voting Gap: Marital Differences in American Voting." *Public Opinion Quarterly* 51:335–43.

———. 1995. "Democracy's Feast: The 1992 U.S. Election." In *Democracy's Feast: Elections in America,* ed. Herbert F. Weisberg. Chatham, N.J.: Chatham House.

Weisberg, Herbert F., and April Kelly. 1997. "Families First in the 1996 Presidential Election? Soccer Moms and the Married as Target Groups." Paper presented at the annual meeting of the Southern Political Science Association, Norfolk, Va., 5–8 November.

Weisberg, Herbert F., and David C. Kimball. 1995. "Attitudinal Correlates of the 1992 Presidential Vote: Party Identification and Beyond." In *Democracy's Feast: Elections in America,* ed. Herbert F. Weisberg. Chatham, N.J.: Chatham House.

References

Weisberg, Herbert F., Jon A. Krosnick, and Bruce D. Bowen. 1996. *An Introduction to Survey Research, Polling, and Data Analysis.* Thousand Oaks, Calif.: Sage.

Weisberg, Herbert F., and Stephen T. Mockabee. 1997. "Attitudinal Correlates of the 1996 Presidential Vote: The People Reelect a President." Paper presented at the annual meeting of the American Political Science Association, Washington, D.C., 28–31 August.

Weisberg, Herbert F., and Samuel Patterson. 1998. *Great Theatre: The American Congress in the 1990s.* New York: Cambridge University Press.

Weisberg, Herbert F., and Charles E. Smith Jr. 1991. "The Influence of the Economy on Party Identification in the Reagan Years." *Journal of Politics* 53:1077–92.

Welch, Susan, and John Hibbing. 1992. "Financial Conditions, Gender, and Voting in American National Elections." *Journal of Politics* 54:197–213.

———. 1997. "The Effects of Charges of Corruption on Voting Behavior in Congressional Elections, 1982–1990." *Journal of Politics* 59:226–39.

Wilcox, Clyde. 1992. *God's Warriors: The Christian Right in Twentieth Century America.* Baltimore: Johns Hopkins University Press.

———. 1995. *The Latest American Revolution? The 1994 Elections and Their Implications for Governance.* New York: St. Martin's Press.

Wirls, Daniel. 1986. "Reinterpreting the Gender Gap." *Public Opinion Quarterly* 50:316–30.

Wolfinger, Raymond E., and Steven J. Rosenstone. 1980. *Who Votes?* New Haven: Yale University Press.

"Women and Men: Is a Realignment Under Way?" 1982. *Public Opinion* (April/ May): 21–32.

Wright, Gerald C. 1993. "Errors in Measuring Vote Choice in National Election Studies, 1952–1988." *American Journal of Political Science* 37:291–316.

Index

Index

Schneider, Edward J., 253
Segal, Jeffrey A., 187
Senate, 184
Shanks, J. Merrill, 46, 56
Shapiro, Robert Y., 146, 150, 151
Significance, statistical, 244, 248
Silver, Brian, 244
Simon, Adam, 43
Simon, Rita J., 151
Size of government, as measure of ideology in election study, 54–56
Smidt, Corwin E., 56, 246
Smith, Charles E., Jr., 5, 19, 86, 163, 247
Smith, Tom W., 146
Smoking, as related to 1992, 1996 election results, 59–60
Social benefits, and the vote, 60, 80–81
Social issues, and the vote, 59–60
Social psychology, 89, 90–91, 92, 243, 249
Social Security, as campaign issue in 1996, 58–60
Socioeconomic status, correlated to voter turnout in 1996, 32, 35–39
Soft money, 128, 187. *See also* Campaign spending
South: gender gap in, 147–49; voter turnout in, 32–33
Southerners, and party coalition, 165–80
Specter, Arlen, 8, 9–15
Stanley, Harold W., 6, 19, 67, 162, 163, 164, 252
Stimson, James A., 52, 163
Stokes, Donald E., 4, 19, 45, 94
Stroh, Patrick, 89, 249
Sullivan, John L., 243, 244, 248
Sundquist, James L., 6
Supreme Court cases, 127
Survey questions, closed-ended vs. open-ended, 88–93, 98, 246, 247

Tau$_c$, 245
Taxes, as campaign issue in 1996, 58–60
Taylor, Murray, 9–15
Taylor, Shelley E., 91, 92
Teixeira, Ruy A., 25
Television, in 1996 election, 126–42
Theiss-Morse, Elizabeth, 193, 206, 207, 210
Thermometer ratings: of Clinton by gender, 157; determinants of Clinton's, 157–61; polarization of the Clintons', 121; for political parties, 48; and popularity of presidential party nominees, 13–15, 62–63; for presidential candidates and their wives, 115–16,

119–21; for prominent Republicans and other political leaders, 14
Thomas, Sue, 161
Tomlinson, Andrew, 5, 19
Tufte, Edward R., 6

Unemployment, and the vote. *See* Economy
University of Michigan, 3–5

Valentino, Nicholas, 43
Van Assendelft, Laura, 112
Verba, Sidney, 25, 42, 102
Volatility of electorate, 20
Voter mobilization, 34–40
Voter registration, 29–31. *See also* National Voter Registration Act
Voter turnout: accuracy, 243–44, 250; attitudes correlated to, 34–40; and the economy, 102–3, 104–8, 110; change from 1992, 40–42; in 1992 election, 23; in 1996 congressional election, 188; implications of decline in, 42–44; at individual level, 31–40; model of, 36
Voters: and interest in 1996 election, 23–24, 138; knowledge level of, regarding House members' policy positions, 221
Voting: and religion in 1996 election, 56–57; in congressional election, 207–9; roll-off, 26

Wald, Kenneth D., 56
Waldholtz, Enid Greene, 218–19
Wayne, Leslie, 128
Weisberg, Herbert F., 3, 4, 5, 6, 7, 15, 19, 45, 66, 161, 163, 191, 243, 252, 253
Welch, Susan, 157, 194
Welfare reform, voter attitudes on, 59–60
Westlye, Mark C., 46
Whites: and 1996 congressional election, 188–93; and support for Congress in 1996, 199–201
Wilcox, Clyde, 56, 146, 151, 161, 253
Wilson, Timothy D., 92, 246
Wirls, Daniel, 146
Wolbrecht, Christina, 193, 206
Wolfinger, Raymond E., 46, 102, 107, 150
Women: and party identification, 169–72; role of, in society, 52–54. *See also* Gender; Gender gap
Wright, Gerald C., 250

Zaller, John, 101
Zavoina, William, 248

271

About the Contributors

Herbert B. Asher is a professor emeritus of political science at The Ohio State University, where he is also counselor to the university president. He is the author of numerous articles and books, including *Polling and the Public: What Every Citizen Should Know, Presidential Elections and American Politics,* and "The Perot Campaign" in *Democracy's Feast.* He is a member of the Ohio Ethics Commission and is interim director of the John Glenn Institute for Public Service and Public Policy.

Paul Allen Beck is a professor of political science and chair of the department at The Ohio State University. He is author of *Party Politics in America* and coauthor of *Electoral Change in Advanced Industrial Democracies.* His most recent research focuses on intermediaries in election campaigns—especially the relative influence of the media, personal discussants, and political organizations on national voting choices—in the United States and cross-nationally.

Janet M. Box-Steffensmeier is an associate professor at The Ohio State University. Her work has been published in *American Political Science Review, American Journal of Political Science, Journal of Politics,* and *Political Analysis.* Her research interests include campaigns and elections, legislatures, public opinion, and political methodology.

Barry C. Burden is an assistant professor at Louisiana State University. His work has been published in *American Political Science Review, American Journal of Political Science,* and several edited volumes. His research interests are political behavior, Congress, public opinion, and methodology.

J. Tobin Grant is a graduate student in political science at The Ohio State University. He is studying voting behavior, legislative politics, formal theory, and statistical methods. His current research interests include campaigns and elections, legislative behavior, and coalition formation.

John H. Kessel is a professor emeritus of political science at The Ohio State University. His analyses of campaign politics include *The Goldwater Coalition, Presidential Campaign Politics,* and *Presidential Parties.* He is currently completing a book on the presidency.

David C. Kimball is an assistant professor of political science at Southern

Illinois University. He has published articles in *American Political Science Review, Journal of Politics,* and *Social Science Computer Review.* His research interests include congressional elections, divided government, public support for government institutions, and interest-group lobbying.

Dean Lacy is an assistant professor of political science at The Ohio State University. His research on elections and public opinion has appeared in *American Journal of Political Science, Journal of Theoretical Politics,* and other journals and edited volumes. He is currently completing a project on nonseparable preferences in politics, funded by the National Science Foundation.

Carl McCurley is an assistant professor at East Carolina University. His work has been published in *Political Geography Quarterly, Political Research Quarterly,* and *American Journal of Political Science.* His research interests include congressional elections, voting behavior, and racial politics.

Steven R.L. Millman is a Ph.D. candidate in political science at the Massachusetts Institute of Technology. His research interests include the study of formal institutions of government (especially Congress), ideological determinants of electoral behavior, trust in government, and the implications of nonlinear models in research design.

Stephen T. Mockabee is a Ph.D. candidate in political science at The Ohio State University. His research interests are voting behavior, public opinion, survey research methods, and legislative politics.

Jeffery J. Mondak is an associate professor of political science at Florida State University. He is the author of *Nothing to Read: Newspapers and Elections in a Social Experiment.* His articles on congressional elections have appeared in *American Journal of Political Science, Journal of Politics,* and several other journals. His research also examines social groups and networks, political knowledge and awareness, media, political tolerance, and public opinion toward courts.

Joseph Quin Monson is a graduate student at The Ohio State University. His interests include mass political behavior, legislative politics, and survey research methods.

Anthony Mughan is a professor of political science at The Ohio State University. He is author of *Party and Participation in British Elections* and coeditor of *Political Leadership in Democratic Societies* and forthcoming *Senates: Bicameralism in the Contemporary World.*

Stephen M. Nichols is an assistant professor of political science at California State University, San Marcos. He has published articles on electoral politics in *Journal of Politics, American Politics Quarterly,* and other journals. His areas of interest include public opinion and mass political behavior.

Richard G. Niemi is a professor of political science at the University of Rochester. He is coauthor of *Civic Education: What Makes Students Learn* and coeditor of *Comparing Democracies: Elections and Voting in Global Perspective.* He has written numerous articles on political socialization, voting, and legislative districting and is currently doing research on legislative term limits and on a number of civic education topics.

Barbara Norrander is an associate professor of political science at the University of Arizona. She is author of *Super Tuesday: Regional Politics and Presidential Primaries* and coeditor of *Understanding Public Opinion*. Her research on partisanship and presidential nominations has appeared in *American Journal of Political Science, Public Opinion Quarterly,* and *Political Research Quarterly.*

Samuel C. Patterson is a professor emeritus of political science at The Ohio State University. He has served as editor of *American Journal of Political Science, Legislative Studies Quarterly,* and *American Political Science Review.* He has been a Guggenheim Fellow, a Fellow at the Center for Advanced Study in the Behavioral Sciences, and a Fulbright Distinguished Lecturer at the University of Bologna, Italy. He is coeditor of the forthcoming *Senates: Bicameralism in the Contemporary World.*

Peter M. Radcliffe received his Ph.D. in political science from The Ohio State University. He has presented conference papers on campaign finance, public opinion, and political parties. His research interests include political organizations and parties, political behavior, and political methodology.

Charles E. Smith Jr. is an assistant professor of political science and co-director of the Social Science Research Laboratory at the University of Mississippi. His research interests include public opinion and voting behavior, judicial politics, and political methodology. His articles have appeared in *American Political Science Review* and *Journal of Politics.*

Harold W. Stanley is a professor and chairman of political science at the University of Rochester. He has published articles on parties and elections in *American Political Science Review, Journal of Politics, Publius,* and other journals. His books include *Voter Mobilization and the Politics of Race* and *Senate vs. Governor, Alabama 1971.* With Richard Niemi, he edited *Vital Statistics on American Politics 1997–1998.*

Andrew R. Tomlinson is a graduate student in political science at The Ohio State University. His interests include mass political behavior, political psychology, research design, and statistical methods. His current interests focus on applying principles of political psychology and formal theory to the study of American voting behavior.

Herbert F. Weisberg is a professor of political science at The Ohio State University. He has coedited *American Journal of Political Science.* His recent books include *Great Theatre: The American Congress in the 1990s* (coedited with Samuel Patterson); *An Introduction to Survey Research, Polling, and Data Analysis* (coauthor); and *Democracy's Feast: Elections in America, 1992* (editor). His forthcoming book is *Classics in Congressional Politics* (coeditor).